THE
BOOK
OF
HELP

THE
BOOK
OF
HELP

A Memoir in Remedies

MEGAN GRISWOLD

RODALE

NEW YORK

Published in the United States by Rodale Books, an imprint of the Crown Publishing Group, a division of Penguin Random House LLC, New York.
crownpublishing.com
rodalebooks.com

RODALE and the Plant colophon are registered trademarks of Penguin Random House LLC.

Grateful acknowledgment is made to the following for permission to reprint previously published material:
Charlotte Sheedy Literary Agency: "Crows" by Mary Oliver from *New and Selected Poems Volume 1* by Mary Oliver (Boston, MA: Beacon Press, 1992), copyright © 1978, 1992 by Mary Oliver. Used herein by permission of the Charlotte Sheedy Literary Agency.
University of Texas Press: Four lines of the English translation of "Sonnet SVII" from *100 Love Sonnets: Cien Sonetos de Amor* by Pablo Neruda, translated by Stephen Tapscott, copyright © 1959 by Pablo Neruda and Fundacion Pablo Neruda, copyright © 1986 by the University of Texas Press. Used by permission of the University of Texas Press.

Library of Congress Cataloging-in-Publication Data is available upon request.

ISBN: 978-1-63565-220-8
Ebook ISBN: 978-1-63565-221-5

Printed in the United States of America

Book design by Nancy Singer
Jacket design by Jessie Sayward Bright
Jacket and interior illustrations by Aitch

1 3 5 7 9 10 8 6 4 2

First Edition

For all those who've ever needed a lantern.

And for all those who've been one.

This world is such a little place. Just the red in the sky
before the sun rises. So let us keep fast hold of hands
that when the birds begin, none of us be missing.

—*Emily Dickinson, 1861*

CONTENTS

ABOUT
ME

I wasn't raised, exactly. Well, I was, but more like raised through sets of instructions to prepare me for worst-case scenarios rather than for, say, life. Fair to say I overtrained for crises, even. Everyone knows that habits of childhood are hard to break. So it turns out—not to brag (and I'm not sure this is something one would ever brag about in the first place)—but if it's out there and in English, I've probably tried it. And technically speaking, I shouldn't even limit it to English. I've tried a few things in Portuguese.

What's the *it*, you ask? That remedy, that discipline, that modality, that thing it ain't cool to admit you've done at the Ivy League mixer. I've logged some fifteen thousand hours *in search of*, spanning forty years and six continents. My search has included (but is not limited to) ways to become less neurotic, to become less of a romantic, to develop emotional intelligence, to get over childhood conditioning, to get out of my own way, to find my place in the world, to be successful in love, and to generally attempt to become more evolved—one nano-micro-millimeter at a time.

It's said when doing anything, a nearly alchemical event happens right around the ten thousand-hour mark—you become an expert of sorts. So I suppose, in an unintentional way, I will declare myself an expert searcher.

Whether this drive was due to particularly odd/searching parents or my own sensitive nervous system and anxious mind, I found myself at a young age with an emotional sensitivity that, for a good long while, felt more liability than asset. I was trained early—for good and for bad—to look outside myself for something that might help me have a smoother relationship between me and me. At birth, my parents assigned me a Christian Science practitioner; by age seven I asked Santa for my first mantra; by twelve I began taking weekend workshops on personal growth. By twenty-seven, I tried to go the academic route, figuring I shouldn't overlook the traditional means to develop. I indoctrinated myself into the halls of Yale Graduate School. By thirty-two, I was a classical acupuncturist. Compulsive? Probably. Freak show? Maybe so. Or, perhaps, from a kinder vantage point, I'll call it an over-the-top existential curiosity.

In spite of my great intentions, by age thirty the family I had chosen, the one I created, exploded (although is getting arrested more explosion or more implosion?). And for all the training I received, the tuition fees and mantras and first-aid readiness, nothing prepared me for handling what came my way.

The point: at my darkest hour, if somebody had told me the surefire way out of my predicament was to ditch my clothes and run naked around Balboa Island backward under the full moon singing "God Save the Queen" in Castilian Spanish, I'd have done it.

You might think I'm being hyperbolic. I'm not.

Nude, clothed, upside down, right side up—you name it. And the following, a record of my attempts and experiments to become a more loving, more awake, more durable version of myself. I think of it like an off-trail log of the landscape of one person's interior.

And this particular log is informed by my affinity for the edges of the bell curve, not the middle. That's my bias. I'll own it here, right up front. I'm drawn to experiences and stories that are the most private, the most embarrassing, the most cringeworthy, the most taboo, the most—how can I say?—the most from the underbelly of our experience, the stuff our culture seems to give us the least permission—and least words—to put words to. Like those times at the end of a party when the really good stuff happens, when most everybody has gone home, but a core set of stragglers is just getting started, telling their deepest-darkest, cracking themselves open on the kitchen floor, all in a huddle, after the coffee or all the beer or the only decent dessert has run out.

So in these pages, you will find me reporting from that place, and that place in me, because that's where I've learned the most, from others and inside myself. And when I wasn't learning, I notice it's where I've felt the most alive. I hope to add in some small way to the great canon of experience where, for one reason or another, the unsayable was suddenly okay to say. If you are anything like me, you could use a little more of that. A little more breathing room, to make life more bearable, more true.

THE TERRAIN

MENTAL WORK
Metaphysical Malpractice
Christian Science
Transcendental Meditation
Transactional Analysis
Color Reading
Past Life Family Tree
EST Training
Atlas and Axis Adjustments
THE ANTI-CANDIDA DIET
Shaklee Shakes
Reflexology (with Grandma)
THE SIX-DAY ADVANCED COURSE
Christian Mysticism
The Aller-Diet
The Anger Process
The Forum
Reading Maya Angelou
Volunteer for EST
About Sex Seminar
The Ballet Dancer Diet (Not the Eat-Cotton-Balls One)
Self-Government Workshop
Read the Greeks
Watch Movies with Happy Endings
Solo Camping
WILDERNESS EXPEDITION SCHOOL

Read the New Testament
The Lawrence Ongoing Class
Feldenkrais Method
READ *A PATH WITH HEART*
Lead Climbing
Craft a Five-Year Plan
Get Engaged
Pilates
NASM Certification
The Episcopal Chapel of Transfiguration
Biodynamic Gardening
ASHTANGA YOGA
Astrology of Wedding Day Assessment
Rolfing
Camp with the Chilean Military
WFR CERTIFICATION
Feng Shui
Study Permaculture
Traditional Chinese Medicine
Mountain Instructor Course
Shiatsu Practitioner Training
Classical Five Element Acupuncture School
Hellerwork
Read the Old Testament
Tai Chi
Graduate School

Qigong
Harville Hendrix
Sea Kayak
The Artist's Way
Study the Upanishads with Freeman and Taylor
Shamanic Journeying
Windows of the Sky Treatments
PLANT SPIRIT MEDICINE
Castor Oil Treatment
Drumming
PRACTICE WILDERNESS RESCUE
Reading bell hooks
Ayurvedic Medicine
Blood-Type Diet
Practice Joel Fuhrman's *Eat to Live*
Cordyceps out the Wazoo
McDougall Plan
Take Raw TCM Herbs
NAET
TRUENORTH HEALTH CENTER
Korean Hand Acupuncture
The Bad Vegetarian Diet
CREVASSE RESCUE
Tui Na
BECOME A DOULA
The Five Rhythms
Reading Elena Brower

Marry Yourself (with a Ring and Everything)

PALEO DIET

Acutonics

Naturopathic Medicine

Speak Spanish

Vegan Diet

Eat Sour Things

Depossession Treatment (Dragons)

Paleo-Vegan Diet

The Dosha Diet

Narrative Therapy

Water Ice Climb

Spirit Burial Ground

The Shock Diet

MAST Pants

STUDY THE HYGIENISTS

Emergency Counseling

The Dugan French Approach (DFA)

READING PEMA

Trail Run

The Serious Therapist

The Gottman Distance and Isolation Test

Skate Ski

Consult a Psychic

Toya Hari

Study the Tongue

Window Shop

Self-Portrait Exercises

Chinese Medicine Diet

Zero Balancing

Primal Screaming

Nutrarian Diet

Vipassana Meditation

Grocery Store Therapy

Camp to Save Your Relationship

Salsa Lessons

Get Lost in CureZone

CLASSICAL HOMEOPATHY

Jivamukti Yoga

Consider Breatharianism

Stick Therapy

Consult a Clairvoyant

Form a Book Club

Reading Rumi

MEDITATE WITH THE TETON SANGHA

Sufi Dance

Read *The Tibetan Book of Living and Dying*

Craniosacral Therapy

Tango

Get Rid of Things

Sex Toys

The Ah-Breath Dyad Bonding Meditation

Sing a Cappella to Save Relationship

Ditch Your Own Book Club

Kayak the Broken Group

Psychodynamic Workshop

Naked Breathing

Learn to Drink

Run a Marathon

Study Design

Read Lonny Jarrett

Practice Loving-Kindness Meditation

Read a Pattern Language

Save-Your-Relationship-Camping

Acroyoga

Raise a Field Mouse as Your Own

Couples Counseling

Eat Gummy Bears

Hakomi Therapy

Art Therapy

RUN ULTRAMARATHONS

Gestalt Therapy

Bataka Bat Sessions

Core Power Yoga

ART THERAPY MIXED WITH HAKOMI THERAPY MIXED WITH GESTALT THERAPY

Do Boundary Exercises

Two Therapists Simultaneously

Internal Family Systems Therapy

Learn to Surf

Contemplative Psychotherapy

Talk to Pillows

Tylenol PM

Vedic Astrology

Take Singing Lessons

Watch a Boatload of Television

PRACTICE NONVIOLENT COMMUNICATION

Gratitude Lists

Network Chiropractic

Collect Platform Shoes

Acupuncture Clinical Internship

Surf Nicaragua

WORSLEY ACUPUNCTURE CLINICAL INTENSIVES

Xanax

Sound Bathing

Nia Teacher Training

Get Thrown Off a Horse

Use White Angelica for Protection

Paxil

Kundalini

Do a Classic Via Ferrata

Byron Katie's "The Work"

Read *Passionate Marriage*
Stop Time (Freeze Your Eggs)
Volunteer at Children's Hospital
CBD OIL
SUP Yoga
Singing Recital
Liver Flush (with Colander and Headlamp)
Hoasca with the UDV
Road Trip
Tonglin Meditation
E-mail-Free-Phone-Signal-Free-Zones
EMDR
Reading Barry Lopez
Colon Hydrotherapy
The Sakara Cleanse
YOGA TEACHER TRAINING
Cadaver Lab
Chanting the Vedas
Three-Day Water Fast
Tell Stories on Stage
Richard Freeman's Bhagavad Gita Intensive
Ear Candling
Live in the Library
Cook SOS-Free Meals
The Enneagram Subtype Study
Write and Perform a One-Woman Show
Date Yourself
Travel Solo (Well, with a Dog)
Go Commando
Theravada Buddhism
Burning Man
Five-Day Water Fast
Fire Rituals
Make Out with Incredibly Handsome Man on Dance Floor
Glacier Travel

Poetry Therapy
Brain Theory Meets Hakomi Therapy
Psychic Surgery
Take a Lover
Take Ultraprevention Tests
Boycott Men
Study Kabbalah
The Clean Program
Thich Nhat Hanh
Navigate Mapless Patagonian Terrain
Chelation
Seven-Day Water Fast
The Blueprint Cleanse
Knitting
Practice Sanskrit Mouth Positions
TAOISM
Crucible Intensive Therapy
Wildfitness
Date Peter Pan (Unintentionally)
BAREFOOT RUNNING
Practice Taking the Twelve Energetic Pulses
Mahayana Buddhism
Open Water Swimming
Valerian Root
Facing Death
Cord Cutting
BUILD A SWEAT LODGE
10-Day Water Fast
Study Hindu Mythology
The Classic Colon Cleanse
Live Communally
Shintoism
The Brown Rice Cleanse
Take Refuge in the Buddha, the Dharma and the Sangha
Study Hospice
Rebirthing

Play Lumosity Games
ULTRAHIKING
Soul Retrieval
Consult "The Secret Language of Birthdays"
TRACY ANDERSON METHOD
Date Like a Man
16-Day Water Fast
Skype Therapy in Your Car
High-Altitude Gardening
Study the Bardos
Un-Facebook People
Sit Shiva
Boxing
Raindrop Therapy
Read and Map Danielle LaPorte's *The Desire Map*
Surf Indo
The AIM Program
TAP AND DRAIN AGGRESSIVE ENERGY
Attend Writers' Colonies
Inject Botulism Toxin into Forehead
Live off the Grid
Ingest Bach Flower Essences
Reading *Ka*
21-Day Water Fast
Climb the Grand
THE HOFFMAN PROCESS
Read Spirit Animal Cards
Take Marie Forleo's B-School
WIM HOF METHOD
Prayer
Hot Soaks, Cold Plunges
The Paintings of Francis Picabia
The Hoffman Q2
Alain de Botton's The School of Life
Meditate with *AGAINST THE STREAM*
Moon Juice Pantry
Astro Bivy

QUICKENING

It is obviously very early.
The light is no more than dusk
that leaks past the edges
of the blinds.

—*Wallace Stegner*

.5

EMBRACING THE BELOVED:
RELATIONSHIP AS A
PATH OF AWAKENING
BY STEPHEN AND ONDREA LEVINE

PURPOSE: I don't just want a good relationship. I want a *great* relationship. And given all that Imago stuff about our family of origin and the relationships we pick, I'd better get cracking. My friend Denise thinks I should do a silent Vipassana meditation retreat. But what with my verbal incontinence, I can't imagine agreeing to a vow of silence for a day, let alone a week. I'd have to be pretty desperate. In lieu of that, I'll read this book.

DURATION: There's the actual reading of the book, and then the subsequent discussions with my husband, Tim, about implementing the exercises in the book.

EQUIPMENT NEEDED: Book, but beyond that, it depends on the exercise. They are largely equipmentless but full of instruction.

AGE: 30.

RELATIONSHIP STATUS: Newly married, and wanting more intimacy. Not sure what I even mean by that. Just know I want more.

COST: $14.95.

LOCATION: Village Bookstore (the best New Age book selection) in Bellingham, Washington.

Oh, my God, I love Stephen and Ondrea Levine. It's my new thing. I can't stop reading their book. I keep thinking her name is Andrea with an *A*, but it's not; it's definitely an *O*. I know because I didn't just buy their book, I bought their tapes too—*To Love and Be Loved: The Difficult Yoga of Relationship*. And Stephen definitely pronounces her name *On-drea*. When I'm not reading them, I listen to them. My friend Denise turned me on to them. I think they're geniuses, like live-action Buddhas meet couples counselors.

My mom was really into Harville Hendrix's *Getting the Love You Want* during a rocky chapter in my parents' marriage. But the Levines seem more . . . what . . . more . . . of my generation or something. And Stephen and Ondrea— unlike most Buddhist-Hindu-Sufi-Taoist-monk types—dedicate their spiritual practice to being a couplehood. None of this celibate monk stuff. They talk about relationships being a tandem climb, where the partners swap leads for a lifetime. I love that metaphor—Tim and I on a tandem climb. That's so what I dream about.

And like all good Buddhists, Stephen and Ondrea (I like to use their first names 'cause I feel like I know them) met in silent retreat—a death-and-dying workshop, no less. Ondrea had been battling a series of diseases for a lifetime and Stephen was a teacher of Conscious Dying. And Buddhists are the bomb as far as death-and-dying stuff goes. Ask anybody. Anyway, they met, they fell in love at this silent retreat. The first day, before dropping into unabating silence, they went around that classic circle, sharing the "what brings you here" talk. After the talk, Ondrea headed back to her tent, where someone had left a note on her pillow that said: "I love you and would like to take care of you and your child for the rest of your life." And Ondrea instantly knew who had written that note.

And the rest writes itself. The silent retreat culminates with a Sufi dance— because if you were a death-and-dying silent retreat, wouldn't you end that way too? A wild spinning dervish sending you straight into ecstatic trance? And mid-dance, their eyes locked and they danced away from that Sufi circle together and have never left each other since. And as any Buddhist Cinderella story should go, both had made peace with being alone indefinitely, each imagining themselves odd enough nuts to never run into somebody else as odd as they. And let's be honest, how big is that death-and-dying dating pool anyway? And as soon as their kids were out of the house, they decided to take relationship as spiritual practice up a notch or two, living in retreat only with each other in New Mexico. (Maybe that's what my parents should have done. Or what Tim and I should do now, when we're just getting started.) But Stephen and Ondrea simply taught what they learned. And you know, typically, Buddhist monks aren't the best advisors to couplehoods. So, for long-term couple stuff, give me Stephen. Give me Ondrea.

.75

STEPHEN AND ONDREA
TELEPHONE READINGS

PURPOSE: One step further. To study and discuss the book with what I call my Designated Spiritual Friend, Denise.

DURATION: These can last hours.

EQUIPMENT NEEDED: Two phones.

AGE: 30.

COST: Free.

LOCATION: Bellingham, Washington (me), and Wyoming (Denise).

Denise and I are on the phone yet again, reading aloud from *Embracing the Beloved*. It's dark outside. I sit in Tim's and my new (old) house, largely empty, minus a bed and a dresser or two. We're still moving in and don't own much furniture.

Tonight, I wait for Tim to return from a business trip to Colorado. He's helping some organizations get on their feet. Tim and I met in Patagonia, on a semester-length wilderness training program I took after graduating from Columbia. I had waited tables at a Berkeley, California, microbrew pub and saved all my tips for the tuition in a pretty white box I hid in my pantry. It was worth every penny. I fell for not only the wilds of Patagonia but my first real love. Tim is kind (and not just average kind; like, exceptionally kind) and handsome (not just regular handsome, but this humble-shy-strong-tall-perfectly-coiffed-with-a-hint-of-disheveled-sun-bleached-blond-haired-all-American-meets-aquamarine-blue-eyes kind of handsome) and not just regular smart, but Ivy-League-got-accepted-everywhere-he-applied smart; and not just polite, but sweet-old-school-New-England-beyond-gracious polite. He's the most grounded, generous man I've ever met. We once played that game Would You Ever and the question was, "If you could save an endangered species by spending a year immobilized in a full-body cast, would you?" Not only was his yes emphatic, I thought we might soon be shopping for splints, plaster, and bandages. And he's kind of a late bloomer, like I am. We've followed each other around ever since—from Chile to graduate school.

And here we are, five years in and newly wedded, fresh off the glow of our crunchy-modern-hippie-wedding-in-the-tall-grasses-at-the-edge-of-the-wild-Similkameen-River, where we said our (of course) handwritten vows, barefoot and bathed in Mary Oliver (his) and Pablo Neruda (mine)—all hay bales, riparian, and Northwest-y—surrounded by our friends and parents and respective older sisters.

But tonight, while I wait for Tim in our little saltbox house, Denise and I do what we do frequently: examine our relationships as if the men in our lives are mere case studies rather than actual human beings. We'll often violate any confidence in the couplehood if we confidantes think it will help us get to the bottom of it. *It.* We analyze our men, dissect them, hoping to make sense of this life stuff, this love stuff. Never realizing that this, too, can take us further from our partners, turning them into objects. But we pat ourselves on the back and call this intimacy, as if talking about it is the same thing as doing it.

So Denise and I are deep into hour two of our little impromptu intimacy phone workshop. I read my favorite bit:

> The distance from your pain, your grief, your unattended wounds, is the distance from your partner. Whatever maintains that distance, that separation from ourselves and our beloveds, must be investigated with mercy and awareness.
>
> The mind creates the abyss but the heart crosses it.

"God, that's brilliant," I say. I'm sure I tear up. "So the less afraid I am of my own pain, the closer I'll feel to Tim. I love that idea that the heart crosses the abyss our minds create. God, that's good. And I love that word *beloved*. I want to start using it: my beloved."

And so it goes. We cry over how gorgeous it is, how sensitive and deep and misunderstood we are, and, in turn, how much we misunderstand our partners; we say our *I love you*s and hang up. The world's problems nearly solved on the phone tonight. Maybe tomorrow we'll redraft the Palestinian peace accord.

I expected Tim home by nine p.m. Now it is ten. Then eleven. Then twelve. I start pacing our dark house in loops. This isn't like Tim to be late, let alone not call. To keep myself occupied, I watch Jay Leno interview Hugh Grant. The last time I saw him on the show it was following his arrest for getting a blow job from a prostitute with an exotic name. And everybody asked, "Why in the world would someone want to get a blow job from Divine Brown, when he had Elizabeth Hurley at home?"

And now it's after one a.m. and I get a phone call from Tim. He tells me he is in jail.

"As in *jail* jail?"

"Jail," he repeats. "I was on my way home on I-5 and saw a woman stumbling by the side of the road near our turnoff. I stopped and offered to let her use my phone. But then the police saw me and thought the whole thing looked suspicious and I got arrested."

And I think: *Helping a woman stumbling? With him, possible.*

"Tim, are you telling me the truth? Because you *know* you can tell me the truth. I can take it." I speak calmly and clearly. I mean it.

"Yes, I'm telling you the truth," he says.

I offer to start making calls for assistance and attorney friends. We're nothing if not annoyingly overeducated with similarly annoyingly (but loving) overeducated friends. But Tim refuses the help.

"I'll be fine. I am *fine*. Don't *do* anything," he says.

"But how will you get out? Is this your *one* phone call? Do you get *another* phone call? Or is that just the movies . . ."

"I don't know. I'll be fine. I'm fine." His voice, firm.

I make those calls to trusted lawyer friends anyway. I call my mother too. Despite it being the middle of the night, I know she will answer and can snap to full consciousness on a dime, no matter how deep her sleep. I need to help, and harness more help where I can. My mom adores Tim. She will help me think this through.

When Tim and I hang up, I head straight to the bathroom. Without going into too much detail, turns out there's some truth to the expression "having the shit scared out of you." I spend an impressive amount of time there over the next seven hours. I keep thinking about *Embracing the Beloved*. I pace our nearly lampless furniture-free house through the night, hoping the phone will ring again. It doesn't. After dawn, I get a call from a strange female voice that tells me I can pick Tim up at the jail in an hour. I put together a goodie bag of sorts, with a snack and a warm wet towel so he can wash up.

When we imagine the geography of our cities, we don't often imagine where the jail is. But it's usually in the middle, with other civic buildings. So while I'm not sure where the Bellingham jail is exactly, I do know where the library is, as Tim and I had taken my mother there for her to compare it with our family's other favorite city libraries just that week. In our family, books were sacred and given far more easily than hugs. Reading aloud a good book was far more natural for Mom than maternal touch. So a good library? Fantastic.

I look up the jail address and get Tim's goodie bag, remicrowaving the washcloth one last time so it will be warm, like they provide at overthought restaurants between courses. I head downtown.

After a few wrong turns using the library as landmark, I pull up to the loading zone. I see Tim standing in front of the jail, wearing the suit he married me in. The vintage olive green coat over his arm, white sleeves rolled up. He looks older. He'd always looked so young for his age. My friend Nessa since second grade has always called him Opie with a Bod because he has such a sweet innocent face atop one spectacularly broad chest. But there he is, my beautiful husband, looking like the saddest person in the world. My heart breaks for him. I know, whatever has happened, that I love him, can see his beauty—the way he steps into the car with a certain extra quiet self-consciousness, a certain asking for permission. I also know—as sure as I know my own name—that whatever his truth, I have zero interest in *ever* adding to the look of suffering and shame I now see before me. My only hope, in fact, is to lessen it. This, the only clear thought I've had between last night and now. Amid the mystery, only one clear thing. My role as his wife and partner: to support the navigation through whatever waters he finds himself. Or through whatever waters *we* find ourselves. I picked this boat. He picked this boat. *We* picked this boat. But neither the waters nor the weather can ever be predicted. Herein lies the tricky part—having some agreement on whose waters one or both of you are in.

We start driving south on I-5 to get his car. He directs me to keep driving past the route home. Glancing back and forth between him and the road I ask, "I thought it all happened right before our turnoff. Why are we heading way down here?"

There is a vast silence. My stomach drops.

"Let's just wait to talk about it when we get home," he says.

Oh.

No.

ROOT

Every person in the house felt that there was no sense in their living together, and that the stray people brought together by chance in any inn had more in common with one another than they . . .

—*Leo Tolstoy*

1

MENTAL WORK

PURPOSE: It's our family slang for a Christian Science thing. When most people call the doctor, Christian Scientists call their practitioners, who perform "treatments." They study and think spiritually on your behalf.

DURATION: Depends on the practitioner. There is no formula, and treatment can be done by telephone or via e-mail.

EQUIPMENT NEEDED: The ability to pick up the phone or send an e-mail. I'm too young to do either.

AGE: 4 months.

COST: Somewhere around the $25 mark. As therapies go, it's remarkably affordable.

HUMILIATION FACTOR: None. That I know of.

LOCATION: Corona del Mar, California.

I'm 119 days old, and I can't breathe. Well, technically I'm still *breathing*, but it's shallow, labored, and rapid. My parents are frightened. Four-month-old little me is doing what? Crying like a maniac, kicking my chubby feet, and pumping my fists up and down?

It's been going on for hours. They've called the pediatrician and have tried everything he's suggested. I've been held upright, patted on the back compulsively, filled with steam in the bathroom, rocked, and cooed at (that last one isn't medical), but still, nothing.

The doctor has told them if my respiratory rate gets above sixty, they're to bring me into Hoag, the hospital where I was born. My dad has been timing my breaths with a stopwatch. In the decades to come, he will put a stopwatch to most anything—between the flash of lightning and the subsequent rumble of thunder, the number of minutes we meditate as a family, the length of presidential debates. Today, it's my breath.

But what I don't know about my dad yet is that because he is a born-and-raised Christian Scientist, the philosophy of his upbringing and adulthood is a little hazy on this life-or-death stuff. They kind of think death doesn't *actually* exist—nor pain, suffering, nor even the idea of difficulty. Maybe better said, they think death can kind of exist, but awkwardly, sort of illogically existing and not existing simultaneously, and only if you understand that in the end these messy little things like pain and death don't *actually* ever happen. More misunderstood metaphor. How's that for a what's-the-sound-of-one-hand-clapping Advanced Placement Zen koan?

So even though my dad, as a "fallen away" Christian Scientist, is game to count my baby breaths in a practical way, the thing is, there's a not-so-small part of him that doesn't—at his foundation—believe in death or illness or pain. Not for him, not for me, not for any of us. I know that's a little bit nutty thing to say here at the get-go because death is, you know, *death*. But from my understanding, as mostly an outsider to the religion (but with, admittedly, fairly good seats) when it comes down to it, if anything painful/medical/bad/scary/negative/bloody/broken/sad/upsetting/nauseating/vomitous happens, well, within this philosophy, none of that is *actually* happening, because—and this is the tricky part—we're all perfect and well at all times.

In the coming years, my dad will say out loud and with his silence, "Life is real. Death, an illusion." And so it follows, illness, problems, pain, an illusion.

So I'm 119 days old and this is my family. And these rapid breaths animate my lungs. We've hit sixty-three breaths per minute. So we load up the Griswold Family Truckster (our green wagon, wood paneling? or maybe Mom's old Mustang?) and head to the hospital. But we haven't just called the doctor. My parents have called our practitioner too. Her name is Margaret and she lives in Santa Monica, California. Calling the practitioner *and* the doctor isn't a proper thing for a traditional Christian Science couple to do, as doctors are a big no-no. But my parents aren't traditional. You'll see.

But it's this Christian Science metaphysical thing that got them together. David (my dad) and Joyce (my mom) met through my mother's practitioner, who helped her cure her ulcerative colitis. While Dad was the disillusioned Christian Scientist, Mom was the newbie. She had come upon the religion when the doctors labeled her condition incurable. She turned to Mary Baker Eddy, a nineteenth-century woman riddled with disease until she began to see a connection between her thoughts and her health. The way I figure it, Christian Science was the most alternative health care Mom could get her hands on in the late 1950s. So Mom read a lot of Mary Baker Eddy and her untreatable condition vanished. That would give anyone pause. But to my mom, unlike many by-the-book Christian Scientists, doctors weren't a big no-no. Western medicine just hadn't been able to help, so she'd gone searching.

So before hopping into the Griswold Family Truckster, Mom and Dad hadn't minded making that call to Margaret. They welcomed it. She'd do Mental Work on my behalf while they drove me to the emergency room. They wanted all the support they could get for their infant in distress.

From the view of a Christian Scientist, people fall sick when they forget the absolute perfection of God. So had my four-month-old self forgotten something already? If we were each "whole and complete," like they said, how had I made a mistake like getting sick already?

And if I'd *already* made a mistake at 119 days old . . .

2

LISTEN TO MARGARET LAIRD TAPES

PURPOSE: To become more spiritually clear.

DURATION: An hour-plus, easy.

EQUIPMENT NEEDED: Cassette player. Ours is a small Sony.

AGE: 5.

RELATIONSHIP STATUS: Daughter. Younger sister. Kindergartner.

COST: Free.

HUMILIATION FACTOR: Even at five, I feel some sense of shame for eavesdropping.

LOCATION: Corona del Mar, California.

Joyce and David often sit and talk to each other in their soft cream-colored velvety chairs in their bedroom. They can spend hours in there talking to each other. He, with his ever-present yellow legal pad; she, with a box of Kleenex. It doesn't always sound so good.

"Joyce, there is the Principle of Unconditional Love and we, in my estimation *(meaning she, I suspect, 'cause it sounds like he's mad)*, need to practice it more fully. Did you hear what Margaret said just now?"

"Wait, a minute, wait a minute," Mom says rather excitedly and positively. "There's this other idea that I hear in her words, that I'm just scratching the surface of . . . that . . . I can barely taste or get my words around . . . wait, yes, yes . . . about showing your . . . . wait, I haven't quite got it, let me . . . Let's listen to the tape again . . ."

Then there's a pause, and I hear this rather garbled, fuzzy voice (I'm hiding outside their room) now from the tape. Margaret sounds about eight hundred years old. And none of what she's saying makes any sense. It's like they're listening to a sorcerer or a foreign language. But with words like *Principle*, and *mortal mind*, and the *Scientific Statement of Being*. And *meaning* and *Truth* and . . .

They stop the tape.

"You hear that, you hear that right there?" Mom says again excitedly. I hear that garbled rewind and it starts again. Back with eight-hundred-year-old Margaret.

To be honest, it's not all that interesting. The only interesting bit is that I have no idea what they're talking about, which pulls at me. I don't like to feel left out of a conversation, even at five. Even grown-up conversations. Our next-door neighbors, the Spellmans, they don't talk like that. Their dad is a pilot for United, and goes and comes a lot. But talk meta-something-or-other? No way. Their house is full of four kids and laughter. Around here, I mostly hear this meta stuff. Because our family's kind of talk carries on through dinner.

My mother's dinner tables are works of art—centerpieces, literary themes with small books and objects corresponding to an idea—love, animals, holidays, nature, and so on. Beyond that, everything must be on a nice dish: whether pewter, or hand-thrown pottery, or lacy china. If we're hurried and need ketchup in a plastic bottle, we must hide it on the floor. But if the dinner table changes, their velvety-chair-meets-dinner-table conversations don't.

Next, my mother will be talking at the table about the way my father's left thumb sticks up when he eats with his right hand, means something.

"See that, David?" she says, pointing to his callused thumb while looking over her glasses at him, just as he overlooks his to her. I'd always liked his hands: strong, but they moved so smoothly when he did stuff.

"I've been reading that your thumb position means anger." Yes, she says something about anger. And then this word *defiance*, which sounds, I don't know, not good. Then she'll start talking about her own thumb.

"See how mine . . ." Now it seems like Mom is trying to joke, but it doesn't seem all that funny to Dad, who's starting to breathe strangely. "You see how mine is tucked inside my fist, all squelched and hidden?"

I look over at Dad and back to Mom. Dad starts these really long *Hmmms* under his breath, his square jaw clenching.

I look over at my own thumb and wonder at what it's doing. Mostly it just looks messy and as if it has been involved in a little too much Lawry's seasoned salt. I look at my sister's thumb. Renee and her ten-year-old blue-eyed, wavy-blond, freckle-nosed self is looking down at her food, saying nothing. Her left, noneating hand rests quietly out of sight.

3

TRANSCENDENTAL MEDITATION

PURPOSE: To cultivate a calm and open mind.

DURATION: Two times a day for twenty minutes.

EQUIPMENT NEEDED: I want a pint-sized kaftan.

AGE: 7 and a good reader. I'm really into *Harriet the Spy*.

RELATIONSHIP STATUS: The younger of two daughters in a four-person family. Plus one golden retriever. One cat.

EMPLOYMENT: Second grader. A full-time position.

COST: No idea what it cost for a kid-sized mantra back then. Now it costs $1,500-ish for an adult.

HUMILIATION FACTOR: Low.

LOCATION: Santa Ana, California.

It is Christmas. I've asked Santa for a mantra. While Mary Baker Eddy, Margaret Laird tapes, and Transactional Analysis continue to circulate our house, Mom still culls for more disciplines. Now we are on mantras. My sister wants one too. And Santa has granted us each our wish. My mother has made an appointment for my sister and me at the Transcendental Meditation center. I saw her write it down in her jumbola Bible-y book where she keeps all the important stuff.

It isn't your typical stocking stuffer. Even *I* know that. Usually in my stocking I'd find Silly Putty or a clove-covered orange shoved into the bottom. But I take my Christmas requests of Santa seriously. I'd thought about it for a while.

It started like this: Mom had been heading into the dining room regularly for twenty minutes a day. She crossed her bird legs in one of the dining room chairs, set a timer, and closed her eyes, her thin frame erect. Renee and I were to keep it down while the timer ticked, but I had to peek. I'd slide open the pocket doors as quietly as I could and peer in. It didn't look like the most comfortable position, all crossed up in that chair.

The first time she set the timer, I hung around the kitchen and waited for her return. When the bell rang, she did.

"What have you been doing in there?" I asked, reaching for an Otter Pop out of the freezer without asking.

"It's called meditation," she said, her voice filled with bubbles.

"What's it do?"

"It calms my mind." She stood over the sink washing her hands, tidying up to make dinner. New York strip steak. She hadn't caught on to the Otter Pop yet. Fine by me.

"Where'd you learn to do that?" I asked, hopping up on the counter for the scissors to open my Alexander the Grape purple pop.

"I went to the Maharishi and he gave me—"

"Maha-what?" The outside of Alexander felt sticky. I licked the plastic. I hated sticky hands.

"Maha-reee-sheee," she said turning to face me. "It means *teacher.*"

"Oh. And what did he do? What did he give you?"

"I asked him for a mantra."

"Why him? And what's a . . . why is he the teacher?"

"Some say he's wise. That he knows about the mind. Our crazy human minds . . . People might think you're too young to understand, but I don't. It's something to help you in your relationships. If I can give you anything, I hope it's that. Because you know, Megan"—she pauses for some of her own pretend sign language, her delicate fingers fluttering around her head—"when any of us has a problem, the best we can do is *never* look for someone else to fix it. The only person who you can *soothe* you is *you*."

Mom gazes out the side yard window as if looking for something, brushing her hair back behind her ears with a wet hand. At forty-five, she has decided to grow out her blond and go gray. She will grow that beautiful bright gray hair of elegant older models. All that gray made me worry. My parents were older than everybody else's.

"Have you fed Chumley yet?" she asked. Chumley was our golden retriever. It was Chumley's side yard. Chumley was her girl. Her right-hand woman. Her Godhead. Her Trueblood. Her peeps. Chubby and dignified.

"What does he know, exactly?" I asked.

"Megan, look at the mess you're making. Do you know what time it is? You're going to ruin your dinner."

"So this Maha—" I asked as she wiped me down head to toe at the sink. "Does he teach kids?"

"Not sure. You would need your own mantra."

"What's a mantra?"

And the questions went. I imagine Mom grew tired of them but did her best to answer. For all my parents' complicated talk with each other, they shared a nearly inexhaustible energy for dialogue. It made them both incredibly patient and engaging with questions, even a child's. Far more patient than any other parents I knew. And perhaps I understood that by asking them involved questions, I could get more of the contact I craved.

"Your mantra is a special phrase from the Maharishi. And the word itself, a secret. It's only for you. Or in my case, only for me. Would you please go find Chumley?"

To me it all sounded like magic. Feeling calm sounded good. I didn't know what she meant about the crazy human mind, though. Very mysterious. Like, why would you sit doing something that looks like nothing? There had to be more to it. So a mantra shot to the top of my Christmas list. If Mom liked it, maybe I would too.

I don't know how I knew this, but between my parents' two velvet chairs, the tapes, the groups of one kind or another Mom would bring into the house, a bunch of things about the world were going on that I didn't really get. Although I did already know life did not feel so easy—not inside myself anyway. Like, a new friend named Jennifer Jacques had invited me to my first big birthday party. My parents didn't know her part of Costa Mesa very well, the next town over, so we looked it up and did something they called a *dry run* to her party the day before. When the next day arrived, we knew exactly where to go. Present in hand and right on time, I knocked on the door. Turns out the day we'd practiced was the actual day of the party. I missed the whole thing.

Our house felt like that sometimes—like I'd just missed the party. I looked for clues about where that party might be, or at least how to move along without making dumb mistakes. I wondered if one clue might be what Mom did right beyond those pocket doors.

Christmas came and went, and Mom, Renee, and I drove half an hour (past Disneyland, if memory serves) to get it. From the freeway, I looked wistfully at the Matterhorn, fairly certain my mantra was not going to be *log ride* or *funnel cake*.

Renee was quiet. She, this other mystery I wanted to unravel. Much quieter than our neighbors or I, not as excited to play outside, like the Spellmans. Sometimes I would camp outside her open door, hoping to be asked in. I tried not to look too desperate. To play it cool. Other times, less cool.

For the mantra, we arrived at a rather plain office with an ugly brown couch. Two men greeted us who looked nothing like the Maharishi—no beard, no billowing robes. They looked more like twin Ken dolls. I had a Ken; you could glue small stickers on him in different facial-hair shapes—beards, mustaches, sideburns. These two looked like Kens with big sticker mutton-chop sideburns, brown suits/orange turtlenecks. Even to my seven-year-old self, I thought they looked like the geeky guys that pretty Marcia from *The Brady Bunch* refused to date.

One of them signaled a shy Renee into a smaller room. She obliged, pressing her Christmas purse to her chest like an airplane flotation device. The other Ken gave me some crayons and paper, asking me to draw a picture. I guessed that the drawing must be key to the mantra, and I intended to make my best picture ever. I sat on the couch and drew my favorite: a house with a chimney, curtains in the windows, happy people, a tree with a swing, a large yellow sun in the sky.

"Can I go to the bathroom?" I asked Mom.

"Do you really have to go?"

"I could hold it. But . . ." But I was bored.

"Then hold it. It will only be a bit."

Renee came out of the room and sat back on the couch with some relief. Purse, no longer gripped. Shoulders, relaxed. The Kens now invited me into the mystery room.

"Megan, we will give you what we call a *walking* mantra. We think it's better for younger people, such as yourself, to walk and meditate instead of sit."

"So no sitting?"

"That's right."

"No timer?"

"That's up to you."

Ken One looked at my hand-drawn masterpiece. I hoped they liked it. There seemed to be some deliberation. I felt like I was waiting to be picked for kickball. Ken One said something to Ken Two. They nodded and then spoke.

"Megan, your mantra is *Ing*."

"*Ing*?"

"Yes, *Ing*."

"*Ing*?" I asked again. For clarification. I moved *Ing* around in my mouth. Silently, of course.

Ing was a sound I knew something about. I knew about swim-ing, play-ing. So I accepted *Ing*. (Not that I knew how to reject.)

"Your sister—being five years older—has a different kind of mantra. She will sit with hers. Mantras are sacred, uniquely yours, and only to be known by you. More powerful that way."

That was it. Finished. I felt an urge to bow or at least bob my head like *I Dream of Jeannie*'s Jeannie. Once home, I took my word out for a spin.

"Ing. Ing. Ing," I announced to our driveway. My Spelman buddies, Julie and Tracy, were out on their bikes, but this was serious. No time for chitchat. I waved and kept going. I focused on the ground.

"Ing. Ing. Ing." I exited the neighborhood past the mailbox. I often tried to peer in to see the letters inside that big blue box. Sometimes I dropped in mustard flowers for the postman. An unexpected party favor in what I imagined as a very boring trip. No time for that now.

"Ing. Ing. Ing." I pressed on.

"Ing. Ing. *Ing.*" Past the neighborhood pool and the power plant across the street. It buzzed and crackled.

"Ing. Ing." I was to use *Ing* for twenty minutes a day. I figured I was at twenty minutes. I asked myself, did I feel different?

I wasn't sure. But maybe, just *maybe*, I found it a little relaxing. It gave me something to do, just with myself. Sometimes I said it over and over on my bike. I didn't set a timer or anything. I'd just say it. Renee said I shouldn't do it on my bike.

I was irritated not to know Renee's word, dying to feel her word inside my head. But she refused. For decades, I attempted to extract her mantra. At twenty-eight, I was still at it. As adults, Renee and I remained as different as night from day, as if we had developed our differences in direct opposition to the other. Like one attenuated argument. Her introvert to my extrovert. Her voluptuousness to my skinny. Her short hair to my long. Her silence to my jokes. Her tidy wallet to my junk show of a purse. Her red state to my blue. Her solitude to my pack of girly friends. Her solid to my gas.

Okay, forget that last one, her kestrel to my hummingbird.

Around twenty-eight, we were driving to LA together to pick up God-knows-whom from the airport.

"Renee, would you please, *please* tell me your mantra. Who's it going to hurt? It's not like you even *use* it."

"No, Megan. It's the principle," she says, clipping me. She lays a bit heavier on the gas pedal. We're pushing seventy.

Jesus, all this talk about Principle. *Principle* with a capital *P.* I was sick of it. I eyed her purse. Something about her tone made me want to root around in there for private things.

"And you never know, I may want to use it later. No kidding, Megan."

"Come on," I say, giving her shoulder a bit of a punch.

"Ow, Megan, that hurt!" She kind of growls, then punches back.

And so begins a round of bizarre—and not pain-free—fisticuffs. A rapid-fire one-arm boxing match. Her stupid Coach purse between us. Renee, with the advantage of her dominant right arm. Mine, a paltry left. We mutually unload on each other's shoulders as we accelerate past a Hyundai, a Honda, or a Lexus or two. I'm getting scared. Then, snap, as if some invisible force of reason hovers atop Renee's car, we each retreat. It's not over, but we've realized this is idiotic.

I still wanted to know her word. Yet I could feel her refusal as if bolted to the driver's seat. The car. The road. The molten lava beneath the earth. She was pissed. She seemed as wedded to the secret of the mantra as if it were our grandmother Deany's wedding ring.

It always scared me when Renee got angry. Her *No* door had always closed far more tightly than mine. I wasn't sure I even had a *No* door.

It terrified me, infuriated me, and had my secret admiration all at once. I always craved a wide-open-door policy with her. But nobody likes a door forced open, least of all Renee.

But as Renee headed north up the 405 from Newport to LAX, it occurred to me. I could break the family code without her permission. While I couldn't control whether Renee told me hers, no one prevented me from telling her mine.

To be fair—to give Renee a running start should she choose to bolt—I announced:

"I am going to tell you my mantra."

I had grown weary of so many rules. That's the thing about every discipline. There's often a format, a belief that if you don't follow the structure to the tiniest detail, you won't get maximum value: mantras are private. *Om* is the most perfect sound in the universe. Never lay a sacred text to chant on the floor. If you are in a seminar, always wear a name tag. Put your name in the upper-right-hand corner of every essay. Do what scares you. Make a life plan. Don't make plans, stay in the moment. Just breathe. No, scream. No, cry or hit something. But don't lose yourself. Never do yoga on the full moon. Walk clockwise around a temple. Don't eat protein and starch in the same meal. Always begin the day with fruit. Don't eat any fruit. Never utter the word of G_d. There is no God. There are multiple gods. To be a good acupuncturist, "check your stuff" at the door. Bring all of you. Never do work on the Sabbath. Don't carry anything in your pockets. Consciousness is constant work. Accept Jesus. Read the Bible. There is no suffering. Acknowledge suffering as a noble truth. Tread lightly on the Earth. Leave no trace. Make your mark. Get noticed. Travel silently through life. Attend to the needs of others. Follow your bliss. Suppress. Express. Withhold. Let go. Let it in. Get off the grid. Join the marketplace. Go toward the light. *Hadn't I heard enough?*

"My word is *Ing*," I told Renee. "Ing. Ing. Ing. Ing."

"No, no . . . Wait, what?" She stammered. "That's your *word*?" Her voice, nearly a groan.

"Ing. Ing. Ing. Ing. Ing."

"Wait, no. Honestly, that's your *mantra*?" Renee's eyes widened.

"Inggggggggg!!!"

"No, that can't be. That's *my* word. *Ing* is *my* mantra," she said angrily.

Turns out we shared a secret.

God. We must have more in common than I thought.

4

TRANSACTIONAL ANALYSIS

PURPOSE: To feel good. To do good. To not feel bad. To not do bad.

DURATION: Less of a measurable time thing. More of a way of thinking.

EQUIPMENT NEEDED: *I'm OK—You're OK* by Thomas Harris, 1969.

AGE: 8.

RELATIONSHIP STATUS: Younger sister; best friend to my neighbor Julie Spellman.

EMPLOYMENT: Mostly spy work around the neighborhood, etc.

COST: Nothing monetary.

HUMILIATION FACTOR: Depends on when you give up, I guess.

LOCATION: 2801 Blue Water Drive, Corona del Mar, California.

I want a Warm Fuzzy. Mom says the easiest way to feel a Warm Fuzzy—instead of a Cold Prickly—is to give one.

"You can't control what anyone else does or gives, but you can control what *you* give." She says this a lot.

I want one for Renee. But my delivery ideas aren't working out so great. A drawing? A song? A game?

Renee and I are upstairs, doing what Dad calls supervising ourselves because they're both at work. She, at the Children's Bookshoppe; he, at his machine shop and office.

I walk down the hall and look into Renee's room to check for occupancy. I need her permission to enter. Those are the rules. The Cold Prickly rules.

She has a kind of big closet, more like a little room. There's just enough space to sit in it surrounded by her shoes and clothes. I love how her closet smells. Kind of like warm food. It just smells like her, kind of strong but soft. Dad says he loved how his dad smelled because even though he had strong BO, it meant that his dad was near.

Renee's closet feels like that. Like she's near. I hang out there sometimes if she's not home. Or I'll look at her records, or lie on her bed, her yellow-and-green comforter our grandmother Deany made her. I love to look up and see what she sees, just the popcorn ceiling really, just like mine.

But right now, she's in—in her rocking chair, under a stained-glass window she made that reads *Renee's Comfy Corner*. She's knitting. She might love rocking even more than knitting.

"That looks cool," I say. "What you're making. Can I help?" *That seems like a Warm Fuzzy, right? Helping?* "Maybe I can hold the yarn and you can restring it around my hands."

"Not now." She keeps rocking, not looking up, her auburn locks hiding most of her face. "I just need to be by myself."

I don't like this idea. *Ever.*

"Can't I just come in and watch?"

I sit down as if there's a line at the door. Like in *I Love Lucy* when Lucy and Ricky divide up their apartment with tape, and never cross into the other's side.

"No, Megan. Just no." She seems mad.

I sit outside my imaginary line, just outside it.

"Are you sure?" She doesn't answer. She keeps rocking. Knitting and rocking.

I draw pictures in the carpet. A house. A tree. My name. Her name. I kinda want to look like I'm busy, like I'm not embarrassed she doesn't want to let me in.

I can be here if I wanna be, right? The hallway is a free zone. She doesn't own the hallway.

But what if . . . your person doesn't want a Warm Fuzzy? How do you give it anyway? She looks sad. Like she feels cold and prickly. Like the yarn is the most interesting thing in the room. And she must be cold; she's knitting a hat. Maybe I should just sit here and figure it out. Or maybe she'll change her mind. Let me cross over.

Mom says it's like the book says, that no matter what, I'm okay, you're okay.

I don't think I feel okay if she's not okay. And she doesn't look okay. Okay?

5

COLOR AND PAST-LIFE READING

PURPOSE: To find out the auras and past lives of our extended family.

DURATION: A series of readings take place at our house.

EQUIPMENT NEEDED: Psychic/aura people say we each have an aura that radiates roughly twelve inches beyond the body with a preponderant color. As for past lives, they say we each have had many lives and that some people on Earth can see/read them.

AGE: 8.

RELATIONSHIP STATUS: Depends on which life we're talking about. Do fairies have relationships?

COST: No idea. Grandmother Deany footed the bill. Based on contemporary knowledge of psychic fees, I bet the psychic got a few hundred dollars. People shuttled in and out all day.

HUMILIATION FACTOR: The entire family's doing it, so barely any. But we aren't shouting it from the rooftops or anything.

LOCATION: Our house.

There's a line forming up the stairs past my room. Mom and Deany have made a whole day of this for our extended family on Dad's side. I have a lot of relatives, we northern European mutts. Three aunts and fifteen cousins. Not that everyone is here, but it's a good showing. It's like voting day, but with each cousin waiting for a turn to enter our den instead of a booth. Mom has put a whole spread out replete with nibbles and fruits, so it feels more like a party. Despite not having a lot of parties (we of the David and Joyce Griswold clan kind of keep to ourselves), Mom knows how to make people feel welcome and is always genuinely interested in her guests.

Our dog, Chumley, is known to have gotten a few paws in some of Renee's and my birthday cakes, so I'm to monitor the back door to make sure it's closed. I head out with Chumley to think. I just had my turn with Nancy, our aura and past-life reader. She is large, gray-haired, and (I privately suspect) in love with my aunt. Nancy's teaching my aunt Glady to see and read auras too. Nancy wears a purple blouse with fanlike arms to either make room for her girth or to conjure a large winged mammal. Aunt Glady has a build like Nancy's, but with a masculine twist. While Mom is tiny, my dad's sisters are taller and larger. So when Aunt Glady laughs, her belly shakes. She always sounds about two minutes from expiring. I suspect it's all her cigarettes.

But to the readings: my mother and father had been lovers in the time of the pharaohs. My father left Egypt to travel with Moses. Mom stayed behind as a slave. Their timing, Nancy said, was a bit off. Dad had to follow his teacher, the aforementioned Moses. And Mom felt loyal to her Egyptian queen.

Mom says Dad going off to follow Moses sounded like him. Being game to cross the Red Sea and all. I had some trouble picturing him with a beard and dusty sandals in a gunny sack robe. He was more of a close-shaven, properly combed, suit-and-tie kind of guy. And he didn't smell dusty. He smelled like the metal and oil of a machine shop. Red Sea or otherwise, she says, he gets very excited about his next big business idea. Mom isn't as into taking risks. That's one of the things they talk about in their chairs. They pretend like they aren't trying to change each other. But I know what it sounds like when Mom or Dad is upset with me. And they often sound just like that.

In a different past life—I expect a few centuries later (Nancy wasn't big on the time line)—Mom and Renee were fellow Buddhist-Taoist-Shinto nuns together in Asia. I'm not certain of their exact denomination, but they were nuns and friends and somewhere on the Asian continent and shared a nun lifestyle. I bet they were good nun buddies. Mom would love the nun homework, and my sister would have excelled in the prayer position. And they both adore ponchos. Deany had one life with my mother as well. I'm jealous.

As it turns out, a few lives back, my father had killed my aunt Glady, which to Glady—never a huge fan of my father—this explained a lot. They'd been fighting silently for years. My father, the black sheep, leaving the family valve business and church. I got a different sort of past-life update.

I settle into our giant leopard beanbag. Nervous to hear, I tuck my arms under my knees, not all splayed out like normal. Nancy's in a chair, as I think if she got down in the bag with me, she'd never get out. I imagine she knows this.

This beanbag is still the heart of our house, where Mom read us *Winnie-the-Pooh* and *The Wind in the Willows* and every other great book she brings home from the Children's Bookshoppe, where she's worked for years. We're getting into older books like *Bridge to Terabithia*. It's so cozy that Dad sometimes falls asleep when we're doing it.

"You were a fairy," Nancy says. "A blue fairy. Fairies often live on or near mushrooms. . . . Do you like mushrooms?"

"What?"

"That means this is your first time on planet Earth."

"My first what?" I look up at her quizzically. If I were bolder, I would ask to start over.

"Megan, I'm getting . . . this is your first time on the planet, what we call Earth. There are other names, but . . ."

"What? Did you ask if I like mushrooms? I don't like eating them, particularly. But I . . ."

"Yes . . . Do you like mushrooms?"

"I have dreamed about them . . . about . . . being upset when people kick dirt on them, like ones on edges of trails with spotted tops . . ."

". . . Ah . . . yes. I see." Nancy was closing and fluttering her eyes strangely.

"Did you say this is my first time here? Are you sure it isn't *Renee's* first? Or my Mom's? Maybe Deany's?"

Maybe my aunt Donny. Dad's oldest sister was downstairs. She always seemed a little arty and out there, with lots of floral, laughter, and oil painting.

I loved how she laughed. I liked her. I didn't know if I felt *like* her but I *liked* her. I didn't like this alone business.

"I won't talk about others but I can tell you, I'm getting this strongly."

Why is it I have to be the only one new to the planet? It matched how I felt, but I didn't like hearing it. I don't want to sound like I think I'm special, because I know everybody is, so I don't like this topic—feeling different. But when I feel sad, my crying feels big and comes out with a roar. When I laugh, it comes louder and faster than the rest and seems harder to stop. When I don't understand something, I *really* don't understand, and my questions are always longer and more complicated. It's embarrassing. I don't particularly like this about myself. I mean, sure, it feels good to laugh. But I often seem to feel things are funnier when funny, sadder when they are sad, and more confusing when confused. I worry I tire my parents out. But I can't seem not to ask. When I try to be quiet, I seem to not do that as unnoticeably as the quiet people. Suddenly somebody wants to know why I'm so quiet.

When I told Mom, Dad, and Renee at dinner this new-to-the-planet stuff, they slowly nodded. Mom said, "Of course. That absolutely makes sense."

They laughed and looked at each other like they'd heard something that made them feel really smart. I didn't like thinking it was all that funny. Feeling exposed, I studied Renee. More than laugh-y, she looked downtrodden, as if her sandy blond waves would droop from the discussion. Looking back, what I guess Renee heard was: *Megan is different, Megan is special.* All I heard was: *Megan's on the outside, trying very hard to get in*, wherever *in* is.

What do they mean that *it absolutely made sense*? And what about this other aura stuff? Nancy says I'm a Yellow. But everybody else was far cooler colors— Blues and Violets. Nancy says Yellows want to bring joy to others and have tremendous energy. Drawn to creative endeavors, supposedly Yellows pick fields like writing, comedy, healing arts, outdoorsy stuff like park rangers (honestly, specifically park rangers?), and athletic pursuits. They often have more than one profession in their lives as they like variety and are health nuts. And their biggest fear? Abandonment.

Also, Nancy explains Yellows are natural healers—something about that unusual volume of energy. Apparently, I can put it to good use. She instructs me rather ominously:

"One last thing," she says as she leans down into the beanbag and into my eyes. "Should you ever find yourself near a car accident, put your hands gently on the injured party ever so subtly."

What am I supposed to say: "Stand back! I'm a Yellow"? I should be writing this stuff down. *Energy. New to planet. Hands.*

I'm not totally alone on the fairy front, though. Deany says she has a guardian angel named Kesela who has saved her from numerous mishaps. I'm not sure I believe her, but I kind of do. She mentions Kesela often, like it's the most normal thing in the world. If Deany wasn't an actual fairy, at least she knew one. Angel, fairy—what's the difference. And like me, Deany's loud, and her laughs are big and slobbery. And she tells the best stories. Among them: a near fall off a cliff before Kesela yanked her to safety. Maybe being a blue fairy is something like that. And I *did* have that dream about mushrooms . . .

But if I was a blue fairy, I didn't understand why I was a Yellow-aura human now. To get the most out of the deal, I brought Nancy a big baseball-card stack of my friends' school photos. Mom said if there was time, Nancy could run through the photos to identify my friends' auras. I wasn't sure I believed this color business, but how did you prove there *weren't* auras? My scientific method: to see if the description of the colors matched my friends. Most of my friends were Blues, which is supposedly somehow opposite of a Yellow. My entire family is Blue, except Dad, who's Violet. Blues are super spiritual but have a hard time taking love in or something. They say Blue parents unconsciously try to get their kids to be dependent on them. Violets are visionary and powerful, and kind of out there. Yep. That fits. I try to remember the formulas of the color wheel. Nancy says it means my insides are the same as what my friends and family show on the outside. Like Blues are emotional and nurturing, whereas Yellows hide that direct care and emotion and help by being entertaining or bringing energy to the group. Blue sounds better—more serious. I would rather be a nurturing Blue than feel like I'm loud or from another planet, or too bright and Yellow like the sun, and make people squint or turn away. I don't want to be forgotten, but I'd rather not stick out, either. I fear I'm too much. Like I came out of Mom raring to go and I'm too loud, too sad, too happy—too too.

At least I'm not a Crystal. Grandpa Don is Crystal. Crystal is like *no* color, which is bad. Nancy told Deany that Grandpa Don is in denial of his color—which makes him Crystal somehow. But apparently there's a cure for it. Deany makes him sleep in pink sheets to compensate.

6

EST CHILDREN'S TRAINING[1]

PURPOSE: It's all a little hazy now. I'm supposed to come out of this different.

DURATION: Four days.

EQUIPMENT NEEDED: Name tags, uncomfortable conference chairs, and a vivid imagination. Lucky me.

AGE: 12. The age range is 5 to 12. The bulk of the kids are on the young side.

RELATIONSHIP STATUS: A guy named Peter asked me to *go* with him. I didn't answer right away. He got impatient. I told him if he didn't like me enough to wait for my answer, then the answer was no.

EMPLOYMENT: Standard chores—room cleaning, dishwasher, homework, piano.

COST: Around $500.

HUMILIATION FACTOR: Has real potential.

LOCATION: Phoenix, Arizona. Some industrial park. Classic conference room arranged theater style: a stage, a sketchpad, an easel, and a director's chair for the trainer.

---

[1] Aka the Forum or Landmark Forum Education; the names and offerings have changed over the years.

Mom and Dad have finished their EST training in Newport Beach, California. The vibe of it? Honestly, a little culty minus the Kool-Aid. Werner Erhard is the founder, and our family will become friends with one of his brothers, who is tall, likable, and not able to keep it in his pants. EST stands for either Erhard Seminars Training or "it is" in Latin. Their training takes place at the Orange County Fairgrounds. I go to their graduation. It is all very smiley. Apparently, the course entailed various confessions to secret abortions or somebody not feeling connected to their father, and this has produced a bond among the graduates that I don't fully understand. The stated goals: to be more effective in relationships, make better decisions, develop integrity and awareness. Done in a group of seventy-five to two hundred people.

By the time graduation rolls around, I feel the "enthusiasm" from the staff to enroll new people. High-pressure sales; even at twelve, I can feel it. So I'm all signed up to do it. Maybe I'm game because I've always loved the fairgrounds. I love how you can smell the horses.

A few months later I sit nowhere near the Orange County Fairgrounds, but in Phoenix with a roomful of kids in my own training. My mother likes to say I choose to do these things for myself. Admires me for it. But really, does a cow in the herd choose to get branded? My mom believes in the Unique Cow, the *Jonathan Livingston Seagull* Independent Cow that chooses to fly (or moo) their own way. We have that Seagull book all over the house.

Days earlier we (Mom, Dad, Renee, my friend Kimberly, and her far hipper and much younger parents Gary and Marilyn) had driven our Bluebird motorhome to Arizona to do it. My family's idea of a vacation.

Now settled into the Children's Training, Joanne the trainer introduces us to our next exercise: the Danger Process. To conjure what most scares us. I know that one easily: finding my parents dead in some freakishly twisted car accident.

I've always worried about that—my parents dying before I'm grown. Kimberly's mother is about twenty years younger than mine. Maybe I worry because my mother has gray hair. Nobody's mother has gray hair. It makes her seem more fragile than other mothers.

Joanne tells us to pick a spot on the ground, lie down, and get talked through the Process.

"First, we need for you to create a safe space to go inside yourself should you become too frightened."

I build a white room with beautiful textured walls with deep swirls. My version has four large windows—one on each wall. And somewhere—inside or outside the room—is a palette of rainbows.

"Please bring the danger up now. Bring up your issue. What does it feel like? What does it smell like? What does it sound like?"

On my back in the dark, the carpet feels itchy and smells like plastic, but in my mind, I conjure the crash. The call from the police. Me slumped over my parents' corpses trying to will them back to life, yet unable. The crash site. The smell of gasoline and burning flesh. The sound of the cop cars and ambulances. My parents trapped within the twisted metal of their sedan. Firemen attempting to pull them out with matching Jaws of Life.

"What's the feeling? Express the feeling. Do you need to scream? Make that sound."

What kids lack in emotional experience they make up for in imagination and lack of inhibition. Within minutes, a room full of children cry and beg for help in the dark.

The momentum builds and soon, really, the most terrifying thing happening in the exercise is the bloodcurdling screams and sobs coming from seventy-five five- to twelve-year-olds. Chaos of the highest order.

A chorus of "Mommy! Mommy!" weaving through "Daddy! Daddy!" With your standard "Help!" as a refrain. The all-important "No!" like a baseline anchoring us to the floor. Put it together and you've got a cacophony of "Mommy, No, Daddy! Help, help me!" shooting up from the carpet, ricocheting across the room, and crashing back into my chest. Pure bedlam.

Somehow Joanne has to wind this fucker down before some five-year-old has an aneurysm. It takes longer to calm everybody down than it did to ramp us up.

"Okay, now let's go back to our safe spaces. That's right. Very good. Very good."

Some kids keep crying. The room feels smaller than it did before. I have no idea how long it lasted. It could have been half an hour. It could have been two. The lights get turned back on as kids slowly get up. The little ones rub their eyes, wiped out. I'm exhausted. If I were a valve, somebody opened me all the way up, and I feel bigger, wider. More water or emotion had pumped through me than I'd ever felt. Maybe it was okay to have all that emotion I spent so much time trying to keep organized. In the strangest way, I took up more space or could feel the edges of my body more clearly now, which I found oddly relaxing, especially for someone who feared feeling too much. But if the valve had opened, I couldn't tell if I'd closed it back up right. I thought I might still be leaking. Shouldn't they have shown me how to close it? I kept picturing those Jaws of Life—feeling so alone without my parents, wondering why I couldn't get to them. And then I remember. My parents weren't, in fact, dead, but would pick me up at the end of this session tonight. That's the weirdest bit. It's all so intense and then it's dinner. I don't feel wrapped up. I feel raw. But not just raw. I'm hungry.

I hope we go for Mexican. Maybe they'll take us back to that spot in Old Town where if you walk in wearing a tie, they cut it off and hang it from the ceiling.

7

FAMILY COMMUNICATION EXERCISE

PURPOSE: No bloody idea. We practice whatever technique Mom and Dad learned in this weekend's metaphysical and/or self-improvement workshop.

DURATION: Varies. Typically, one to two hours.

EQUIPMENT NEEDED: Chairs, clock. Timer—even better.

AGE: 13.

RELATIONSHIP STATUS: We have a trampoline in our backyard, so a lot of the neighborhood hangs out here. I try to play with Renee, but she still keeps to herself mostly. So I hang out with my friends Brett and Nessa.

COST: Free. But the original seminar probably cost around $300.

HUMILIATION FACTOR: Moderate. You can only be so embarrassed by your family.

LOCATION: Our living room.

My mother has informed us that tonight we'll have a family seminar in the living room.

"Since your dad and I finished the communication workshop, we thought we would work on our communication, what with our second Pinch challenge."

The Pinch: our word (aka understatement) for a financial hardship in a failed business venture of Dad's when I was little. We're in our next one. Dad dreams of alternate fuel possibilities and cheese. He's leveraged it all (the house, his small business, our savings) to build a cheese whey factory to produce both ethanol and cheese. It requires Danish investors, Irish technology, and, for some reason, the purchase of Desi Arnaz's ranch in Corona, California. To say my father is risk-friendly and my mother risk-averse would be an understatement.

It's weird between my parents. Each seems afraid that the other is in charge of their fate as a couple. It's like a confusing game of tennis where nobody can figure out whose turn it is to serve. Maybe if we actually *did* things together (you know, *activities*) instead of talk about *communication* ad nauseam, we (or maybe they) would actually feel closer, but nobody's asking me. Not yet, anyway. Maybe I'll bring it up at tonight's workshop.

Mom gathers us in the living room, directing us like a hostess on a game show about to display the prizes behind curtain number one. The room is being remodeled, but slowly—so it's a bit of a construction zone. Out of money after phase one, it's now a project in two parts until we can afford phase two. My mom has chosen a thick Mexican tile but was sick of the pea-soup-green carpet (I don't blame her), so she's ripped it up. So we sit in a cement-floored living room on a pea-soup-green couch surrounded by velvety green wallpaper.

Renee and I settle in because we know the drill. We know we are going to be here for an uncomfortably long time. I'm guessing an hour and a half, two tops. My aunt Donny says as a family, we spend more time talking about where we'll eat dinner than they did about where, or if, my cousin Kenny would go to college. Despite the ribbing, I'm putting my hope in the workshop. Doesn't wanting to connect mean we *are* connected? I hope so.

"So now," Mom says with a formality in her voice as if leading a roomful of *actual* seminarians, "we're going to do an exercise in simultaneous dialogue. One of us will call out colors and the other will match the calls. The goal: to pay so much attention to our partner that the exact same words will come out of both our mouths simultaneously."

"David," Mom asks, "should we go first?"

Dad clears his throat.

"Is there anything about the exercise," she asks Dad, "that you would like to add?"

"Hmmmm." (He makes this sound a lot.) "I believe that our judgments can really get in the way of truly listening and prevent us from understanding *what's really going on*." Those may be his four favorite words. (My parents like to talk in code. Now they are talking about each other.)

"*Exactly*," Mom says. "And people can feel highly unsupported when they aren't heard."

Dad sits down on one of the dining room chairs he's dragged in across the cement. Mom follows. They face each other, the knees of their jeans almost touching.

"So your father will call out colors and I will open myself to say the exact same words to really *hear* him."

Dad:	Blue.
Mom:	Blue.
Dad:	Blue.
Mom:	Blue.
Dad:	Yellow.
Mom:	Yellow.
Dad:	Green.
Mom:	Green.

They're building speed.

> Blue.
> Blue.
> Orange.
> Orange.
> Green.
> Blue. I mean green.
> Green.

And then it happens. They are speaking colors in unison. No longer two blues, but one. One yellow, one green, one orange—said in stereo across Windsor chairs. They stop and look over at Renee and me.

"Why don't you two try it now?" Mom asks, her hands presenting the chairs like Vanna White. Renee's eyes dart when nervous, as if surveying any scene for safety. She's darting.

While speaking in unison is odd, I like the idea. Like a trance. We take their seats. Dad sets his stopwatch. Ready. Set. Go. I focus on Renee's mouth. I feel like I'm at the starting blocks of a footrace, but with lip gloss. She begins the color shouts as we stare at each other: red, red; green, green; blue, blue.

I feel this anxiety, this heat, this adrenaline inside me as I stare only at her mouth as it forms these words. The staring tonight is less intense than some of the other exercises we've done. With this one, we don't have to stare in silence into each other's eyes. With eye-focused exercises, I've stared so hard at my sister's face, it would distort. Her perfectly straight elegant nose would start to grow. Her dusting of freckles blurs.

Her bee-stung lips inflate.

On the upside, this is the most time we've spent together in a while. If we had to stare at each other shouting the color wheel for quality one-on-one, fine by me.

But tonight, amid the red and the green and this blue, there is a nanosecond of a moment where my sister and I look at each other and smile underneath our serious faces—just to each other. While we live down the hall from one another, we're normally worlds apart. Yet now, without ever saying a word, and despite the miles of distance between us, there is an understanding.

That we are caught in something odd—earnest, but odd. And each of us knows the other will follow along as best she can. If we perform the exercise well enough, perhaps it will help bring these silently warring parties closer to a truce. This is part of our unspoken sisterly pact. One part of each of us hopes this workshop will somehow help our family, and the other is a silent bond like hostages with a shared fate.

The job is not merely to endure the debrief, but to find ways to bring the exercise to a unified and pleasing end. Renee will do so with silence. I will scan the debrief for points where Mom and Dad might agree. If anything my father says sounds remotely similar to what my mother says, I echo like a Greek chorus.

Tonight the crevasse between them feels too wide. No point in even my best Greek chorus. It would only echo the distance. I look down at my Miss Piggy watch. *The Love Boat* is on. I'm missing it. I love *The Love Boat*. No conflict that enormous vessel can't cut through. One hour, four plotlines, and everything always works out in the end—and partway through, everybody gets time by the pool with a pretty umbrella drink.

"Joyce," my father says, "what we need to come to some understanding about is that we each have our own highest sense of right."

Oh, God, it's the Highest Sense of Right talk. I look down at my watch again. I notice a small scratch on the face. I hadn't noticed that before. My perfect little watch is no longer pristine. *How did this happen? When did it happen?* I'd been trying to be so careful.

"Can I please be excused?" I ask.

Dad looks startled, so focused on talking, I suspect he's forgotten anybody else is in the room.

"May you . . . ? Joyce, are we good with letting them go?"

Mom is caught up in something. The last fifteen minutes have gotten thicker. The nights always get thicker.

"Yes, you may go," she says, not looking at us as she lifts her glasses to wipe her eyes. *Why is there never Kleenex around when you need it? This room is definitely in need of a box.*

"Joyce, what you don't understand . . ."

"But David, not to be negative, I just . . ."

We will leave my parents as we do—to their words. Renee and I exit and head down the stairs to the family room. We both want to know what cruise director Julie McCoy is up to. She's so cute and bubbly. We don't yet know that in real life she's addicted to cocaine.

It's commercials. But we still have a half hour of Mazatlán to catch. Maybe I'll go bring a roll of toilet paper back into the living room. Maybe I can skulk in, make the toilet paper delivery to Mom and skulk right back out unnoticed.

It could go either way. All I know is neither Renee nor I utters a word. About any of it.

8

CONSCIOUS TERMINOLOGY

PURPOSE: Refers to a practice, like many in our house, to make our behavior more self-aware. Specifically, this describes the term *Communication Withhold*: an act of nonverbal antagonism wherein one party opts not to share some piece of vital information with a second party.

DURATION: A constant. A day-in, day-out, year-in, year-out sort of thing.

EQUIPMENT NEEDED: A tolerance for terms and phrases you can't find in the dictionary.

AGE: 14.

RELATIONSHIP STATUS: I like going to high school dances, but that's it. Dancing. No making out. My own rule.

COST: Free. But the seminar where the phrase was taught cost a few hundred dollars.

HUMILIATION FACTOR: Low. More fear than embarrassment.

LOCATION: Anywhere where we talk to each other (house, car, grocery store, elevator, etc.).

The day my father fell off the roof, my mother was convinced it was because he had a *Communication Withhold*. This term was regularly thrown around our house as readily as other families called out that it was time for dinner.

At any one time, one or all of us were in a seminar gathering new terms. The main goal was to make new life commitments. The most common: a circular commitment to enrolling new people. I'd signed up to do a weekly evening of cold calls to unregistered seminarians. Like fund-raising for the Red Cross minus the charity bit. The whole thing conflicted me. On the one hand, I felt pride in working alongside full-fledged adults. On the other, I was bursting with shame for being extremely ineffective at my job. My fourteen-year-old voice didn't help. I was even more ineffective at hiding how badly I wanted to be good at something that simultaneously made me feel dirty. I was terrible at pretending (the adults were far better) that we weren't pressuring people, when we were. This was my Withhold. The enrollment manager insisted it wasn't sales. Rather, we were *helping others see the possibility of themselves.* As fishy as it smelled in that sterile office, I kept repeating my manager's words, thinking that if I dug deep enough, the pressure vibe would drop away and both caller and callee would be transformed. Like magic. Like alchemy. Water into wine.

Another Withhold: I wondered if all this business explained why I chose to memorize every lyric in the musical *The Music Man*, a story about a people-pleasing con artist and the sincere people who put hope in his tune.

I wasn't sure if I was connee or conner. But all four of us found ourselves in a chorus of awkward proclamations in the name of self-betterment. We were *manifesting possibilities* and *stepping into openings* in lieu of more intimate talk. Getting close to difficult emotions was merely the awkward bit to make way for our new life-changing commitments. Perhaps it was perfect for us. We worshipped at the Church of Ideas. Not that I was sure what our ideas were, but ideas kept us from dealing directly with our tender underbellies. We didn't have to address why Renee was holed up in her room or why Dad had to chase his next big idea, or what drove Mom to search. Or how I nominated myself the clown who tried to joke and prod about our messy emotional stuff.

Honestly, church sounded easier. With less recruitment. If my religion was to register strangers or develop wit to attempt connection, my mother's was more visceral. She had committed to *not* take pain pills or antibiotics in the middle of a urinary tract infection. Like me, I suspect she imagined if she/

we dropped deeper into whatever-it-was-we-were-dropping-into, then her/our pain would vanish. Perhaps her motivation was an homage to her doctor-free Christian Science ideas—a trait Mom and Dad still shared. They could both have twins-y severed torsos in an auto accident and decide to just lie there in the road indefinitely, agreeing that the severing was just a mild misunderstanding.

But I worried. Mom felt fragile in a way I didn't fully understand—so willing to wrestle alone, turning only to disciplines and classes. It didn't seem right for her to endure avoidable pain, like the UTI, for no reason. But you aren't supposed to counsel your parents. *Everybody* knows that.

Yet I admired her earnest humility. We repeated with fondness a family war story about the time she withstood a multihour verbal firing squad of one when a seminar leader insisted she acknowledge she was a *bitch* for requesting a bathroom break for the entire group. She must have uttered the phrase "I *get* that I'm a bitch," at the trainer's prompting dozens of times, in dozens of tones, each announcement more sincere than the last.

To me, a proper Communication Withhold might be Mom not saying, "I don't know how to get close to you, Dave, but I so love you." Or Dad not admitting, "I'm furious, Joyce, that you don't support my business risks." Or mine could be, "Could we make some family friends or just do fun stuff together? Plant a garden? Have a barbecue?" Instead we withheld.

But when it comes to Communication Withholds, sometimes falling off the roof maybe *is* just falling off the roof. My father went up there to put up Christmas lights. He was dressed in his rather tight blue sweat suit, stretched across his generous girth, upon which my sister had embroidered the words *The Big Cheese*, with a large piece of Swiss cheese appliquéd across his chest.

From inside the house my mother and I heard this startling:

Rumble, rumble, smash. Rumble, rumble, smash.

He rolled off the first roof, landed on the second, then tumbled down through the clothesline, the trash cans, and then onto the twelve-foot wooden ladder that somehow broke his fall.

We ran out toward the ruckus and found him on his back, moaning, with the large piece of cheese heaving up and down as he struggled to regain his breath. And my mother, more frightened than angry, standing over him in her *Apple a Day* sweatshirt, yelling to my father's belly cheese:

DAVID, I'M CERTAIN YOU HAVE A COMMUNICATION
WITHHOLD. I'M CERTAIN THERE IS SOMETHING YOU
ARE NOT COMMUNICATING WITH ME. AND BECAUSE
YOU DIDN'T COMMUNICATE WITH ME, YOU CHECKED
OUT AND FELL OFF THE ROOF.

But my father—with the wind knocked out of him, his glasses catawampus—
appeared hard-pressed to think of what that little tidbit of communication
could possibly be. And my mother—because she was *not* a bitch—helped him
limp to the bed anyway. Because that's what you do when someone you love
falls off the roof.

But you do have a living room seminar the next day to get at the Withhold.

9

FANTASIZE

PURPOSE: Something Mom and I do to entertain ourselves.

DURATION: We do this all the time. Takes anywhere from twenty minutes to two hours.

EQUIPMENT NEEDED: Car for cruising.

AGE: 14.

RELATIONSHIP STATUS: It's mostly Mom and me. Dad travels constantly in pursuit of his cheese whey ethanol factory dream. And Renee's off to college.

EMPLOYMENT: Still cold calling.

COST: Our hobby is free. It's why we especially like it.

HUMILIATION FACTOR: Quite its opposite.

LOCATION: Newport Beach, Balboa Island, Laguna, and anywhere else we find ourselves.

"Shall we take one more tour around the block?" Mom asks me. We have this conversation nearly every day. Might be the favorite time of day for both of us.

Since I can't drive yet, she still has to drive me everywhere: school, ballet five days a week, volunteering for EST, visits with friends. I like being her co-pilot, near her warm smell, like slightly overcooked English scones with hints of dried apricot.

Every time we enter our neighborhood, this is what we both want to do: look at houses, often the ones just in our small neighborhood, but we also branch out. And for any house that strikes our fancy, we can linger for some time.

We imagine we live in every one, but we have our favorites.

How would you redo the door, Megan? Might that one have an airy kitchen? How would it be to have an English library? Wouldn't that be the perfect place for a hammock? If it were ours, shouldn't we do a Dutch glass door there? Do you remember if that one has a pool?

She's always done this, and I happened to like it, so we started to imagine together. She taught me things. About design. About her.

"When I was little, we moved all the time, you know, because Daddy kept running out of money. So back-forth, back-forth between California and Ohio, and since Daddy was still drinking, and Mother was trying to get him sober, I spent a lot of time alone, wandering my neighborhood, imagining where I might live. Those big old screened-in porches, the dormered windows, old ice-boxes at the front of the house where Daddy would deliver the ice."

"He stopped drinking at some point, right?"

"Yes, such a kind man, but it never quite came together for him. Mother worked to keep us afloat, and soon we'd all work. You know, with Grandmother Kosier and her charity shop. It's where we got all our clothes. She's the one who taught me how to dress well with no money. I tried to make our houses look nice in that same way. Mother wasn't very tidy. So I got tidy for all of us."

"Did you like your childhood much?"

"Hmm. Good question. What with all the moving, I just had my two best friends in Ohio that I had to leave when we came back to California. I never had friends as fun as Margaret and Marianne again. I think that's when I tried to kill myself." She says this rather matter-of-factly.

"What?"

"Oh, I've never told you about that? Yes, well, I tried to strangle myself with a terry-cloth towel, and it wasn't very effective, so I just stopped . . . I don't know how serious I was . . ." She kind of starts chuckling. I'm not sure I believe the chuckle.

"Mom . . . that's crushing. Did you ever tell your parents?"

"No, I was young . . ."

Didn't that make it even worse? I mean, I'd had some hard days, but I'd never contemplated—let alone attempted—to cut off my airway.

"Mother was busy sobering up Daddy on and off, and Ted and Phyllis were so much older . . . I had my dog, Trix, and my cat . . ."

"You are killing me Mom. *Killing me.* Do you think you were depressed? Did you ever make more friends?"

"Oh, sure. By high school, our Baptist youth group, I learned to have some fun, but it wasn't until after I recovered from the ulcerative colitis, before I met your dad, that I started to learn to have fun. You know, I wouldn't have met your dad without the colitis. My new Christian Science friends, Harold and Ivy, taught me to camp, plan a picnic. Through them I met your dad. He sure was a lot of fun. Boisterous, charismatic, confident." She says *was, was* a lot of fun.

And like usual, after we take the full run around the neighborhood, she slows as we pull up to our own house.

What does it mean that my mom tried to kill herself with a terry-cloth towel?

"Should we go one more time?" Usually we both answered yes. A guilty pleasure. We always lingered longest on our own front drive.

I imagined my mother would love to create her own new house, and put her aesthetic to the test. But that wasn't happening anytime soon. We were leveraged in cheese. No harm dreaming, though. We'd drive to Laguna Hills and imagine a tree house, to old LA and look at big Spanish ramblers, to beach houses along the cliffs of Corona del Mar.

"More than anything," she'd say, gazing up at our house dreamily, "as a girl I imagined I would someday live on a ranch, in Wyoming, with lots of dogs and animals and wide open spaces. And maybe now, I'd make it modern, not what you'd expect in Wyoming at all."

10

ABOUT SEX SEMINAR

PURPOSE: Explore issues of sex and sexuality.

DURATION: Ten weeks. Three hours a week.

EQUIPMENT NEEDED: The seminar leader has a manual in front of the room. This is one manual I would like to get my hands on.

AGE: 15.

RELATIONSHIP STATUS: Distant boy crushes. Movies with girlfriends. Ballet class. Time with Mom.

EMPLOYMENT: My job making Country Fair Cinnamon Rolls on Balboa Island doesn't cover the tuition. My parents support one seminar a semester. They think of seminars like other families think of piano lessons.

COST: $225.

HUMILIATION FACTOR: Warming up.

LOCATION: Newport Beach, California (another office park).

I did the *About Sex* seminar years before I actually kissed a guy, let alone had sex. This was a detail nobody seemed all that concerned about at registration.

As for taking a seminar about sex? I was an open-minded prude. I would talk about the topic plenty—I just didn't plan on doing it anytime soon. Sex looked like being under the spell of a man—and seeming out of control or rendered speechless with doe eyes; none of it looked appealing. I was wrapped up tight. Love looked messy. Not to mention, I was shy about my body. I was all about ballet and the discipline of it. Didn't think of my body much beyond that. Oh, except masturbating. I knew how to do it, and felt insanely guilty about it.

"Who would like to share their first sexual thought?" Michael, the small Spanish seminar leader, asked us. I'd heard that his tall girlfriend, Margaux, who had about five inches on him, used to be a model. It sure looked that way.

I meekly raised my hand. I knew I likely would get called on. There was some novelty in being the youngest person in the group. An assistant handed me a microphone.

"I remember my first romantic thought. I'm not sure it was sexual. But there was this guy in my class. Ross. He was so cute. So smart. He sat behind me in Mr. Jones's eighth-grade homeroom, and I imagined what it would be like if he kissed my neck. Or if he leaned the slightest bit forward, how it might be to feel his breath on my neck."

"Admit it, Megan, your thought of this kiss, led to thoughts of . . ."

"I don't think I . . ."

"Sex," he said.

"No, I'm not trying to say . . . I think I wanted to *kiss* him. Dreamed of his kissing me."

"But didn't you also imagine *sex*?"

I started feeling hot. I could feel this welling up of my eyes, but I wanted none of that. I swallowed it down. I was pretty skilled at this. I knew what was transpiring with this seminar leader. My response didn't fit into whatever was in that manual. Someone is supposed to admit they wanted to sleep with somebody else. But that wasn't my first thought. I mostly thought about Ross's lips.

"I wanted to kiss him."

"By wanting to kiss," Michael said with certainty, rocking up onto his toes for emphasis to the rhythm of his syllables, "you, Megan, wanted to be sexual, which means sex. You aren't acknowledging *what's so*. Sex is *what's so*, for all of us." That was a common expression: *to acknowledge what was so*.

He scanned the crowd for a new candidate. "Now, who else can share their first sexual thought?"

I looked around awkwardly for a seminar assistant to whom I could hand back the microphone.

11

THE SIX-DAY ADVANCED COURSE

PURPOSE: They never spelled out what we'd be *Advanced* in. Mom and Renee took the course together a year ago, and Dad, the Executive Version. They each looked happy and lighter in their *After* photos. Way happier than their *Before* photos. I want my face to look brighter too.

DURATION: Six days.

SCHEDULE: Wake. Run. Follow the Pritikin diet. Do volunteer chores. Enter Seminar Room. Be in Seminar Room until God-Knows-When. Exit in wee hours. Sleep. Repeat.

EQUIPMENT NEEDED (NOT EXHAUSTIVE): The ever-present name tags, running shoes, climbing gear (for the ropes course), audio equipment (to play the *Rocky* theme song on our final run), scissors (hairstylists came from San Francisco to give us new looks to transform us into our new, shinier selves).

AGE: 16.5.

RELATIONSHIP STATUS: Single and happy. There is a lot about high school to love. With friends from different groups, I can sort of fit in anywhere.

COST: $750+.

HUMILIATION FACTOR: Go big or go home.

LOCATION: Marin County, California. Some old camplike facility.

This is Day-I-Don't-Know-What of the Six-Day Advanced Course, an advanced training in the hills outside Napa Valley. I would be the fourth Griswold to get through it. We sleep in bunk rooms; we have seminars from sunup to sundown. As a group of teens, we hail from more affluent and progressive parts of the Bay Area, New York, and Los Angeles, with a few stragglers from other parts of the country and Canada. Most of us enrolled because our parents have done this, and through invitation or coercion, we are to have a life-changing week.

Day Two is Stand-Up/Sit-Down Night: to explore our relationship with authority. As the trainer instructs us to "Stand up. Sit down," we do exactly that—stand up and sit down for an hour or more.

If you get pissed off or have an easy time of it, no matter—observe your reaction. The next night is scheduled for some other topic, like *Authenticity*. A guy raises his hand to talk. From his presentation, you can tell he is not at the top of the Six-Day clique hierarchy. He has a feathery blond mustache, with even more feathery blond hair, and a comb in the back pocket of his tight brown OP corduroy shorts. He is not cool. I, myself, am not at the top of the cool pile either. But neither am I uncool. I would describe my position as cool-neutral. My guess is that this guy's lack of coolness will work against him.

He stands up and takes the microphone. He has something they call a Burning Share, a share that burns so hot inside him that it needs to be let out. Like a fart. But he's nervous. The trainer, sensing his hesitancy, tries to help.

"I want you to know this is a totally safe space, and we are here for you. You are safe and these people are your partners. And really, you're giving us this gift because if it's something you've gone through, I *guarantee* you someone else has gone through it too. You will be helping them. There's no judgment here."

"I've done some things I am not proud of . . ." Feather Man says.

"Yes, yes, we all have these things . . . please continue."

"Well, I've had sex . . ."

"Yes, you've had sex. Please."

"I've had sex with . . . I've had sex with . . ."

"Remember, you will be helping *all* of us."

"I've had sex . . . I've had sex . . . I've had sex with . . . a Shetland pony."

The room goes silent for a half second. And then erupts into raging, uncontrollable laughter. The trainer himself looks shocked but pulls it together—

trying to look like he's heard this all a million times before. I see the wheels of his mind turning to somehow convince this guy that we are not laughing *at* him. A tall order because there is no doubt, we are laughing *at* him. He tries shaming the audience into silence.

"Your other partners only laugh because of their immaturity. They are not laughing *at* you."

But no matter. One hundred minds picture this guy with the feathery hair. And then we picture a pony. Not a stallion. Not a horse. But a tiny, cute, petting zoo pony.

Adding to this image is the knowledge of how hard-pressed the trainer is to deliver on his guarantee about how if Feathers has gone through it, somebody else in the room has gone through it too. I'm fairly confident that Feathers is the only person in the room who has had sex with a miniature horse.

The next night's seminar was supposed to be Sex Night. I'd heard from Mom and Renee that they show three screens of pornography simultaneously for us to "confront our issues around sex." How titillating. Three different screens—a triptych of porn. I was looking forward to it. They skip over it entirely. No Sex Night. No porn. No triptych. I suspect they assumed this horse business would cover it.

But five days have passed and I haven't experienced my Breakthrough yet. And I won't leave here without it. I have this idea about what a Breakthrough requires: pure humiliation, utter fear, and *100* percent chance of embarrassment. Should I withstand the heat, I imagine the release and salvation to follow. (I came up with this fabulous plan myself, *thank you very much*.) I will be reborn into a braver, stronger version of myself. This is no small assignment. I've been racking my brain. I finally come up with something worthy of a share. Now I just need the opportunity to share it.

We've spent the afternoon roaming around the room in slow motion, assuming *Karate Kid*–like postures for some Samurai Leadership Something or Other. We gather to review our insights as Samurais. I have no insight. In my mind, no insight would be as effective as purging myself. I want to be like Shetland Pony Guy—without the pony part.

I raise my hand. The trainer calls on me. We have two trainers. The one who talked to Feathers has a gentle, relaxed air, not to mention he looks like a movie star. This trainer is arrogant. And squatty. With the high voice of a tenor.

"What, Megan, what would you like to share about the Leadership Process?"

I fiddle with the edges of my skirt while I stall. "Um, I don't so much want to say anything about the Leadership Process. But I have a *Burning Share* . . ."

"Oh, a Burning Share. Well, yes. Yes. Go on. We have a lot of material to get through, but go ahead." He looks away impatiently. We're off to a bad start, but I suck it up, grip the microphone, and take a big breath.

"I want to say that I've masturbated. I've masturbated in the shower. I have masturbated in the tub. I have masturbated in the Jacuzzi. (Nobody's brought up masturbation yet. I think this might be good for the group.) I have looked at *Playboy* . . . at *Playgirl* . . ."

"Excuse me, *Megan*."

"I've masturbated in the . . ."

"Excuse me, Megan. Excuse me, Megan . . ." He interrupts my list. I won't be stopped.

"One time I took off my . . ."

"Megan. Stop." Squat Man calls me to a halt with his Bryan-Adams-on-a bad-day voice.

"Once I found some porn in my parents' closet. It was Germa—"

"Megan, we *all* have things we feel shame about. Seems best you move on."

Best I *move on*? Was this guy going to blow me off? They spent like an hour talking to the guy about the horse. And now because it was some *MINOR* masturbation guilt, he wasn't going to give me the time of day? This might have been the Leadership Exercise, but Feathers got to talk about the horse during the Integrity Workshop. They treated him like a brave soldier, recounting the horrors of war. The man had fucked a horse, for Christ's sake. He wasn't a hero.

Squatty requests I sit down. I start sobbing. I wasn't even tormented in the right way. I wanted to confess and come out the other side clearer, brighter. I felt more alive when I thought somebody knew the worst in me.

12

THE RETREAT WORKSHOP ON SELF-GOVERNMENT

PURPOSE: Develop skills of self-government. To be more self-actualized, self-disciplined, self-reflective. A lot of words that begin with a *self* and a dash.

DURATION: Five days.

EQUIPMENT NEEDED: Pen and paper.

AGE: 17.

RELATIONSHIP STATUS: I haven't mentioned it, but I won a ballet scholarship a while back. My patron sees something in me. But I've given it up. I loved it, but there's too much stress with Dad gone with work and Renee finishing UCLA. I think my time is better spent on things like autonomy. Yeah, autonomy. Mom's super into it.

COST: Somewhere more than $500. But less than a thousand.

HUMILIATION FACTOR: I don't feel humiliation so much as guilt.

LOCATION: Lovely-Rural-Spot-Popular-with-Retreat-Leaders-Everywhere. Breitenbush Hot Springs meets Taos, New Mexico, meets Alice Waters. Trying to keep it vague. Not interested in throwing anyone under the bus.

Mom started a new training. In Self-Government with a capital *S*. I'm not sure what it means—well, I know what *self-government* means, I looked it up—but I'm not sure what it means to learn it. It's a new teacher she found through a friend of a friend. His name is Lawrence, and he's some sort of authority. He has a short retreat, then an ongoing class. Mom did the retreat and headed straight into "The Ongoing." Marilyn from our Phoenix EST trip is doing it too. They say it's *really* different from what we've done.

I've signed up for the Retreat and so here I am with Mom. No pressure, but Mom thinks it might inform my thinking on what's next—with college looming and all. It's got the familiar name tags and chairs, but this feels more . . . *academic*. Tables in front of us with pen and paper. I love that we'll be writing. Not that I know *what* we'll be writing.

And I love that Lawrence is this refined, rather starched-shirt version of a seminar. We're reading his book, tracing the development of Western philosophy. How did we get to thinking the way we do? How did religious thought lead to thinkers like Plato, Rousseau, Nietzsche, and Freud? If my last seminars felt like a mishmash of jazzy phrases, this feels far more intellectual.

Here's the only problem. If my seminars and Six-Day Advanced Course aren't a *cult*, then why do I feel incredibly guilty for doing this retreat? So guilty that I'm missing an afternoon session for fear I'm crossing into enemy territory, or in the very least a competitor's camp. Even *I* know there's only so much personal-growth business to go around. I don't want to lose my friends there, but truth is, I've found some cracks. Like, how can you teach a whole seminar on integrity when you are doing not-so-integrity-ish things? Not that Mom and I have told anyone, but because we host seminar leaders in our house, occasionally we see the leaders' private lives more than most. Mom runs our guest room like a mini B&B, which the seminar leaders find homier than hotels. But with the last leader we hosted, I was awakened in the night by some pretty loud moaning. Alarmed, I woke Mom and dragged her upstairs to listen with me. Definitely *sex* sounds. With my detective self in full swing, we confirmed an additional car parked out front—with custom Arizona plates I recognize, some variation on the word *karma*. No joke. And I happen to know our Karma driver is the married enrollment manager who leads my Phone-Enrollment Night.

After Karma departed before dawn, upon changing the bed later in the day, Mom and I discovered that—like Cinderella—Karma had left something behind. A big black-and-white polka-dot plastic hoop earring. I would recognize Karma's jewelry anywhere.

So if Integrity teachers have vow-breaking sex with married people, and if I heard anti-anger teachers yelling in the hall on Enrollment Night, well, I'd tolerate a massive guilty stomachache during a retreat to try something new. So here I am. Lawrence says he understands my seminar loyalty and stomachache. And that no one has taken his class so young, so if it doesn't speak to me, there's no problem with leaving. But I want to hear what happens with Freud and something called the homunculus. I want to finish Lawrence's book. To see how it ends. Or, maybe, how it begins.

13

OUR BODIES, OURSELVES

PURPOSE: Angela Phillips's quintessential guide to, um, our bodies, ourselves.

DURATION: It's one of those books I think I should keep by the toilet. A true reference text, especially if you're interested in seeing women rocking a '70s bush in black and white.

EQUIPMENT NEEDED: A hand mirror, I suppose. Not really required.

AGE: 17.

RELATIONSHIP STATUS: I'm 17 and have had, like, two kisses, tops. One involved tongue.

EMPLOYMENT: Country Fair Cinnamon Rolls Bakery. I roll out the dough in the window. My parents are extremely proud, as if I'm performing quadruple bypass surgery.

COST: $19.05 in paperback.

HUMILIATION FACTOR: Is mortification the same as humiliation?

LOCATION: 405 Freeway, Costa Mesa, California.

Our family is driving somewhere. All four of us. My father is at the wheel of our butter-colored, gray-market diesel Mercedes. With all his stressful work trips to Europe and the strength of the dollar, it was an expense we could swing. My mother and I are in the back seat (we both prefer it), which means Renee is in the front shotgun position, where she likes it. Right hand to Dad. While she's quiet, she's quite identified as being a formidable driver. She can help keep Dad on the road, or at least some part of it. Hopefully, the right. He drifts left when bored.

Which leaves my mother and me to our conversation. There's no obvious segue with us. We jump wherever the other goes.

"I'm concerned about kissing. And my level of performance."

"Hmm. Interesting. Say more."

(Now, keep in mind, Dad and Renee are about four inches away from us, but there is not a peep that this is a tidbit of conversation that either of them wants to be a part of.)

"Well, there's nothing particularly romantic on the horizon, but I figure I should be prepared." (My junior high and high school obsession, Ross, still has absolutely zero interest in me. But my mother is big on preparation, so she'll get this. When we visit Lake Tahoe, for some reason she practices rowing a decaying rowboat from the dock to the buoy—all of fifty feet and back, until her thirty minutes are up—prepping for some nautical Armageddon.)

On the preparation front, my mother wants me to know more about life than she did at my age, hence the *Our Bodies, Ourselves*, delivered oh-so-subtly to my desk a few months ago. But there's nothing in there about kissing. Menstrual flow, absolutely. Home births, of course. The occasional tipped cervix, sure. Tongue placement in kissing, not a word.

"I think kissing is a feminist issue," I say. "Don't you?" I look at Mom quizzically. Yet certain that I state the obvious. And if I go intellectual, this may mask some of my performance anxiety on the matter. "I mean, shouldn't I *know* what I'm doing in that department so that life or whatever goes smoothly? Shouldn't all girls know about these things? Why don't they teach this in health class?"

"Well, Megan, sure, yes, yes, feminist, I suppose. Now what do you want to know exactly?"

"So if a guy leans in, at what point do I close my eyes? And do I tilt my head right or left? I mean what if I go right and he goes right, but I don't know because I've already closed my eyes?"

"Hmm. Let me think." My mother mulls this. She starts tilting her head to herself. Right, pause. Then, left, pause. (Again, nothing coming from the front seat. We might as well be on different planets. Renee's pretending not to hear; I'm *sure* of it.)

"Fair questions, Megan. Now, I'm no expert, but seems to me the logical thing is to keep your eyes open long enough to see which way he's headed. No sense bobbing your head in the dark. Knowledge is power, so get as much as you can before closing. Then I suppose close your eyes after mouth-to-mouth contact."

Mouth-to-mouth contact. Got it. "Then what?"

"Well, then softly open your mouth—well, if he does, maybe. Well, just be receptive, as it were."

Receptive. Okay. "Receptive to his tongue or his mouth or what?"

"I suppose open to either. I mean, if the idea appeals to you."

If the idea appeals to me. "Do I start moving my tongue around? Like a certain direction? I heard not to go crazy like a windmill or anything."

"It's a bit of a . . . a bit of a dance."

"A dance. Well, what sort of dance? A cha-cha? A rumba? A waltz?"

"Maybe a tango. They say the tango is like sexual chess." My mother draws out the *shhhhhh* syllable in the word *sexual.* Sex-*shhhhhhew*-al. Always has. Makes me squeamish.

"Well, I don't know how to tango, and I don't play chess."

"Let me see. A tango of the mouth. A tongue-go." She surprises herself with a small laugh at her own joke. "Shall I just show you? Shall I kiss you? Maybe for practical purposes, that would be easier?"

Whaaaaaaaaat??????? What did my mother just say to me??? Shall she just show me by kissing me?

"For *practical* purposes? *MOM!* Are you nuts? That's disgusting. That's like child molesting, you realize that? You'd be, like, molesting me."

"Molesting you? I'm just trying to be helpful."

"You know that it's not, like, *normal,* to offer to French-kiss your own daughter, right?" *How is it that I'm having to explain this?*

(No reaction from the front seat. Surely, if anything was going to get a rise out of those two, it would be this.)

"I'm just trying to be helpful, Megan. It wouldn't mean . . ."

"It wouldn't mean what? Oh, yes, it would. It would absolutely mean that!"

Thank God I know this is not okay. Think of the therapy, or the Child Protective Services investigation that a gesture like this could spark. What does it mean that this doesn't even faze my mother? Should I be concerned? Why isn't anyone else in the car saying anything? There are four of us in the car, are there not?

"Barf. Barf. Barf. Mom, I'm going to pretend like you never said that. Like never ever. Never ever ever. And I'm never telling anyone you just offered to French-kiss me. Seriously, do I really have to explain this?"

"Oh, Megan, I just want you to have the information you want, and I don't know how else to get it to you."

"In the very least, you could have offered to pantomime with a pillow or something. Or a small sponge or . . . a mirror. Why jump straight to a live demo here in the car??"

"Okay, well, we don't have a pillow or a sponge or a mirror here, now do we?"

My sister pushes my father in the forearm; he's starting to drift. He must be nodding off.

Nodding off. During this. I, myself, want to go unconscious. *Why am I the only one hearing this conversation? Or am I? Is it one of those if-a-tree-falls-in-the-woods-when-no-one-is-around-does-it-still-make-a-sound situations? Like, if I'm the only one who heard it, did it actually happen if I would prefer to think it didn't? AND does it still count as crazy or, minimally, an avoided crazy if I'm the only one to hear or know?*

I'm embarrassed for my mother. And ashamed. I feel pity, and sympathy, and heat and sorrow. All these states rise in me. And I swallow down something like a silent wordless scream. I can't talk about these things. With anyone. These are the things I do not say, feelings I do not describe. Protecting my mother from judgment from anyone else feels more important than just about anything. I try to make it funny instead.

I will not kiss again for another three years.

14

THE ART OF SEXUAL ECSTASY

PURPOSE: A love and ecstasy training manual for Western lovers by Margot Anand.

DURATION: It's quite a big book.

EQUIPMENT NEEDED: Don't get me started.

AGE: 20.

RELATIONSHIP STATUS: None.

EMPLOYMENT: Temping and waiting tables while home from school.

COST: It was a gift.

LOCATION: Balboa Island, California. My parents have moved since I started college.

I'm really not sure what to make of this one. Dad has given all of us hardback copies of *The Art of Sexual Ecstasy*. Not that Dad knows my sexual status (I'm still a virgin), but they know Renee's. When she was first home from college, years ago now, I had stumbled upon the contents of her quilted Pierre Deux purse (honestly, what legitimate reason did I have to be rooting around in there?), and inside I found an unused pregnancy test. Upon finding the test, I confronted Renee and she didn't so much confess as rightly refuse to answer. But she has a terrible poker face—a trait we share. Her eye-darting is her tell. Her eye darts said yes. With this revelation, I ran to my parents' closet, locked myself in, and wept. *(Why??? Was unmarried sex naughty? Bad with a capital B? Parent-disappointing?)* I wept until they returned home from their seminar, when I emerged from their closet blurting it all out in some bizarre epileptic fit as if it were normal to confess my guilt about her sex life as my own. I hated keeping secrets, not understanding the difference between dishonesty and discretion. Much to Renee's horror, it became a family affair to wait for the results of that little blue stick (negative). If I were Renee, I don't know if I could ever forgive me.

So needless to say, daughter sex hadn't been a family topic for some time. And I had nothing new of my own to confess. Hadn't even had a boyfriend yet.

And to be clear, when I say Dad has given *all* of us a copy, I mean it goes beyond our nuclear family. It's his new favorite gift. He recently gave it to my cousin Connie for her wedding. I wish I could have seen her face when he hand-delivered it. (Yes, I think he hand-delivered.) She married a very fresh-faced, incredibly innocent-looking Christian Science practitioner. Come to think of it, maybe that's how this all started. Since Christian Scientists don't exactly think they have physical bodies, what with matter being an illusion and all, maybe Dad thinks he got ripped off because no one ever taught him about his body.

According to the table of contents, Dad must think I should open my inner flute, heal my yoni, and deliver a nice Anal Healing Massage (although the last one doesn't get covered till Chapter 10).

If this all comes together right, after I've learned Feathering and the PC Pump, then I can Ride the Tiger, Shoot the Crown, and eventually graduate into Riding the Wave of Bliss. I have no idea how to approach this verbally, let alone physically. I'm gonna take this one in silence. I don't think I can use humor as a psychological salve with Dad on this one. Well, that's what my yoni told me.

15

INTERNATIONAL WILDERNESS TRAINING COURSE

PURPOSE: To be the leading source and teacher of wilderness skills, serving both people and the environment.

DURATION: Courses vary in length from a month to a semester.

EQUIPMENT NEEDED: A staggering gear check at the branch in Chile. While much can be rented, you are required to buy your own polypropylene underpants. At home, despite my new backcountry-travel-light philosophy, my mother has insisted I buy my own dresser so I know I'm starting my own life, not continuing theirs. I now own an Ikea maple veneer dresser.

AGE: 22/23.

RELATIONSHIP STATUS: Started dating a guy named Lowry about 3 minutes ago. He thinks I'll travel to Patagonia and fall for an instructor. How ridiculous.

EMPLOYMENT: Princeton Review SAT instructor and waitress.

COST: At the time, a semester course cost about $4,500.

LOCATION: Cochrane, Chile, where we will bag our rations and stage our gear, then travel for two days on one very bumpy dirt road to the heart of Patagonia.

FIVE MONTHS POST–COLLEGE GRADUATION PRE-COURSE

Location: The Wedge, Newport Beach, California

After saturating myself in my collegial political philosophy texts and Lawrence's classes, I know I need to make more than just theoretical sense of what Rousseau saw as a corrosive overdependence on what others think and what others think of us. And somewhere in the back of my eyeballs, I not only feel this but also sense what Plato calls the shadows on the cave, where we humans are chained to a cave wall since childhood, unable to see the full nature of things. Instead we merely see shadows on the walls, the closest we'll get to seeing reality, that is, unless—and it's a big *unless*—we figure out how to unchain ourselves from the cave. But honestly, I don't need a college degree to tell me I need help with my own cave, or some sort of cave extraction. My mother and father keep growing more distant from one another by the day. How can I merge the out-there metaphysical musings of Dad about physics and dwarf stars with the very close-to-home nature of my mother's desire for safety and reassurance from her spouse? And why couldn't I *really* have a boyfriend? Don't I want one? Why doesn't love find me?

I want to turn my world upside down. Like taking one of those glass balls with water and glittery snow inside it and giving it a really good shake. I have this idea that climbing around on glaciers and paddling across big, broad water and speaking a language not native to me is what it would mean to be shaken up.

It's been a stressful couple of years finishing college. When my parents dropped me off as a freshman, they dropped me off together. But Mom drove back alone. Needed time to think, she said. Now they've sold the family home and they're living part-time in Lake Tahoe and part-time in Newport. Dad comes up to visit when he can. They don't call it a separation, they say they're just avoiding capital gains by establishing a new residence. But it still seems like a separation. I wish they'd get on with it, if that's where they're headed. As much as I think about my future, I don't yet know how to unravel my future from theirs.

They don't like this international-wilderness-backcountry-thing. I have a talk with Dad on the Balboa Peninsula so we could walk on the Wedge. As we walk, he goes on and on about my not being dreamy. But I don't think it's dreamy, what I want right now. I want to feel raw, and pushed to my limits, and extreme. Like I used to feel when I danced. I crave intensity. Something larger than me. Larger than this little world of haze, this post-college-what-am-I-supposed-to-do-now kind of gloom. The kind of gloom that makes you want to eat Twix bars in the Gelson's grocery store parking lot (hypothetically, of course). I didn't thrive in college. I survived college. I'm embarrassed—humiliated, even—to admit that I merely survived. I endured a certain solitudinal loneliness I didn't even understand. I was supposed to be happy-go-lucky and seize every exceptional opportunity that could come my way with an Ivy League deal. Instead, I nursed myself with romantic movies, alone, always alone in dark theaters on the Upper West Side of Manhattan; with popcorn, falafel sandwiches, and large carrots; with bagels and strange health-food-store bran cookies; with calls to my mother. I nursed myself with these small pleasures. Could I even call them pleasures? Little stopgaps between the solitude of waking, walking to class, coming back to my dorm room; all the while, wishing I were an Orthodox Jew—they seemed to have the best social life, their own cafeteria, and group weekend trips for Shabbat. In my occasional social moments in the halls of Columbia, I pretended to be far jollier and smoother than I ever felt. But I mostly performed for an audience of one. Me. And even *I* didn't believe me. But I did know I missed what I used to be. I missed myself. I missed my mother. Our strange twosome. The long talks, the bad TV, the seminars, and slow drives critiquing our favorite houses. I missed what we were. I missed what we all could have been. All four of us. If only.

"Megan, as for this wild-whatever travel idea, consider it a mere concept, which may be getting in the way of your *thinking*. See this cup here?" *Oh, no, here comes the Cup analogy.* He raised his empty recycled coffee cup, one from a cupboardful he collected and reused from Starbucks.

"This *cup* is not a *Cup*. It's a collection of molecules, of energy. It looks like a cup. We *call* it a cup. But it's our concept *Cup* that gets in the way," he said while pointing to his temples when he said the word *concept*. "Do you see what I'm saying?"

I kept walking, in silence. Head down, looking at my sneakers in the sand. "Um, not exactly . . ." Usually I pretended he made sense to please him.

Cup. Energy. Molecules. Wilderness course. How you gonna dot-to-dot that one together, Megan. I can't find the thread. It just sounds like a thumbs-down to my plan.

My job, normally: to be the Emperor-Has-No-Clothes Kid. The Truth Teller, the Joker in the King's Court to tell him with levity when something didn't make sense to anybody else. But I was weary of interpreting his abstractions. I'd been in the what-is-he-really-saying-I-don't-think-even-*he*-knows-Metaphor-Deciphering-Olympic-Training-Camp for as long as I knew how to speak. Despite decades of rigorous verbal gymnastics, and getting closer than most, I'd never even gotten close to winning a medal.

Maybe the cup thing is about Starbucks. The only part I *do* get? He won't be magically offering to kick in on my Rocky-Mountain-High tuition.

We both turn to stare at the beach, our faces toward the set. The Wedge was famous for the way the waves seized up and broke so close in. And when they break abruptly without peeling down the line like today, they call that *closing out*.

"There's work to think of," he went on. My father hadn't believed in college. He went to work for his father after his brother was killed in World War II. Dad loved college. But that luxurious option was taken two years in.

As for getting a job, I didn't mind working. I already had a job. Two, actually. It wasn't about that. It was this larger thing. This question of being alive. How to be really alive. In my Lawrence class, he says we must learn to be pragmatic. Be realistic. But isn't part of youth being encouraged to dream?

"But Dad, I'm paying for it *myself*. I'm not asking . . . I'm not . . ."

I trail off. I stare at the stormy winter set rolling in. My body vibrates as I struggle to ignore my dad's critique. I don't like misbehaving. I'd had the summer jobs, the good grades, the on-time and under-budget graduation. But there's this voice inside telling me it's essential to break out of fixating on pleasing the people around me. So I carry around the goddamn brochure of the backcountry trips I can't afford.

I carry it everywhere. In the car. In my purse. To the gym. On the elliptical. In the bathroom. In the break room at work. At night, before studying the brochure again, I stuff my tip money in a white paper box to gather the tuition. I study each catalog picture with the seriousness of a scientist dissecting a corpse. It's as though I believe that some part of me that needs resurrecting will be found in those photographs. Something about the harsh-looking weather, the thick storm gear. That stormy weather matches something in my interior. And if I am ever going to do anything with my life, I feel like I need to wrestle and make peace with those dark forces. Or at least begin the conversation properly. Introduce myself. Boldly. Instead of this meek, moping, rule-following type who has forgotten what it means to say boo.

ELEVEN MONTHS POST-GRADUATION

Location: Cochrane, Chile

It's six months since the Wedge Chat with Dad and I've earned my tuition serving one tremendous amount of beer. But waiting tables couldn't feel further away from what I'm doing now at the wilderness program's home base, a small farm tucked under an escarpment not far from Cerro Castillo. I discuss with Liam, our tells-it-like-it-is-even-if-it's-embarrassing-head-sea-kayaking teacher, how many tampons I'll need for the next three months. He looks at my mother lode of Tampax and asks, "Do you *honestly* need *this* many?" I guess I look as though braced for the tsunami of all menstrual cycles.

And some six weeks after the tampon discussion, my backpack rests squarely on my hips, its weight evenly distributed between the massive straps around my waist and shoulder blades. Weighing upward of eighty pounds, it is more than three-quarters of my body weight. A challenging load, made more so by the fact that I'm 3,000 percent confident I broke a couple of ribs two days ago when a horse threw my mountain instructor Tim and me during a river crossing. I've been hiding it, pretending I'm barely injured. I don't want to be medically evacuated. And eight hundred milligrams of ibuprofen four times a day is making it all possible.

Up until the horse-throwing moment, I had been gobbling up any conversation with Tim—the shy, sometimes playful, yet confident mountain-expedition head teacher. We could have talked about lawnmower repair and I would have been riveted. I mostly enjoyed holding on to him on that horse—feeling his back close to my chest. We talked about primates and rock climbing and poetry and spotted hyenas.

This one conversation was worth the broken ribs—all the more reason not to evac to see a doctor. *What do they do for cracked ribs, anyway? Don't they just heal on their own? Maybe the backpack will compress them back together.* I will not leave voluntarily. Difficulty taking deep breaths and the hideous pain I feel lifting my arms pales compared to the joy brought by my first seventy-five days in the Chilean backcountry. So Vitamin Ibu, it is. My life has begun.

Seventy-five days of firsts.

First transport in a cattle truck instead of a bus. First chart. First 1:50,000–
scale map. First time knowing the difference between a chart and a map. First
condor. First time planning an off-trail route. First self-assembled kayak—
heavy with a month of food. First compass bearing. First fjord crossing. First
campsite search at high tide. First miscalculation of high tide. First flooded
tent at two a.m. First time to run out of food before the resupply. First resupply.
First off-trail travel. First moraine. First plastic boot, first crampon, first ice
axe, first glacier. First self-arrest. First snow anchor. First ice climb.

First herb bread made from scratch by twiggy fire. First *calafate* berry.
First puma. First time to lead a group. First travel above tree line on unmapped
mountain passes. First getting lost—like, really lost. First accidental wander into
Argentina. First river crossing. First maté. First coffee, for that matter, but the
best kind—South American, and thick like espresso, with a dash of wild mint.
First glacier lily salad. First bivy. First Southern Cross. First biting black flies.

First seventy-five days without a single look in a mirror. First seventy-five
days without one shower. First seventy-five days sleeping outside. First time I
could feel up close how broad and wild the world is. First time I ate breakfast
and dinner in a family-like group since I turned thirteen. First time not bracing
for when my parents would blow apart.

To know the strange satisfaction (and adrenaline rush) of being truly lost—
not metaphorically lost or emotionally thrown off balance, but geographically
lost, I was oddly comfortable—even if it went on for days in literal mapless terrain through unnamed river valleys and unmarked glaciated peaks surrounding
Mount San Valentín. Suddenly, my external experience matched my internal
one—not just lost on the inside, but technically lost on the outside. For the
first time, my nervous system could rest. And I had company. A whole group of
people navigating along with me.

Navigating difficult terrain requires that you study an environment, learn
how not to become overwhelmed by obstacles larger than you. To cross a river,
timing is everything: wait till morning when the water is low, face upriver, as
directly facing the resistance helps keep you steady. To stay balanced, go slowly.
And look for broad water. Wider sections are typically shallower. Should the
unexpected happen, these spots mean a safer washout downriver. Avoid getting
caught in a strainer.

And to live nomadically with a small group feels natural and deeply sooth-ing. At the end of the day, we remain a herding species. Spending each night together after a hard day of travel and navigation didn't happen in my house or any family I knew. There may be actual magic in making a group a hot beverage with water you went in search of yourself—making each drink how you know each tentmate likes it. And then gathering around the stove in an intimate circle to talk of the day's unfolding, of nothing much, simply easy talk. I think that's what family is supposed to feel like: a group that works together, regroups together, and helps one another make life a little more comfortable—looking out for those around and among you. One person erects the tent; another might lay out the sleeping bags, while the other makes dinner. Protection. Nourish-ment. Comfort. In the end, it's not that complicated.

DAY 75

Location: Lago Esmeralda, Chile

I must be in love because I have diarrhea. I've had it since our Mountaineer-ing Course Leader Tim and I admitted to liking one another here at the end. Despite being college graduates, you can tell we are both idiotic late bloomers. I'm supposed to spend the last day thinking about what I've learned, but all I can think about is when my elbow might brush up against his elbow during our end-of-course *asado*. I'd much rather think about our little conversations on the trail, and how he's earned the respect of everyone on the course. While we students, from the beginning, ran around like overwhelmed gear-laden cartoon characters—all sweaty and disorganized—Tim always exuded this quiet confi-dence, teasing us over our concerns without patronizing.

Before our shy meeting under a large poplar, where he gave me my final mountaineering evaluation, I had taken to wearing sunglasses even in the shade for fear he'd catch me staring. So handsome—that strong jaw, shockingly blue eyes—like he walked out of the turquoise waters of Belize and straight into a Patagonia catalog. He wrote poetry and was a Stanford graduate, but he was also what I pleasantly experienced as a good-guilty-Stanford grad, not tak-ing the privilege of his education for granted. His presence had an unusual calm and young innocence; free of edges and dark corners. Such a lighthearted teacher; I was transfixed—whether watching him build a snow anchor or talk about puma behavior. He lent me a collection of essays by a writer named Barry Lopez. I can't get enough of it. Especially this chapter about a migration of Arctic snow geese in Oregon. The way they can ride and bank on the wind in tight unison by the thousands. A single flight can last thirty-two hours. When one of them falls sick in formation, a few will drop down and fly with them until they recover. Or die. The stories are so gentle but there's this incredible power to them. Tim is like those stories. I can feel it.

Sometimes I thought we caught each other's eyes, but I couldn't tell for sure. Ever since we were thrown off that horse, it felt like something changed. And under that shady poplar, I had no sunglasses to hide behind. Tim cleared his throat.

"Well, Megan, you've done well." He passes me my multipage evaluation. I scan the course report card. On a scale of one to five, nearly all fours, fives, and a few threes.

"Camping, great. Safety, a four. Handling that evac and river crossing, nice contribution. Ropes and knots skills, just fine. Great expedition behavior. Good group participation and leadership. I know that small group when you were leader at the end of our last ration was rough, with Brent's fall and knee injury."

"Well, thank you," I say bashfully. This isn't like me, not able to find a good joke opportunity.

"To be honest, Megan, the instructor team and I discussed whether I was in the best position to evaluate you, as, well . . ." He looks down back at his papers, "I really . . . like you. So I worried I might be biased. On the other hand, perhaps because of that, I've gotten to know you better than the other instructors. And I think they trust me to be fair, regardless of those additional feelings."

Additional feelings. I blush. I feel about ten years old. I start pulling grass nervously.

"You say you like me?" I ask, looking at him quickly and then shooting my eyes back down to the safe green grass. "Like, *like*-me like me?"

"Yes. *Like*-you like you." We gaze a moment longer than is proper. We grin. It's quiet, but there's a lot going on. I feel heat in my chest. And on my face. Out of what looks like composure mixed with timidity, he adjusts his arms in his lap, extends his legs out in front of him, sitting up quite straight. I speak.

". . . I like you too. I mean, it's special because you know, everything has felt so big here. So *new*. And then this. I didn't think I'd come down here and meet a boy. I mean a guy, I mean a man. It's like . . . finding out you really like cinnamon and you hadn't even known what cinnamon tasted like before . . . Does that make sense?"

Cinnamon? Why am I bringing cinnamon into this? God, I wish I were smoother.

He smiles. I babble. "Clearly I've been spending too much time with the group spice kit."

We grin like fools. One big smile bouncing between us. So now it's official—we like each other. It sounds so eighth grade. I suspect we're both young like that, inexperienced like that. I've taken to daydreaming about Tim and snow anchors and coyote love poems.

And after seventy-five days under one moon, one sun, I learn something else: what it feels like to fall in love. Here at twenty-three, for the first time. With another sunset over Lago Esmeralda comes the course's end, and my first moonlight kiss. Maybe it's the mountains, or my new skills, or the hard-earned sense of self-reliance, or the blush of first love, but my life, my insides, have never felt like this. Magic.

And that first shy kiss? It took place on that last day—that seventy-sixth day—when Tim was no longer my instructor. The entire course laid our sleeping bags out under the stars. Tim put his bag near mine. It felt so bold and scary. While everyone around us slept, I could see Tim lean forward, his tan face and timid smile framed by wild mountain hair and his three-month beard. All this, easy to see in the moonlight. He was so close, I could smell his vanilla mint lip balm.

"I want to kiss you, but I'm scared," he said.

"Me too. But there's no rush. We have plenty of time," I said nonchalantly. Inside, I'm terrified. I tucked my face a wee bit into my bag.

That seemed to put him at ease. He leaned toward me, his thin green sleeping bag now touching my giant orange one. Our lips touched; my body went electric. It all stayed really gentle. He smelled like hard work and wood smoke.

On that seventy-sixth day, we began—secretly proud we had followed the "post-course understood kissing rules." Because, in addition to his patient demeanor and a cardiovascular efficiency so great he never seemed to break a sweat, Tim was one of those guys who wanted to do what was good and right. And I really liked that about him.

16

TAKE AN IN-TOWN JOB: WILDERNESS EXPEDITION FOOD MANAGER

PURPOSE: Dive into this romance with Tim *and* work toward (maybe) becoming a wilderness teacher. Work up the outdoor education employment food chain (from the bottom).

DURATION: Expeditions run year-round.

EQUIPMENT NEEDED: To get an in-town job, it helps to have been on an expedition. As for the job equipment: standard commercial kitchen along with eight million plastic bags.

AGE: 24.

RELATIONSHIP STATUS: I hate the stereotype I'm fulfilling: taking a job I'm overqualified for so that Tim can take his dream job in the next town over. Other than that, I'm excited about my little innocent, still-new relationship.

COST: I'm paid a salary and provided housing.

LOCATION: Bellingham, Washington.

I am twenty-four years old. This is Tim's and my second summer together. The first year, he followed me to Laguna Beach and we rented a little place together (!!) while I waited tables and studied for the GRE. And this summer we are living in staff housing (a mix of moldy old wall tents and newly constructed Quonset huts). It means a lot of communal living with in-town staff and the cooler mountain teachers and guides heading out on trips. Turns out, I like the built-in social life of sharing communal kitchens, bathhouses, and a large gathering room. I even like the smelly tiny TV room everyone crams into on weeknights. When I'm working or cooking in the group kitchen, I listen to a lot of Ani DiFranco. Tim turned me on to her.

> All that steel and stone
> are no match for the air, my friend
> what doesn't bend breaks.

I work as the food manager for a wilderness branch in the Pacific Northwest. I am bagging food for an expedition going to the Waputik Range in the Canadian Rockies of Alberta. They head out tomorrow. Tomorrow the counters of this room will be overflowing with bags and bags of pasta, pounds of black beans, and hot chocolate. I'm thinking about sneaking in a surprise tube of pesto for the instructor team. And I am listening to this Ani DiFranco song. You see, I don't want to be like steel or stone. I want to learn how to bend in the wind.

And the world is wide open to me. I am smart. I am capable. I am kind. All my limbs work. And my hair isn't half bad. I am in love with a young man who's trying to step into the adult world, like I am. We look and feel young for our years. I learned how to navigate a family (sorta) but haven't the first clue how to navigate the world in a way that makes an impact. Not in a way that thrives. Not yet.

And I'm worried. The worry is sourceless, directionless—other than inward—and it pervades everything. I worry about my future, my family, a career, what I'm meant to do, how we're meant to live, what it means to die, what it is to commit to this young man. These are big questions, but bagging flour gives me a lot of time to think.

Tim passes by and gives me a quick kiss, pulling a square of dark chocolate for me out of the pocket of his Patagonia jacket. Or was it his perfectly pressed khakis? We'll make dinner together in a couple of hours.

After I clock out, I'll head to the open-air shower house and soap up under the sway of enormous Douglas firs. I will breathe in their sweet aroma. But the shower, it won't be enough. I can't wash out this worry.

17

GRADUATE SCHOOL

PURPOSE: A program to award advanced academic degrees. Maybe mainstream education is the better way to go.

DURATION: Two years.

EQUIPMENT NEEDED: Because it's Yale with a capital Y, I bet I won't have time to shop, so I buy all my food in bulk from Costco in Seattle and drive it across the country in my truck

AGE: 26.

RELATIONSHIP STATUS: Head over heels. Or head over hiking boots. Tim and I have been following each other across the globe: Chile, California, Chile again. He'll come with me to New Haven after an Arctic expedition. Then we'll commute back and forth while he's at Brown for grad school too.

EMPLOYMENT: Graduate NPR intern, full-time student.

COST: Staggering. We've just skyrocketed past any seminar thus far. That piece of paper from these Ivy-covered guys isn't cheap. Deany wants to help. And I'll sell my truck after I get my Costco food to New Haven. Dad doesn't believe in graduate school, or its tuition. He cuts it close anyway, so better not to ask.

HUMILIATION FACTOR: Low. It's plain interesting to be among so many smarty-pants.

LOCATION: New Haven, Connecticut, and Providence, Rhode Island.

His face. That's what it is. It's so soft. So certain. When Tim looks at me, I feel this sweetness wash over me. And that's a couple years in. I love what he smells like when he's been in the mountains for weeks, when his bright blond beard gets thick, his face tan, smelling like salt and polypro. And I love that he's not only sweet to me. He's nice to everybody.

We spent a day volunteering to teach natural history to the kids where Mom started a reading program for abused children. It's a residential facility out in the desert called Childhelp, near Joshua Tree. To teach birding and ornithology, Tim dressed up as a stork-billed kingfisher and had them identify features of his wacky outfit—goggles, wild climbing pants, colorful gloves. To teach conservation, he brought tiny flags we'd fashioned out of toothpicks for each child to claim and label their own miniature national parks on the property, all while dressed as a Southeast Asian bird. He had them in giggling fits. But it's not only his playfulness and intelligence.

When I first saw him repair an MSR WhisperLite stove in Patagonia, I couldn't stop watching the muscles of his forearms ripple with the movement of his hands. As for being in the mountains together, I would hike forever with him, out in front or in back as the sweep. There's no one I would trust more if lost. When we practice how to build a 3:1 pulley system to rescue a hypothetical tentmate who'd fallen in a crevasse, I know he'd be the guy I'd want to pull me out. And I trust that if the emergency arose, I could rescue him too.

He knows what he wants. Not all these worrying antics I carry. In college, he was a mountain guide in various organizations well before he graduated. He's clear, even in transition. After we got together, he told me he wanted to spend less time in the mountains and more time with me instead. He figured that out so thoughtfully, saying he was ready to direct his experience to help his community. And when he applied to his ideal school, he got into his first choice without fretting. Who wouldn't want Tim in their program? He doesn't treat graduate school like a snobby stamp of approval, but more like a laboratory for the work he'll do.

Am I entering graduate school to become more like . . . him? With a master's in international relations and interest in ethnographic research, I hope to put my secret embarrassing professional fantasies about writing, performing, and designing finally out of my head and focus on something *serious* that helps society. Mom says I'm so good with people, she's sure I am meant to help. *But doesn't art help too?* It's all a little hazy how I'll use this degree. I hope to get as clear as he is.

He's down from Providence. This morning he made me a breakfast of little goofy-faced animals all out of fruit. An apricot with a mischievous grin; a plum, an angry professor; the strawberry like an upside-down Poindexter. He finds ways to make a present out of a meal—a cause for celebration. From his heart to mine. He knows I'm stressed about exams.

I've passed him my paper on social standards and international trade. Did I mention he's the best editor for academic stuff? What more could a girl want than a guy like this, a certain future, and a couple of shiny letters after her name? Sometimes I sense I'm chasing something. But there's a certain safety at this school and with Tim that I cling to.

18

THE LAWRENCE ONGOING CLASS

PURPOSE: To learn the art of self-government. Develop critical-thinking skills.

DURATION: Nine years in.

EQUIPMENT NEEDED: Paper, pen, carbon paper (to keep my own copies of my essays); graph paper (to chart out our hefty Five-Year Plans).

AGE: 26.

RELATIONSHIP STATUS: With Tim.

EMPLOYMENT: GRE instructor, Daily Grill waitress, private tutor, graduate student, retail shopkeeper/stock girl. Secretly, I always believed my clear career would come together after I fell in love. Didn't I learn anything at Barnard? My feminism has too much romanticism.

COST: A few thousand dollars. Many weekends over many months. As Tim and I now share expenses, I'm not sure Lawrence's class is an expense I can justify. Maybe I need to stop.

HUMILIATION FACTOR: Low. It's very academic in vibe.

LOCATION: Hotel conference rooms in Santa Barbara, California, or in upstate New York during the school year.

The Lawrence Years, as I like to call them, distinguish themselves by the sheer scope of the goal: to improve the quality of one's thinking in the same way a PhD in applied philosophy might. These Lawrence Weekends are the main times I see my family.

When not writing essays about the seven cardinal virtues or reporting on our zillion cultural projects to become more well-rounded (music, volunteering, politics, art, exercise . . .), we ask Lawrence questions. If the question is more personal, we can ask for a private conversation at the back of the room—like an audience with the pope. I request to talk to our measured, corporate-looking Lawrence all the time. I look to him for the fatherly advice I never quite get. I know this because in the Santa Barbara class, my father sits in the row behind me, feverishly taking notes.

Arguing with Lawrence isn't allowed. We instead do what he calls "forwarding the relevancy of the discourse." But I push it. More than most. There is something about the messiness of desire and big dreams—strong emotional and romantic instincts that I think Lawrence's pragmatism fails to address. He tolerates me, perhaps because he knows I pay close attention. But I'm a needling force too. I present my question to him at the back of the room.

"How long do you think it takes to really get to know someone? To decide if someone's right for you for the long haul?" I stand next to him in his director's chair. We speak in whispers so we don't disturb the writing period.

"I think it's difficult to hide something significant for more than three months. I think we put on our best behavior—likely more together than our private selves—but that's difficult to keep up for long. It's the whole public/private distinction we're talking about—to learn to be *a singular voice*—where there's no difference between our public and private selves."

Hmm. Three months. Tim and I had been together far longer, and no cracks had appeared, no huge split I'd seen. *He's been as sincere and respectful as the day we met. Our conversations, animated; our goals, complementary. Our sex, young and sweet—perhaps a little simple or sleepy. Maybe the word is* shutdown.

"What about when you learn more about their family of origin? Mine's no picnic, but how much would you weigh their environment?"

"Megan, I don't typically talk from a psychological perspective. I'm only concerned with teaching you the skills of self-government. We can talk about this more, perhaps, but I need you to return to your seat. We're about to start another essay."

Arggh. I hate this format. Humiliating.

I sit down, incomplete. I need a reliable person to talk with. Back on the stage, Lawrence instructs us to write about the distinction between what he calls "talking to yourself" and thinking. Talking to yourself is lower-quality thinking, a mistaken notion that there is a homunculus—a miniature you living inside you—with whom you can talk. Signs of this: brooding and reflexive emotion, rather than the clear-mindedness that comes from pragmatic reflection.

I had too much to think about to make time to think.

Lawrence's essay instructions faded into the background while Tim and his mother kidnapped my cortex. She was famous with all of Tim's friends and colleagues for her Katharine-Hepburn-Meets-Insane-Maine-Accent. Not just southern Maine, mind you, but way there at the tippy top, deep in the lexicon of the diphthong. She was also famous with his colleagues for calling his office at odd times to find out about Tim. A hovering helicopter of a mom. And not just a regular helicopter like a twinkly ECO-Star, where you tour the Na Pali Coast while listening to "Somewhere over the Rainbow." But a seven-blade, 73,000-pound Sikorsky CH-53E Super Stallion. The kind that creates high winds and a lot of noise and throws sand in everybody's eyes. Even in rescue mode, those choppers can disturb anything from dolphins to ant colonies—depending on where they hover. So picture that: a helicopter, high winds, a lot of noise and chop. Then picture Katharine Hepburn with a shorter neck.

To say that Mrs. Anderson (I was not to call her by her first name—was that her old-fashioned New England formality or a freakishly formal rule to distance me?) was extremely proper would be an understatement. Let's put it this way: I'm willing to bet she had to smoke to have a bowel movement. All in cashmere sweater sets, paisley scarves, and monogrammed thank-you notes. I knew where Tim got the good posture and direct gaze. Hers, a haunting one. Once her eyes locked on, they didn't waver.

On our visit, I slept in the guest room. Tim, the room next door. After her divorce, she had crammed all her furniture from the family home into a tiny town house. Nothing fit. The beds were too big for the rooms—as if forcing a life she no longer had. When I awoke and popped in to say good morning to Tim, I wore sweatpants and a large boxy Pirate Surf T-shirt—hardly the outfit of a seductress. He wore boxers and no shirt. I sat on the edge of his antique four-poster bed with wood pineapple finials.[1] My feet rested on the steps up to the bed.

Tim's mom walked in dressed in her white robe. She looked at us and stopped dead. In a flash, she went ballistic.

"Did you two *sleep* together? Did you *sleep* together *last night*? Are you *sleeping together* in *my* house?" She gasped and shrieked in a way I'd never seen a person do. *How did she ramp up so fast?* We went from zero to 317 in two seconds.[2]

Tim sat frozen while she shrieked through her sobs:

"I wasn't *spying*!! I came in looking for my *eyedrops*. If I don't get my *eyedrops* my eyes seal *right* shut. Megan, *what* are *you* doing in *here?*"

On autopilot, I stood up, groping for a pineapple to steady me. *Holy shit. This must be what passing out feels like.* The room telescoped. With Tim still calcified, I tried to calm her.

"Mrs. Anderson, I *swear* we weren't doing *anything*. I came in to say hello." Tim hadn't moved. But his chest and neck were breaking out in splotches.

She ran out of the room, down the stairs, and locked herself in her powder room. I could hear (frankly anyone could) her moans and sobs. With Tim still frozen, I decided to check on her. I tiptoed down the stairs and stood at the door. The crying eventually diminished. But she was still in there. I caught a whiff. *A menthol slim? Huh, maybe she's trying to smoke one out.* I headed back upstairs.

"Tim, not to point out the obvious, but I don't think I'm the right one to come to her aid here. I'm obviously the upsetting bit. I think you'll have to do something." He didn't smile or not smile so much as remain immobilized.

Back in Lawrence's class, half the essay period had passed. I had three pages on the Mrs. Anderson thing.

---

[1] Pineapple: The Colonial symbol of hospitality.
[2] 317 miles per hour: speedboat speed record.

Possible Actions:

1. Call her regularly to get to know her.
2. Have her know me so she stops thinking of me as her son's harlot.
3. Discuss with Tim how he coped with a sexually repressed mother.
4. Handle my concerns on my own. If I was to learn self-government, should I really expect Tim to provide relief?

Screw the essay. I'll turn in these notes, or write something fast at the end.

A few days after the locked powder-room incident, I tried to tell his mother a sweet story about Tim, to normalize things:

"So this one night we were dancing with some friends after work . . . and Tim wasn't enthusiastic, but he knows I love to dance, so he danced anyway. Mrs. Anderson, he was so . . . his eyes fixed on me like a lifeline. But I knew from his expression and awkward moves, it wasn't fun for him. I said, 'Tim, you should only dance if it feels free. If it doesn't, you don't have to. I can dance on my own . . .'"

Her eyes drilled down on me. I drilled back. But like a game of chicken, I would swerve first. "I just mean to say that . . ."

She interrupted. "Megan, I really don't know *why* you'd think he would want to dance with *you*. He *never* wanted to dance with me."

Huh?

Well, lady, there's a difference. I don't know how to tell you this if it's not completely obvious, but the two of us, we have sex. The two of you, no. He wants to put his tongue in my mouth and whatnot. You see, loving and sexing and dancing with someone you love is not the same as dancing with your mother. Got it?

But I said nothing. I again asked Lawrence about it:

"If I—from my Chair of Self-Government—want to evaluate a possible mate, what sort of questions might I ask?"

"From your observations, is he a good man? Do you respect his values?"

"Absolutely. Sometimes I almost think he's too good, like he's trying to make up for millennia of global inequity all on his own, being a privileged white man. There's this uprightness to him. People literally stand a little straighter around him. My parents even commented. Doesn't even like to walk down the street carrying nice retail bags. He doesn't want people of more limited means to be reminded they can't shop at, like, Banana Republic. He brings bagels to the homeless, like that."

"How does he care for you?" Lawrence's exaggerated eyes zeroing in.

"He doesn't engage my neuroses, but I think that's an advantage. He's not the most emotionally expressive person. I suspect that's something I bring."

"Do you love him?"

"Yes."

"And he, you?"

"Yes. Sometimes he says he doesn't deserve me. I never understand what he means by that."

"From your Chair of Self-Government, go slow. Keep observing as rationally as you can."

"Okay. I just want to pick well, Lawrence. I want to use my best thinking to pick well."

19

CAMP WITH THE CHILEAN MILITARY

PURPOSE: Point-of-view change. First ethnographic research for graduate school in international relations.

DURATION: Three months.

EQUIPMENT NEEDED: Backpack, boots, tent, tape recorder, food, maps.

AGE: 26.

RELATIONSHIP STATUS: Tim and I have returned to Patagonia.

EMPLOYMENT: GRE and SAT test-prep instructor, waitress, professional graduate student.

COST: Free (minus plane ticket).

LOCATION: Chilean Patagonia, Rio Baker.

While Tim guides some scientists in Antarctica, I'm back in the Chilean backcountry with another large backpack on. I am alone, studying a roadless region—now of interest because it's about to have one. So while Tim and I aren't exactly right next door, at least we share a partial itinerary, the same hemisphere, and some mountain alone time at the end of this. I'm back to interview locals, ranchers, and those involved in the road's construction. The Carretera Austral will be the first road to take residents to southernmost Chile without needing Argentina to get there. The military is building it. Argentina and Chile haven't ever been the best of friends—not so good at sharing. I'm on my way to meet my friend Michelle at a footbridge at the bend of the verdant Baker River, passing along its milky blue—through forests of *coihue* and *lenga* beech and Patagonian cypress, crossing horse trails and *calafate* bushes, all with glaciated peaks out in the distance. It's getting dark.

From behind me, an enormous blue military truck comes barreling down the new dirt road. It stops next to me; the diesel fumes cloud my vision. The truck's hefty driver rolls down his window.

"No good, a woman alone here. Wherever it is you are going we must give you a ride."

"*No te preocupes. Estoy* . . . I'm absolutely fi—"

It appears they see me as a lady in distress, when really, I am just a lady who is late. But I can't refuse. I must say yes in the same polite way they must offer the ride. Chivalry commands it.

"Ramón. Give her a hand. Take her *mochila*."

There is utter certainty and force in his graciousness. Arguing with my graying Chilean Marlon Brando would prove useless.

"*Gracias.*" I smile awkwardly, hoisting my pack to Ramón and then taking his offered hand, pulling me into the cab. It smells of cigarettes, body odor, and diesel. Marlon Brando is chatty.

They drive me to that bend in the river. Michelle never shows. While I'm worried, we had a backup plan, so we'll reconnect tomorrow. Brando refuses to let me camp alone.

"*Absolutamente no. Aquí, no. No podemos permitirlo.*" He must protect me from the sense of danger a woman alone evokes. He now drives me to the military encampment. The next thing I know, Marlon ushers me through camp head-quarters.

"You will have tea and biscuits with the captain. You must be hungry. And tired. This requires tea," he says.

I walk behind Brando through the dark, head down (with giant pack still on) under an open sky, past the entire squad of all-male soldiers who stand at attention for the Chilean version of "Taps." I don't know if I feel scolded or revered as I pass. I look up at the heavens and wonder where Tim is tonight under this map of stars. At the beginning of our romance, we promised to look at the night sky at the exact same time no matter what time zone we each were in. On this night, just a brief glance skyward.

Marlon introduces me to the captain. Large South American mustache and all.

"Come, come, tell me about your travels. We never have guests."

We bounce between Spanish and English as I tell him of my research on the Carretera Austral.

"Yes, everything will change now that we are here. This road will connect them to the world. The very first time for some of them. Providence. Progress. Pinochet's crowning act."

Crowning act? I say nothing. I smile and nod and reach for another biscuit. And now, biscuit in hand, the only thing keeping me from more dazzling conversation (apart from the frequently misconjugated verb) is that I can't stop staring at the giant oil painting behind the captain. It is of Pinochet, the former dictator and general of the army, who seems to stare me down as well. Has this captain, who keeps offering me hot biscuits and rose-hip jam, tortured innocent civilians, crimes for which Pinochet is responsible? I try to avoid Pinochet's gaze.

After enough chitchat to tire even the most fluent of Spanish speakers, my captain says, "I must not keep you any longer. You will take my room. I will sleep elsewhere." All said with a certain fatherly care.

"But I—"

"Nonsense. I won't hear of it. Off we go. This way."

I follow him to his small quarters with its papery-thin temporary walls. The worry of a possible rape now fades into the background. If there were a rape attempt, I figure my screams would be heard through those walls in a heartbeat. I guess whether anyone would do anything about it is another question. Not sure I can picture Brando or anyone else coming to my rescue. I laugh to myself thinking what Mom would say.

"Do you have your backup plan?"

In this case, no. No on all fronts. No to escape a rape, nothing considered without a life with Tim.

Mom loves to think of these worst-case-scenario solutions: the Hillside Strangler in my tween years when Dad was away. I chose hair spray as my bedside weapon for the eyeballs, and jacks on the floor for the toes to slow the Strangler down (apparently, I pictured a barefoot strangler); Mom's plans for my elaborate career as a dental hygienist, despite being at a great college; her emergency snack stockpile everywhere she ventured—always overly healthy, like steamed kamut and almond butter—on the road or planted in any house she occupied. I can hear Dad:

"Thank goodness for the gallons of water she has stored, given your mother's survival choice of jars and jars of salty almond butter . . ."

Back in Patagonia, Captain Non-Rapist offers me his shower shoes for the morning and his music player for my entertainment. In this one moment, amid tiny teacups and stale bread, amid thoughts of thousands of men and women lost to torture, I try to wrap my brain around the fact that the same machine responsible for brutality is offering me shower thongs, a comfortable bed, and a prized officer's music player. Somehow this changes me. The world has never looked more generous, never more cruel. Neither all black, nor all white. Both in the same moment. And my small problems—my missing friend, a heavy pack, the pressures of young love and graduate school—none of this will feel quite the same way again.

20

WILDERNESS FIRST RESPONDER (WFR)

PURPOSE: A national certification to handle emergencies in remote settings: wound management; vital-signs assessment; fractures and dislocations; splinting; patient monitoring and long-term management; spinal immobilization and litter packaging; head/chest injuries; neurological, respiratory, and cardiac emergencies; diabetes; bites; stings; allergies; anaphylaxis; search and rescue; poisoning; lightning; shock; gender medical issues; fecal impaction; cold injuries.

DURATION: Eighty hours in ten days.

EQUIPMENT NEEDED: Tape, scissors, gauze, etc. And a good set of lungs.

AGE: 26.

RELATIONSHIP STATUS: No talk of marriage yet. Although I'm starting to bring it up to Tim with hugely charming frequency (not).

EMPLOYMENT: A mishmash of Yale graduate student, retail shopkeeper, and graduate NPR intern.

COST: $600.

LOCATION: Missoula, Montana, and outside Pinedale, Wyoming.

Back from Patagonia, it seems prudent to be prepared in solitude. I am my mother's daughter. Plus, shhh, don't tell anyone, but I want to work as a wilderness educator. And what's not to love about knowing how to realign a broken femur, splint it, build a litter, and hike that poor bastard to the nearest roadhead? First-aid paradise. There's nothing like blood-curdling yells coming from a patient with a fractured femur. Keeping this in mind during femur-break scenarios, I scream my bloody head off.

"Help *meeeeeee*!!!!! Help meeee!!!!! Help me!!!!!"

My method acting might be a tad overkill, but it's heaven nonetheless. I mean, really, did you know men can get their testicles twisted up *inside* their scrotums? Must be extremely aggressive hiking. Fascinating. Apparently, safety never takes a vacation.

I may be genetically encrypted to handle emergencies. All metaphysical New Age workshopping aside, my parents and Renee each have the same quality. We're your people if you're having an emergency. And we have a pretty broad definition for what constitutes one, so my family is an ace in the hole if you know us. But you likely don't know us because we busy ourselves living from one logistical scenario to the next. We don't, as a rule, have the strongest let's-socialize-like-regular-people skills. It's one of our flaws.

Afraid you'll miss your flight? We'll get you there. Roads closed due to bad weather? We'll get through. Car broken down in the middle of the night? We will locate (and have located) the right people to fix it, waking them without hesitation. Has the airline lost your luggage? We'll talk our way into the aircraft cargo to do a hand search. Need to get a vital message to someone at an unknown restaurant who can't be reached by phone? We'll convince every maître d' to inspect every table at every restaurant. If someone thinks they saw him or her, we will acquire that witness's home number and question them. Have a relative lost at sea and the foreign government refuses to continue the search? We'll find the one off-duty ship with the one bored captain who's looking for something to do. If that doesn't work, we'll procure and then paddle a rubber dinghy ourselves. We don't even need to stop for snacks. We feed on adrenaline. When others' energy fades, we're just warming up. And the beauty: we're so into it, people don't even get irritated. We usually get them caught up in the infectious life-of-its-own energy that an emergency holds.

The Griswolds are not so good with the boring everyday stuff. Picking up the dry cleaning? Yuck. Regular grocery shopping? Who cares. We only like it when we've been collectively digging a hole in the front yard and it becomes obvious we should take a break because a few people have keeled over. Then we will handle both situations efficiently—dropping the unconscious people off at the emergency room on the way to the market. It's probably why we are particularly suited to courses with the word *intensive* or *immersion* in the title. They all involve a certain intensity: an enthusiastic beginning, a grueling middle, a tearful end. Perfect.

So give me that hypothermic head-injured climber in a diabetic coma with testicular torsion and fecal impaction and let's *do* this. If pressed, I know how to curve my finger just so. I never understood the technique involving a metal spoon, though. That must be the advanced course. And I don't think I'll volunteer as pretend patient.

Up next in our WFR: a multihour rescue exercise. We find our victims in various states of shock, covered in the requisite tomato-paste blood with massive head trauma and broken limbs. My assignment: calm a shock-ridden wife who's running around in river-soaked clothes, which we've agreed must be removed.

"Help me!" my patient calls. "Somebody needs to help my husband! He's in the river! Why isn't anyone *doing* anything?"

"Janet, I can assure you we're doing everything we can for Steve. Now," I say, taking her hand strongly, "why don't we get off those soaked pants?"

I've gotten her pants off, but she breaks away. She's running loose with no pants. I chase her through some trees, grab her gently but firmly, and sit her down on a rock.

"Let's get you some dry pants, shall we? Which do you like better, tea or cocoa? We're getting some hot water fired up for you right now."

"But Megan, he's, he's . . . what if Tim were in trouble? Wouldn't you freak out?"

Wow. She's taking this scenario to a whole new level.

"Yes, but the best way to help Steve is to stay calm so we can think clearly. We're going to need your help, okay? Now, which do you prefer? Cocoa or Bengal Spice?"

"Cocoa sounds good."

"Perfect."

Our patient's first-aid scenario "husband" remains in the river with a head injury, wrapped in the burrito method (aka ridiculous amounts of sleeping bags) to prevent hypothermic shock. He looks like the banana in the Fruit of the Loom commercial. But in this case, the large banana-man is currently submerged in a river.

Wife calmed and re-panted, I'm off to locate where to land a helicopter should our runners make good time by nightfall. I'm high as a kite. I don't fret over anything because (even just hypothetically) there's no need to worry the worst *might* happen. It's here.

Mom would love this. As would Renee. She just might not dig the outdoor part. And if Renee's femur were shattered—pretend or otherwise—she would be far more polite about it. And Dad would nominate himself the group's incident commander while orienting the map upside down, passionately sending us not to the roadhead but possibly off a lovely cliff. But with that blind enthusiasm, I promise, the troops would love him for it.

21

FIRST OFFICIAL COUNSELING SESSION

PURPOSE: My parents are getting a divorce. A Federal Express envelope came to New Haven, Connecticut, right before spring break telling me so. It was signed by both of them. I want to talk to someone. FedEx isn't all that conversational.

DURATION: One hour.

EQUIPMENT NEEDED: A borrowed car while visiting the parentals. But where I will go with Mom's car is private.

AGE: 27.

RELATIONSHIP STATUS: Tim's parents went through this a few years ago. I don't know where to put the grief. Our family might have been fractured, but it was mine.

EMPLOYMENT: Full-time graduate student with part-time work gigs.

COST: Reduced rate of $50. She's my friend's mother, and the only counselor I know.

LOCATION: Costa Mesa, California.

The counselor's name was Mickey. As in mouse.

"If I'm totally honest . . ." I told Mickey while sitting in her office, which appeared trapped in the year 1986. Either that, or I had a guest spot on *Miami Vice*.

I wasn't even sure what a counselor was supposed to do. Do they just listen or do they dispense advice? Or both? There should be a rule book explaining these things. I just launched in.

"I think I thought all those workshops might help keep them together, or *us* together. I mean, nobody told me to take them all. That was sort of my idea or the group idea. Like we were all in this boat together and you don't leave a sinking ship. You paddle. Get really smart about this life stuff, this love stuff, any way you can. Then put those skills to practice. Keep the ship afloat. Now what? It's over. I'm a failure. My father says he's 'sorry I choose to experience this divorce as a problem.' He thinks it's wonderful. I wanted to talk to someone who at least thinks it's okay to see it as a problem."

"That's very admirable," she said.

"Admirable?" I ask. "To want to talk to someone? Or to see this as a problem?"

"Neither. It's admirable to want to fix it."

"I don't think it's admirable. I think I'm off my nut."

22

THE ASTRO BIVY

PURPOSE: *Astro:* meaning of or relating to stars. *Bivy:* short for *bivouac*, a lightweight sack that slips over a sleeping bag, rendering a tent unnecessary. While the term *bivouac* is a technical one, it can also describe any time you sleep out without a tent. Add the word *astro* and you've got a night under a blanket of stars on a high peak.

DURATION: One night.

EQUIPMENT NEEDED: One sleeping bag, one pad, one hat.

AGE: 27.

RELATIONSHIP STATUS: In love and so proud to be with Timmy-Tim-Tim yet *also* grateful to be able to do this mountain professional training on my own.

EMPLOYMENT: In process. Working to get hired as a wilderness expedition leader.

COST: Free.

LOCATION: The Wind River Range, Wyoming.

While I've been moving in the wilderness direction, Dad has apparently been privately wooing his married unrequited love from his Christian Science college days (he says it's all in a platonic-family-friendly way) while he waits for his divorce to go through. Her husband is a wheelchair-bound stroke survivor and, like his wife, a hard-core traditional Christian Scientist. Apparently Dad has been writing Metaphysical Open Letters to both of them, and only she writes back. Dad has been visiting and pledging his platonic love for her to the husband and the wife both. The husband must love that. Not to sound crass, but to catch you up, the husband has now died unexpectedly a few months later, and Dad announces her existence to us for the first time, and his plans to marry her.

"Dad, isn't it a little awkward that last week you were the family friend and this week you are the fiancé?" I'm not trying to be obnoxious. I really want to know.

"Oh, Megan . . ." (I think I've blocked out what he said beyond that. Whatever he says, it suggests that I'm not being super positive on the whole thing.)

He's right. I feel for the family. Her grown children just lost their dad. And it's hard to train the Emperor-Has-No-Clothes Kid out of me. I love it about me, and I hate it about me. Both.

But *maybe* (and I promise I'm not trying to be snarky here) if Christian Scientists don't believe in death, maybe the wife doesn't need to mourn? So Dad's on the wedding track. They're planning the event for Mother's Day. Ouch. Our mom.

So Mom is trying to make a new life for herself, single at sixty-five. As for Renee, she's gotten a corgi. I begged her to. I'm thankful she said good-bye to her Napoleonic-complex-know-it-all boyfriend Doug, so she can welcome in someone special. As for myself, I sit in the mountains for the equivalent of a monthlong job interview to become a wilderness teacher. Maybe I'll finally fit in somewhere. I love the mountains. I love Tim. I love my outdoor-loving-natural-history-ornithology-geology-studying-climb-ski-paddle-worshipping friends. When I left for the course, Dad had broken up with his fiancée.

To be honest, it gives me a tremendous sense of relief to not have a new stepmom just yet. The last thing Dad asks me before I head into the mountains: "Megan, what do you think all this love stuff is about?"

I rattle on for at least fifteen minutes, but circle around to clichés and things I *hope* to be true about love.

"Dad, I think you have to love yourself first and not be afraid to be alone for a bit without Mom, without anyone. It might be a great learning."

Who was I to talk? I had grabbed onto Tim like a life raft as soon as he'd kissed me and never considered an alternative.

Unknown to me, Dad's solo learning will last two weeks. But for now, I take comfort in having everything I need on my back, in the company of fourteen equally ambitious outdoor-worker types surrounding me in the mountains.

And tonight, three weeks in, the weather looks like a solid go. It's clear. The sun is setting. It's August, the best time to be in the Winds. The clear sky screams astro bivy. On a full stomach of pesto pasta and a giant hot chocolate, I leave our camp in the fading light. I cross the small creek that gurgles in that way I only imagine happens in the most romantic of gentle summer love stories. I cut through the meadow up to a small saddle. To the left is a bald granite peak that today I can't seem to remember the name of. Despite being in the middle of this monthlong interview, tonight it feels like I am off the clock. I'm not worried about my performance, or the class I have yet to teach, or the epic debrief I had with the instructor team when I failed to descend a climb fast enough in an impending lightning storm. I want my face under the stars. All fifteen of us are buzzing with excitement from the break in routine. Casual chat rumbles softly as the group makes its way up the peak. There's no trail, just one rock after the next—boulder by boulder. All anybody's got with them is a headlamp and a sleeping bag, so we move efficiently. We reach the top in the fading light. It's bright enough to capture a few silly photographs of the group in silhouette. I wonder why I can't live up here, gazing at the expansive view to the west where the range fades to prairie. I select the perfect spot, snuggled in a rock alcove with a view of the stars so vivid, I'm certain no movie, no light show, no performance will ever compare. I don't know if I believe in God, but if I did, I suspect God would live here. Or if not live here, then she would certainly consider this spot when feeling particularly spiritual. I wonder whether my molecules are being rearranged in response to the beauty. The beast in me feels soothed. In this moment, life isn't just bearable or a mixed bag. It feels full and round and tingles everywhere. I feel my toes curl with excitement at the bottom of my bag. I let my eyes peek out from under my hat but keep everything else covered in my womb cocoon. I feel like I am six years old, with that volume of glee that threatens to blow me apart with happiness.

And then I see it. A flash of light. And then another. It's lightning. The flashes are moving. Closer. I won't make the same mistake twice. Which means we must descend. I scramble for my headlamp. Without speaking, the entire group has gone into retreat mode. It's understood the bivy is over. I wonder whether the nature of the divine is to only get small vibrant tastes. Maybe the point is to savor it like one special chocolate wrapped in fine paper, rather than a box of them in bulk. Maybe it's better this way—to leave one wanting more. A reminder that life, even in its full pageantry, can be gone in a flash.

23

TRADITIONAL CHINESE MEDICINE

PURPOSE: Concerned primarily with the external causes of disease: Wind, Cold, Damp, Heat, Dryness, and Summer Heat. These cover anything from aches and inflammation to sluggishness to pathogens that wander and change. My diagnosis: Liver Qi Stagnation with Dampness and False Heat. My pulses: wiry.

DURATION: Weekly treatments when treating both acute and chronic conditions.

EQUIPMENT NEEDED: The telltale sign of a TCM student? They appear to be wearing a hemp-ish outfit purchased at the health food store.

AGE: 28.

RELATIONSHIP STATUS: I wonder why it looks easier for my father to plunge into marriage than for me.

COST: $20 at student clinic.

LOCATION: Bastyr University, Kenmore, Washington.

Dad has remarried. Happened as soon as the divorce was final. He did it while I was finishing my wilderness guide's course. When it began, like I said, he was single. At the end, another Federal Express envelope greeted me—this time with a small note and a wedding photo. Good old FedEx. It's a nice picture of the two of them—big smiles and fancy clothes. He's in a new gray suit and she, a silvery ball gown, like a nonanorexic inaugural Nancy Reagan. Now, the fact that I don't know the people standing on either side of them is more than a little disconcerting, but there it is. I think the people beside them are my new stepmother's Christian Science practitioner and his wife. Not sure.

I'm out of Yale. Tim has proposed. I was standing in my kitchen in New Haven when it happened—in my ratty pink sweatpants, my go-to study outfit. Tim calls them my depressed pants. He stood in contrast with his crisp button-down and J. Crew khakis. While I puttered over cereal, he put his two hands out toward me.

Two fists. Like a shell game.

"Pick a hand," he said.

I picked his right. He turned over his hand, opened his palm, and there it was. A solitaire diamond ring. His mother's ring. I looked up and down between his face and his hand, stunned. He smiled nervously, almost apologetically, with a diminutive tilting of his head side to side, like a metronome.

"I don't understand. Are you—are you asking to marry me? Is that what this is?"

Was it unkind of me to make him spell it out?

He nodded yes.

"Wow. But I thought, I thought we weren't talking about this stuff. The three-month moratorium . . . to not push the marriage question like I was."

He shrugged nervously. And as if it were just another day, he said:

"I wanted to ask you earlier in the weekend, but you were pretty distracted with your UN class with Sylvia. Sorry, but we kind of have to hurry if I'm going to catch the train back to Providence and make my afternoon class."

I nod. Still thinking, he said *ask*. Is it asking if you don't *say* anything?

With the ring still in my left hand, my right grabbed my purse and headed with him to my rusty Subaru to sprint him to the station. We didn't say much in the car. This felt so out of the blue, and so . . . quiet. As he undid his seat belt, I asked:

"If I put it on my finger, could that mean I'm thinking about it?"

I don't want to have my silence hurt his feelings. What if I'm crushing him in my pausing? Maybe that was really hard for him.

"Yes," he said.

I called Mom after dropping Tim off.

"I think Tim just asked me to marry him. It was a little . . . different. He couldn't seem to *say* anything. Is that normal? Is that how this should go?"

Mom adores Tim, as ever. As do I. *I think. I mean I think I do. Why wouldn't I?*

"Oh, Megan. This is what you've wanted. [*Was it, truly?*] Don't overthink this one. Just leap."

We hung up and I called him. My Can-I-Think-About-It phase lasted about an hour. I didn't want to distress him. And Mom was right, wasn't she?

So now we are engaged and live in Bellingham, Washington, and I work as a freelance radio reporter, house cleaner, and mountain instructor. I'm still figuring out how to put my training and interests together. But I don't totally know how to go about it. I kind of want *National Geographic* meets NPR. But more urgently (or conveniently distracting from career questions): my breasts are bugging me. Three weeks of every cycle they ache and ache badly—like giant cantaloupe bruises. The breast search has begun. I try it all: the Anti-Candida Diet (I burst into a spontaneous yeast infection after a bowl of cereal on a predawn hike—screw that); Ashtanga yoga (I practice five to six days a week from six to eight a.m.); Ayurveda (I'm Vata-Kapha); the Blood Type Diet (lots of iodine and red meat; apparently, as an O, I'm a hunter, not a gatherer—sure, that sort of fits). I've gotten Rolfed—yes, all ten sessions. It will help my posture and make my pelvis drop and rib cage protrude, and I will sob like a baby (all these are considered good things); but my breasts still hurt like a mother. Tim thinks my experiments are funny. I joke about my quest all the time. He's not into the searching thing. He says he's happy with himself and doesn't need to change or explore. He isn't looking for solutions to anything. And his chest is fine.

I refuse to believe there's something wrong with curiosity. The world is a big place with lots of creative solutions, especially if I look hard enough and stay curious. So I will try acupuncture. And now, in the student clinic, I've never had a group of people so fascinated to check out my tongue. Either they're easily amused or they don't have televisions. They poke, prod, needle, and give me hideous herbs that stink up the house and ask me if I sweat at night. One intern is concerned I have a goiter. I try to reassure him it's simply my fat neck, which gets fatter under stress. I swear. The fat goes straight to my neck, avoiding my hips entirely. Lucky me. The TCM acupuncture lowers my breast pain by a week. That's something. Just not enough.

24

ASHTANGA YOGA (MYSORE STYLE)

PURPOSE: Yoga is exercise I can do that doesn't require strapping my breasts into an industrial-strength jog bra when PMS rears its swollen head.

FREQUENCY/DURATION: Five to six days a week. Two hours a day, six to eight a.m.

EQUIPMENT NEEDED: A thick mat is nice but not required.

AGE: 28 to present (depending on my mood).

RELATIONSHIP STATUS: I've been practicing yoga because I feel this loneliness sometimes with Tim, or maybe it's only within myself; yoga helps fill me up.

EMPLOYMENT: Wilderness teacher, personal assistant, substitute yoga teacher, freelance radio reporter. How are all these jobs going to come *together*?

COST: The same as going to a moderately priced gym.

LOCATION: Bellingham, Washington.

Do your practice and all is coming.

—*K. Pattabhi Jois*

Mom is completely devastated—Dad marrying so suddenly. I'm trying to get to know my stepmother and her adult children (quite a bit older than Renee and me) and be gracious. She's kind to me, but we speak a different language. She has strong Christian Science views on how the world is, so I'm very careful with my words. I want her to like me. I don't want to step on any metaphysical toes. So no talk of problems, or the body, or graphic humor, or boobs. She's devout. No doctors. No medicine. Vitamins might as well be heroin. No messy talk about emotions or *negativity*. Good luck with this, self, as the messy stuff is about the only thing that interests me.

I hoped to get to know my dad on his own—like really, finally know him. I wanted to somehow pass through (via osmosis?) this formidable energetic bubble that encases and radiates around him. It's clear, so I can see him. But it's like this sphere renders out of reach any closeness, connection, or fatherly something. The bubble of energy is large. It could fill a small New York studio apartment or, minimally, a freight elevator. Yet somehow, my stepmom speaks enough of his language or thinks enough of his thoughts that she's welcomed. She inhabits a similar bubble. I imagine they overlap like a Venn diagram. Or maybe their bubbles kiss. Perhaps because he can't imagine a moment where his bubble doesn't kiss hers, he hasn't let Renee or me see or talk to him on his own. It stings. I build my own routine to help me not think about that all too much. And this yoga is what I've come up with.

It's six a.m. The room is dark and warm. Walking into practice is like burrowing into a seashell, as the students' Ujjayi breath technique sounds like the ocean. Each morning I place my mat right next to Tracy. Our friendship exists in our daily proximity—breathing and twisting into all sorts of postures, side by side. She's further along in the Second Series than I, which means she spends more time with her legs behind her head. And while I stuff my legs behind my neck, and drop into backbends, and bind my hands around my torso this way and that, I'll tell you what my actual practice consists of. Regardless of the warm room, the burning candles, and the roomful of heavy breathers, where it's truly fiery is on the inside.

This is the material of my practice: I feel a lot. I feel a lot a lot of the time. I have a lot of energy, which gives me a lot of time to do stuff and then feel a lot about it. It appears that one of my life's passions has been the following: I seem to like to worry, then criticize myself, then worry some more. Occasionally, I think a couple of really solid thoughts, then I worry some more, then I worry about worrying. Then I judge myself for being a worrier who worries too much. Then I worry about how I judge myself about worrying that I worry too much. Then I worry that I judge that I worry about worrying. Then I just worry. Then I get sad that I wasted so much time worrying. Then I get sad that I feel so sad. Then I am disgusted that I felt so sad about worrying. Then I fantasize a couple of things about myself and then about a couple of other people. Then I work for a while and have a couple of really good thoughts.

And this morning, I don't know if they're good thoughts. I can't stop thinking about—wait for it—my dad, Renee, and my recent trip to SeaWorld. We'd been asking if we could just see him on our own, and we got no after no. Some weird idea he got into his head that alone time would hurt his new wife. I don't know why she would mind, but that's what he thought. Then somewhere in there, SeaWorld came up.

Dad seems to think this trip to SeaWorld can clear up every problem we've had this past year: the way Renee and I worried for Mom, who felt blindsided by the divorce; having the first time we hear of Margie (let alone his plans to marry) be four days after her husband's passing; Renee and I not experiencing our father as particularly compassionate in the divorce terms for a thirty-five-year marriage to a now sixty-six-year-old woman; and finally, his spending the holidays only with Margie's family.

All the while, I'm dying to know him away from all our family drama because I crave something, *anything*, from him. Yet he feels like a Tower of Babel I have not the foggiest idea how to climb. And Shamu is his only offer.

We navigate this sweaty San Diego asphalt parking lot with attendants in orange vests and occasional acne directing us through a maze of RVs. Renee and I follow like we really are ten again, falling in line behind our big-bellied dad in his acid-washed jeans, white sneakers, and go-to shirt with his valve company's logo and a teeny bit of armpit sweat.

I can't decide if it's breaking my heart or if it infuriates me that he sees things so simply. He just looks so cute rushing ahead to beat the line at the ticket window. An attendant offers to take our picture with the walking Shamu. Normally, Dad would say no to this, insisting they are milking us. But today he's game.

Consulting the map, he says, "Now, girls, if we hurry we can see the Penguin Performance. We've got three minutes. Let's go, let's go!"

Obedient girl-women, we start lightly jogging to keep up, passing hundreds of sweaty less-hurried Americans. He excuse-me-pardon-me's himself to the middle of the amphitheater to make sure we have the centermost seats both vertically and horizontally.

"I *do* think this is the best location. Although maybe we can get this gentleman to move down a bit. Sir, would you mind . . ."

Here we go. The man who can't be embarrassed. Who, after our trip to Ringling Brothers Circus, drove our sedan the wrong way up the exit ramp to follow the elephants, becoming the special envoy lead car in a parade of fellow unauthorized vehicles; flashing lights and sirens; my sister and I hunkered down on cue; state patrol at our window.

From the Dolphin Presentation on to the Shark-Tank Diorama, his sprinting routine continues. I'm not sure how much time we will actually spend *together* if this keeps up.

"If I . . . I think we can just make it to the walrus and sea otter show."

Oh, God, I think that's the one where they dress the walrus up in costumes. I haven't been here since sixth grade. This is one of those moments I can't look at Renee. I'm twenty-eight and off to watch a French-maid walrus.

"How about some cotton candy?" he asks.

I can't bear to tell him we're not ten anymore and that Renee's idea of a treat is more in the fondue department or a nice cabernet. And mine, when it comes to cotton candy—let's just say I've never taken the idea of bulimia seriously, but it will force me to consider dabbling.

"Sure, Dad!" we say in unexpected unison, surrounded by overfed families with toddlers digging into corn dogs in the food court. I feel a little sick. I've been watching overtanned trainers dump buckets of tubby dead fish into the mouths of sea life of various sizes for about four hours now.

Renee and I can't bear to look at each other. If we do, we'll have to admit that this breaks our hearts. About fifteen years too late. I don't want this to be true. We love him too much. Each of us wants his attention and enthusiasm so badly, we'd probably jump into the shark tank if we thought it would please him.

So I eat cotton candy, feeling my jeans tightening. Renee eats the pink cloud while glancing around for something like, minimally, a bad beer to wash it down. The tanks of fish, in a weird way, helped, gave us something to focus on.

Upon exiting the park, we stop to pick up our group portrait. Renee and I look surprisingly similar—some mixture of bewilderment and sadness, all underneath toothy smiles. Dad is in the middle with Shamu, looking like he's never seen something cooler than a walking, talking furry killer whale.

Renee and I want to tell him we've had the time of our lives. We'll say something like that. But it's not true. Dad doesn't know how to have all that regular of conversations. And there are about seventeen conversations we're not having: his being back in his family's fold, his rush to marry, Mom's settlement, and, perhaps the hardest to admit, that it seems he no longer needs any of us.

25

THE ONGOING CLASS WITH LAWRENCE (REVISITED)

PURPOSE: Sometimes one must pause to consider whether one's teacher is sufficiently consistent with what's being taught.

DURATION: One weekend a month. And lots of homework.

EQUIPMENT NEEDED: None.

AGE: 28.

RELATIONSHIP STATUS: Earnest (sometimes annoyingly so) questioning student to one comfortably hierarchical teacher.

COST: If I stop studying with Lawrence, it will definitely save me money.

HUMILIATION FACTOR: A top note of humiliation in a chypre of disillusionment.

LOCATION: Bellingham, Washington (a phone call).

Lawrence has been sitting in front of me, on a stage, well above my sight line, for about a decade, month in, month out, year in, year out. He's encouraged me to think rationally, not too emotionally, and to be the same person in private as I am in public. Whether I've learned that way of being is another question entirely. I think I'm pretty good with being my same self in public as I am in private. And given what I just learned about Lawrence, I'm thinking I'm better at that than he is. What I do know is I've never felt that Lawrence understood how with love and human emotion, we're not designed to always act in a measured, rational way. I seemed to be the only person noticing this blind spot in his theories in class. I wonder if I mind. Minimally, it might be time to stop talking to him as an authority figure.

The mighty sure can tumble.

Lawrence has apparently been sleeping with/dating/being intimate with one of his students. Word got out. And so his team of all female staffers are calling all the students to do damage control. Get ahead of the gossip. Control the spin. In case we hadn't heard. And I hadn't.

What bothers me most isn't what you might think. I never expected Lawrence to be a superhero, free of human desire. But I suspect *he* did. For myself, I realize I've been tiptoeing for years around something about spiritual teaching and leadership: that putting yourself at the front of *any* room as an expert—especially in spirituality—is dangerous. I've sat with some sort of leader or another at the front of a room for decades now. And I've noticed that this kind of front-of-the-room power can go to the front-of-the-room-person's head. And more often than not, it does. It seems especially easy for men. Just sayin'. They have the confidence to put themselves there, and often enough arrogance to justify behavior they didn't exhibit before they became a leader. It's about impossible to not start believing the hype you've created about yourself.

For all Lawrence's measuredness, the one thing I was convinced was missing from his *paradigm* was the messiness of love.

So maybe it surprised Lawrence, but it didn't surprise me. He broke his own rule—a class rule—against sexual involvements in the class, and started dating (can you even call it that?) from within his own—from the teacher position, no less. It did not surprise me. Nor did it surprise me (but it did disappoint) that he didn't choose to be intimate with the age-appropriate and intellectual equal—the professor and poet. He picked the young, malleable-hero-worship participant.

So I'm going to exit. No big speeches. Not because Lawrence slept with Jessica, the doe-eyed woman of average intellect. I'm out because I don't like the way I just got spun. His female staffers are complicit. And instead of just owning the facts, they are throwing Jessica's mental stability into question. Calling her the vindictive spurned woman and all that. This crushes me too, as I don't just believe in the brotherhood of man, but the sisterhood as well. All beings. And they just threw one of ours to the wolves of judgment and one-sided narratives.

Lawrence, I suspect you believed you were above error. I never did. I don't want to be taught by someone who doesn't know this. I forgive you your human frailties. I do not condone your speaking ill of a student who put her trust in you.

I'm out.

26

CLASSICAL FIVE ELEMENT LICENTIATE (ACUPUNCTURE SCHOOL)

PURPOSE: System of Chinese medicine to address physical, emotional, and spiritual concerns. Developed over thousands of years, identifying pathways of energy called meridians, which enliven the body.

DURATION: Three years of training. Then clinicals. Then national exams.

EQUIPMENT NEEDED: Uh, needles. And moxa (an herb you burn on the point before needling).

AGE: 29.

RELATIONSHIP STATUS: Engaged.

EMPLOYMENT: I'm ditching the reporter direction. I know it's an insane switch. But in reporting they want me to feel neutral about whatever story I'm covering. And I can't seem to feel neutral. It's cringe-inducing to add more graduate school in a family that doesn't believe in it—and pricey to jump ship like this—but I'm compelled. I don't want to just hear people's heartbreaking stories, I want to help do something about them.

COST: $75 to $100 per session as a patient.

LOCATION: Institute of Taoist Education and Acupuncture, Louisville, Colorado, and Bellingham, Washington.

Follow the nothingness of the Tao and you can be like it, not needing anything, seeing the wonder and the root of everything. And even if you cannot grasp this nothingness, you can still see something of the Tao in everything.

—Tao Te Ching

It started easily enough. On the breast quest, I became a Five Element patient. The first appointment and intake was nothing I had ever experienced. Not only was I asked to elaborately detail every fluid that has ever come out of me, the questions about my family and personal life would give Freud a run for his money.

My mother has moved up to Whidbey Island to be closer to Tim and me, and to her dream of a pack of dogs and a farm. Dad and my stepmother have moved to Lake Tahoe into what we all think of as Mom's cabin. Renee, in Oakland, listened to me and not only got a dog but is taking her first road trip. A big deal. Some outdoor friends that I hope she likes are on her itinerary. She has a new boyfriend, Mark, but I don't think (from my view in the cheap seats) he's kind enough. She deserves to find a real love connection.

With all this swirling around me, I wasn't even sure what *I* wanted. My secret: I dreamed of a more artistic professional life, and I liked the flexibility that working for myself in acupuncture would provide while I figured out the art part. Whatever I eventually fit in creatively, I could still make a living. Plus, I liked the mysterious traditions of Five Element Acupuncture. This was my kind of something. I mean nothing. This was my kind of nothing.

The diagnosing hooked me. Talk about a detective searching for clues. Studying the color, sound, odor, and emotion of each person. It's all about retraining the senses: to see subtle color on a face, smell a constitutional odor, to hear the predominant sound in a voice, to sense an underlying emotion. And no tongue inspection required.

The five elements—fire, earth, metal, water, wood—describe, in metaphor, the cyclical harmony of the natural world, as well as the functions of the body. Five colors from which to choose. Five odors. Five sounds. Five emotions. Categorize each and you're in business. I, for example, am Earth-Metal-Metal, meaning: I'm yellow (at least this yellow stuff is consistent) with a bit of shiny white swirled in (look around the eyes and mouth). My odor is fragrant (think vomit) mixed with rotten (think dead animal or . . . uh . . . feces). My sound: a sing and a weep within. And my emotion? Worry with a little grief for good measure. Yep, that pegs it. Earth relates to the Mother—finding/needing a sense of home. Metal relates to the father, the heavens, a quest for spiritual understanding.

Every element is different. Fire (my mother) smells scorched. Water (my sister) like a tide pool. Wood, rancid (my lovely Tim). Metal, rotten (I've yet to definitively diagnose Dad, but I think Metal). Doesn't this all sound delicious? But here's the hitch: diagnosing is extraordinarily difficult, and the harder you try, the harder it gets. You train to smell with your ears, see with your nose, listen with your eyes, and so on. If you're lucky enough to get three out of the "the four legs of the stool," make a diagnosis, assign an element, and treat the corresponding organs . . . *then* your patient's on her way to glowing health.

Lest you think you're getting off easy, throw in the pressure of getting the proper point location (corrected within the tip of a pen) and precise needle angle and depth, and you must also plan the right treatment, which feels more akin to poetry. Each point is said to have a particular spirit—names like Fly and Scatter, Grasping the Wind, Spirit Burial Ground—but pick the wrong element or point, or do so at the wrong time of day in the wrong season, and your treatment is totally (and this is a clinical term) fucked.

If you don't enjoy the hunt, it's a wonderful way to get an ulcer. No one understands this better than my exacting classmate Coco. She's a delight in contradictions. She can ask the most dead-serious insightful question in class, and then at break time be the one doing a little elfin dance as we circle to eat our overcooked Chinese vegetables. As the Pied Piper of the group, she enacts the best imitations of our stuffiest teachers—their idiosyncratic movements and expressions—turning them up a notch to perfection. She has the self-reliance of a single mother of two teenage boys but will always report the most hilarious moment of the day when she comes up for air. Sometimes, when telling a story, her laughter can get the best of her before she gets a word out. But then, if anyone is having a hard time, she can meet them with utter seriousness and compassion, giving them her razor-sharp focus and kind ear. And if you're lucky, a back massage. That's what she did before acupuncture school. She has all this spirit, even in the face of a massive challenge. She's going blind. For real.

After she began acupuncture school, she learned she has a rare genetic condition called pseudoxanthoma elasticum, which causes the degeneration of her connective tissue, leading her macula to hemorrhage and to permanent loss over time. Imagine, all that spirit in the face of such devastating news. She's flat-out extraordinary.

Picture this: a wood sprite of a brunette with cropped hair, bangs, hazel eyes. A petite former dancer, coming in right around the five-foot-one mark. Although she insists on a good day, there's an additional all-important three-quarters; to look after her eyes, she avoids high-impact anything, so she walks for exercise with this perky gait and a backside you'd kill for, all wearing some de rigueur pretty awful eye-protecting bottle-thick sunglasses. She possesses an internal authority I imagine she was born with and then cultivated in the farmlands of her native Iowa (and P.S., you should know she *made* me call her Coco in these pages because she says her parents gave her a terribly boring name, and the name Coco definitely has that *je ne sais quoi* that she does).

And so the two of us, from whatever forces collided for us to meet, delight in each other. It started when our touchy-feely school assigned us to do a skit on the Fire Element. We laughed our heads off and got the information across (we think). We share a freakishly inexhaustible obsession to develop these highly specific, rather intangible sensory skills. Our shared wonder at the enormity of awakening our senses binds us. We also share hefty self-doubt for how in the world a removed-from-nature human can awaken one's senses like this. Barring a move to the Arctic to live among the planet's best trackers, we want the nose, eyes, ears, and minds of those indigenous peoples, coupled with the knowledge of the best medical clinicians. The Yupik people, for example, have ninety-nine different distinctions for sea ice. We want this sensitivity, but with people. We share the strange combination of receiving top exam scores while scoring highest at feeling forever insufficient.

All this is, of course, made more complex for Coco, as she's losing one of those senses. So the development of her others—touch, smell, sound, and emotional awareness—is that much more crucial.

To be Five Element students means being excited that Coco can smell my confirmed diagnosis as Earth and Metal—fragrant (sickly sweet like an overripe greenhouse or, say, vomit) and rotten (like a discarded ground-beef wrapper or, more classically stated, poop). But Coco deflates to learn that on that day I had donned a lilac essential oil peppered with a bad case of gas. A bottom note, as it were. *Dammit.* And did I mention the twelve energetic wrist pulses corresponding to the twelve organs? Like the rest, push too hard and you'll misdiagnose entirely.

This is way better than becoming a reporter. Fits my detective fantasy too. I get to smell people till I want to puke, stare at faces till a subtle color emerges, and listen to the sounds people emit when sharing their deepest darkest. Then press on the wrist and ask Coco, "What in the *H–E–L–L* do *you* feel?"

Tim thinks it's all a little strange, but he's supportive. So this is what I've become about. If I'm lucky enough to pick the right element, right day, right point for the right person, I get to help a fellow traveler with depression or a busted knee or infertility.

Not to mention, this is another way to understand Tim. He's my well-meaning, well-mannered puzzle.

27

READ *GETTING THE LOVE YOU WANT* BY HARVILLE HENDRIX

PURPOSE: Get better at intimate relationships. More specifically—my relationship.

DURATION: Depends on how many of his exercises you do.

EQUIPMENT NEEDED: The book itself (library). Clothing optional.

AGE: 29.

RELATIONSHIP STATUS: Engaged. We have two blended families. Four sets of parents to visit at the holidays. We're in good company with a bulk of the United States.

EMPLOYMENT: Freelance radio reporter, wilderness instructor, house cleaner.

COST: Free. Mother's advice and library.

LOCATION: Bellingham, Washington.

We marry to heal and finish the unfinished business of childhood. Since our parents wounded us, it is only they who can heal us. Not them, literally, but a primary love partner who matches their traits. With conscious effort and dialogue our Imago love partner is most compatible with us and able to help us to resolve unfinished issues of self-wholeness.

—*Harville Hendrix*

Tim's a Leo. I'm a Virgo. August babies both. Is there anything to that stuff? According to Vedic astrology, I'm actually a Leo. Something about how those Hindus kept time. I've always felt I was very Leo-ish, so maybe I should go Vedic. Let's call it a Leo-Leo couplehood then. And if we're to heal those familial wounds, like Harville says, we definitely mirror each other. We even look similar: light blond hair, angular faces, Nordic athletic types. But shoot, that's half of the Pacific Northwest. I don't know, maybe Harville is full of it.

But now that he mentions it, we both come from two-children families, both the babies of the family with sisters roughly four years older, meaning neither of us went to high school with our sisters. Our fathers, workaholic engineers running their own modest manufacturing companies and machine shops. Both learned their trade from their fathers. So Tim and I each even grew up with the smell of grease and metal shavings. Our fathers divorced our mothers roughly three decades in. And our mothers never seemed to recover. Each father remarried, but our mothers never did. In high school we were popular, but rather straightlaced, with a streak of the nerd academic. As sexual late bloomers, we were both in our twenties before we had sex. We both barely dabbled in dating in college. We were the other's first big relationship. But then regionalism creates some differences. The fact that he comes from Maine and I from California might explain where we diverge. I'm pretty sure his parents didn't call a Christian Science practitioner when he got sick. Leave that to the Californians and a couple of people in Boston.

Here's where we also diverge. I'm no Jenna Jameson, but I think Tim and I are uptight about sex. Our sex is normal, loving, but it's also shy, quiet, and a bit predictable. I mean, everybody in our twosome has orgasms, but I want more.

Maybe Harville can get us closer. My mom says it helped Dad and her. I'm not sure what it helped, seeing as their marriage blew apart, and I'm not sure I ever saw a time they were actually, you know, enjoying each other. But if she said it helped, it must have helped. Hendrix says romantic love is the door to marriage and is nature's selection process to connect us with the right partner for our growth. He says in addition to Mirroring what the other says (aka repeating), capping off with a hint of Validation (like "that makes sense because . . .") and a polish of Empathy ("I imagine that makes you feel . . .") will enable us to better understand one another.

But here's what I really want to do. Harville thinks we should strip off our clothes, stand in front of each other naked, and laugh. He calls it a Naked Belly Laugh. We'll get all naked and vulnerable and bust into something new.

But you'd think I suggested we don space suits and head to Mars. Maybe we're not as similar as I thought. Tim blames the California thing. Is partnering supposed to feel like this? I'm not sure I like this closed-off part of him. But I would never say that out loud, even to myself. He keeps a lot of himself to himself, which I treat like a mystery to solve—a package I can open. Somehow, I think if I'm funny enough or charming enough, he'll come out and play more. So I vote Naked Belly Laugh.

"Nope," he says.

"Nope as in nope?" I ask.

"Yes," he says, making his tenth vat of coffee for the day. "Nope as in nope. You can do this one on your own."

"Well," I argue, "I think the point is to, you know, do it *together*."

I think it's totally reasonable to try together. Sounds vulnerable, sure, but what is sex if not vulnerable? I'd do it alone if I thought it would help, but solo Naked Belly Laughing seems a little silly. Even to me.

28

PLANT SPIRIT MEDICINE
(OR CASTOR OIL PACKS WHILE
DRUMMING)

PURPOSE: Plant Spirit Medicine Shamanism meets Five Element Acupuncture. Huichol Indian shamanism meets Eliot Cowan, a Five Element acupuncturist and creator of Plant Spirit Medicine. I believe it's possible to multitask even in the physio-spiritual experiments.

DURATION: Varies wildly. From minutes to hours to lifelong practice (minus the castor oil).

EQUIPMENT NEEDED: Castor oil, cheesecloth or rags, towels, drum.

AGE: 29.

RELATIONSHIP STATUS: My father has returned to Christian Science. Anything about the body is now taboo. He says my asking about his health is akin to his asking about my sex life. Kind of takes my studies off the holiday dinner table conversation.

EMPLOYMENT: Wilderness instructor, acupuncture student.

COST: CD: $21.95. Castor oil: $8.50.

LOCATION: Tim's and my bedroom, Bellingham, Washington.

Since I can't Naked Belly Laugh with Tim, I'm going to take a deeper solo tack. There's lots of talk at school about Plant Spirit Medicine that blends Five Element Acupuncture with shamanism. I don't have all the equipment, so if I'm to journey solo to the underworld, and a drum is key, I think it's fair (and frankly cheaper) to wear some headphones and let someone else who owns a drum, drum. I refuse to buy a bunch of equipment prematurely.

I'm wrestling with this hormone nonsense. I'm doing my Ashtanga yoga, eating large quantities of vegetables, trying various supplements, boiling Chinese herbs (aka stinking up the house), getting good sleep, working hard, getting acupuncture, and loving on Tim. Still wrestling with Dad stuff, and worrying about Mom. Maybe my breasts are reacting. Did I mention? I still can't talk to Dad on the phone alone. I'm supposed to understand that he and Margie are now one. One.

Maybe my breasts are in protest. While my spirits have improved markedly with all these activities, my breasts are still a beast. I've tried loving them, talking to them (*Come on now, gals, what do you need? How can I help? I appreciate you both, but what's with the pain?*), but they still *kill* (less often, but when they kill they *kill*). So I'm busting out the packs and the drum.

Today's mission: to experience a shamanic journey. In my acupuncture discipline, they also do with plants what we do with needles. But to select the plants for treatment (stay with me here), you must journey to the plants and let them tell you what they would be best used for. Before I journey to an actual plant (like mullein, say, or penstemon), I'm supposed to journey down to the underworld and make a proper introduction. At best, I'll run into my Power Animal, if I have such a thing.

I've spent the last half hour getting everything ready. I have the rags properly saturated and they now cover my breasts. Castor soothes inflammation. And breast tissue discomfort—hormonally caused or not—is aided by decreasing inflammation. I'm lying on about seven towels. I only have one nice pair of sheets that I got from Mrs. Anderson and I'm not going to ruin them with Health Experiment No. 45.

Headphones on, I hit *play*. Tom. Tom. Tom. Tom. *This is an awfully expensive CD, for the rather simple melody.* I am supposed to close my eyes, relax, and *drop in*. I'm distracted by the castor oil. I might have oversoaked the rags. I feel a trickle of oil dribbling down my flank. This is all harder than it sounds.

I'm to picture a cave or tunnel, and take my time crawling down into it. It's dark, rather like *Lord of the Rings* meets *Alice in Wonderland*. Somebody needs to turn on some light.

It's rocky, all right—dark, wet rocks. Water droplets echo through the passage. As caves go, this feels pretty sacred. I crawl out from the cave and enter the forest. Before me stand tall trees, gnarled with a dense canopy above. The light dappling through is rather blue, illuminated by moonlight. I'm supposed to meet someone here. Surely somebody will show. What are the animals I always hear about in shamanic talk? A raven, a bear, a wolf. Heck, I'd settle for a fish. I walk around a while. It appears a rather empty neighborhood. Maybe everybody's out for drinks. What do shamanic animals drink, anyway? I bet absinthe, or gin and tonics. Certainly some of this gnarly bushy stuff is juniper. Maybe there's a pair of little squirrels making moonshine down a hollow or two. I'll have to ask around.

Hellooo! I think to myself. *Anybody here? Maybe I'm trying too hard. Maybe I'm scaring him/her/it off. Okay, I'll try less hard. Less hard.* I walk and walk. *Hey, are those some tracks?* I feel like Winnie-the-Pooh searching for Heffalumps. I don't want to get lost. *Get lost? What am I talking about? Sheesh. Isn't anybody around?* I come upon a little toadstool thing. It's big enough to sit on. *For real, is this a mushroom? Come on, a bluish-lit mushroom toadstool thing? How predictable. If I turn around and see blue fairy wings on my back, I'm blowing this joint. Should I just wait here?* I start tapping my feet. *Must not be impatient, must not be impatient. I'll focus on the drum. Yeah, the drum. Tom. Tom. Tom. Tom.*

I don't see a single creature. Not a bird, not a cricket, not a rabbit. No squirrel speakeasy. *Maybe I'll just relax here for a minute under this toadstool. Just for a minute.* And, you know, well, conveniently for me, I'm already lying down.

I'm so very . . . very . . . Well, I'm asleep. Not that I know that's happening. But the forty-five-minute CD is over. Maybe I *did* go somewhere. Maybe it was like one those mysterious half-sleeps in *savasana*.

I'm tired. I have no idea who my power animal is. Coco's power animal is a horse named Shanti. She must have a gift. I just have stained sheets. I hear Tim coming in. I gather up my swaddle of blankets. Total mess. But my breasts feel better.

The problem with doing so many techniques: it's a crap scientific method.

When I land on one that works, I'm going to have no idea which discipline was responsible.

Tim pops in while I gather. He's been at a meeting. He just gets busier and busier.

"I thought I'd try a little shamanic journeying and figure out this Plant Spirit Medicine stuff. And these"—I say, pointing to a pile of towels—"are for my breasts."

He looks at me quizzically. On our wedding day, I dream of looking like a real-life fairy with a crown of flowers and a gossamer train. Now I look like a greasy-T-shirted, messy-haired, boxer-wearing junk show in need of a comb, a personal shopper, and a decent bar of soap.

"You realize," I ask, "that things are likely going to get weirder around here, right?"

"Yes," he says with an adorable grin. "I do."

In his own quiet Wendell-Berry-reading-clean-shaven-proper-New-England-grooming-earnest-way, Tim understands me. Most of the time he embraces me. He doesn't say a lot at times like these, but I can see it in his grin. I think my oddness gives him a little permission to not try so hard to follow the straight and narrow. I really hope I give him that.

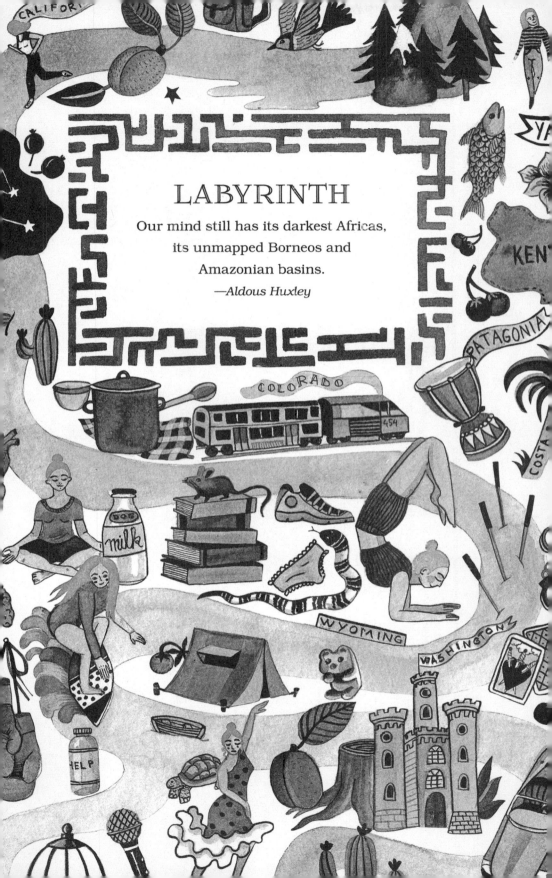

LABYRINTH

Our mind still has its darkest Africas,
its unmapped Borneos and
Amazonian basins.

—*Aldous Huxley*

29

WRITE YOUR OWN VOWS

PURPOSE: Maybe when you come from divorce on both sides, this is what people like us do. Break with convention. Write our own rules. Make promises we can keep.

DURATION: A lifetime to wax rhapsodic about what to pledge.

EQUIPMENT NEEDED: A forceful thrust of faith to put pen to actual paper. A loved one to marry us. Two rings. Summer flowers. And a lot of hope.

AGE: 29.

RELATIONSHIP STATUS: Host and hostess to a riparian love-fest.

EMPLOYMENT: Wilderness instructor, house cleaner, acupuncture student.

COST: I'm wearing a bridesmaid dress, but I love it. My backcountry tent-expert buddies helped erect the borrowed party tent. One of Tim's groomsmen and his fiancée baked the cakes. They are gorgeous.

LOCATION: Hedley, British Columbia.

We stand in a clearing of alder at the bank of the Similkameen River. I hold Tim's hands amid a circle of moss and rocks decorated with berries and leaves that Marilyn from EST has lovingly arranged. I've asked Mom and Dad to walk me to the clearing. But I want to walk down the aisle alone. Feels right. Mom is my matron of honor. And Dad will sit in the front row with Margie, right near Michelle and Scott, our Wyoming and Patagonian equally newly wedded friends.

This weekend will be our first official family event with my stepmom. She's very sweet to me, all dressed in yellow—almost too sweet, like her perfume. I'm not sure how much the affection is for me so much as her love for my father overflowing. I worry for my mother. When Dad arrived, he forgot to introduce his wife to everyone. He was more focused on riding the John Deere tractor at high speeds. So Mom did the kind introductions.

Mom stands next to me in a flowing silk jacket and skirt in a gray that flatters her light tan and blue eyes. My sister stands with me, too, in a periwinkle gown and sparkling blue vintage necklace we'd found together in Vancouver. She's crying.

I feel the moss under my bare feet. Our friends surround us. My schoolgirl friends, Kimberly from EST, and my girls Brett and Nessa and Julie, right there with me. Tim, in his equally bare feet and slightly rolled-up pants, reads the Mary Oliver poem he's chosen.

> From a single grain they have multiplied.
> When you look in the eyes of one
> you have seen them all.
>
> At the edges of highways
> they pick at limp things.
> They are anything but refined.
>
> Or they fly out over the corn
> like pellets of black fire,
> like overlords.

(Crow is crow, you say.
What else is there to say?
Drive down any road,

take a train or an airplane
across the world, leave
your old life behind,
die and be born again—

wherever you arrive
they'll be there first,

glossy and rowdy
and indistinguishable.
The deep muscle of the world.

I tell myself to see the beauty in shy Tim's selection; I admit to no one my unease/question/bewilderment/worry/fear/compassion/disappointment/sadness/concern with his choice and what it means. I read somewhere that crows are the ministers of veiled mystery. They appear to be doing their job. More than mysterious, it was looking pretty darn dark. *They pick at limp things. Overlords. Anything but refined. Drive down any road. Seen one, you've seen them all. Pellets of black fire. Indistinguishable.*

And I read him Pablo Neruda:

. . . So I love you because I know no other way

than this: where I does not exist, nor you,
so close that your hand on my chest is my hand,
so close that your eyes close as I fall asleep.

Then I promise to honor his nature, not press him to share himself, and instead encourage his own pace and style—his introversion. I think my exact words:

"I promise to be like a sponge, to soak up what you offer."

(Yes, folks, you read that right. I wish I could say this was a typo. I vowed to be a *sponge*.[1] My big promise. Keep in mind, I wrote these. My own brilliance, thank you very much. Make of that what you will. Quite a way to book-end Neruda. A *sponge*.)

At the time, as crazy as it sounds, I meant it. I hoped to make Tim feel safe and held so he could open toward me. And he vowed to do what I hoped:

"I promise to share myself—to open without prompting." To let me, Megan, into his private world.

Before placing our rings on one another's fingers, we pass them through our friends' hands to bless them. We kiss. We embrace. I run my fingers through his thick hair. We stare at each other with giddy nervousness and delight. We walk to the bank of the Similkameen and each throw a flower into the river with a wish for the sanctity of hope, the enduring nature of love, and the leap of faith such promises require. I love this day. We will eat cake and dance as an evening fog settles on our tent under the stars, replete with Japanese lanterns and twinkly lights.

---

[1]   Sponge /spənj/ *noun* **1.** a primitive sedentary aquatic invertebrate with a soft porous body that is typically supported by a framework of fibers or calcareous or glassy spicules. Sponges draw in a current of water to extract nutrients and oxygen **2.** a piece of a soft, light, porous substance originally consisting of the fibrous skeleton of an invertebrate but now usually made of synthetic material. Sponges absorb liquid and are used for washing and cleaning (and natural tampons).

30

DOULA CERTIFICATION

PURPOSE: Learn to provide physical, emotional, and informational support to a mother before, during, and shortly after childbirth to help her achieve the healthiest, most satisfying experience possible.

DURATION: Three-day workshop and then subsequent apprenticeship.

EQUIPMENT NEEDED: A pregnant mother in labor. Then ice chips, rice bag, hot water bottle, tennis balls. Frankly, whatever helps get 'er done: Hank Williams, speed metal, Gregorian chanting, nipple clamps.

AGE: 30.

RELATIONSHIP STATUS: Newlywed.

EMPLOYMENT: Acupuncture student, retail worker.

COST: Interning is free.

LOCATION: St. Joseph Hospital, Bellingham, Washington.

A baby was born today. A perfect, small, soft pink little baby. It's not mine. And it's the most perfect creature I have ever seen take its first breath. Correction: it's the most perfect creature I've seen take *her* first breath. It was a girl.

And I, a mere handmaid. Technically, I'm the handmaid's handmaid. I'm still in training. I got the call from the head doula and the next thing I know, I'm putting a rice bag on the lower half of a tall, heavyset blond woman in labor. She's at four centimeters. It's going to be a while.

Truth be told, I want a baby. I want to grow one in my belly. I want the man I love like no other to lie on top of me and, in that perfect moment of connection, I want him to flood me with everything he's got. I want to receive that one perfect sperm that swims that one perfect speed to be greeted by that one perfect fat and happy egg who will receive him and say, "It's about time. Get on in here, my sweet friend. Let's make something happen."

But now isn't the time. While I wonder if it will ever be time, I refuse to mope. That man I love like no other says he's not ready. And really, am I? Being in school again and all? Before we married, he said he was open to having one, then maybe adopting one. But sometimes he gets on his zero-populationist thing.

But what's one more baby in the world? One more baby. And it would be ours. In lieu of obsessing over a baby, I will learn about them, help them come into the world. The birth of my own baby is no more beautiful than any other, and that's the truth.

Turns out the world of doulas, natural childbirth, and midwifery are exactly how I imagined. The granola factor is high, with a fair share of Birkenstocks, headscarves, and handmade long purses. But jeans and T-shirts are represented as well. I'm in the T-shirt/jeans contingency. Although lately I've been feeling a little puffy, so today it's leggings. And as I would imagine, the training, in all its political correctness, resides in a Latino community center, its walls replete with photographs of protest marches, native tapestries, and posters for after-school programs. Our training room smells like someone has been cooking quinoa. And with this crowd, I'm sure someone *has* been cooking quinoa. We'll likely be served the Aztec grain with a side of hemp dip come snack time.

Day One: childbirth education, fine; role-playing as pregnant people, fine;

listening to babies' heartbeats with old-school wooden trumpetlike objects, fascinating; 101 rice-bag, yoga-ball, stretching-ball positions, magnificent.

Day Two: birth stories, riveting. Birth plan write-up exercises, comprehensive. But must they keep showing slide show after slide show of touching births to the soundtrack of crooning women who have lost their way home from Lilith Fair? They're trying to kill me with sentimentality. And it's working. Aren't photographs of birth emotional enough without Joan Baez and Sarah McLachlan? I'm a sucker for these slide shows. Six in two days. Soon I'll require an IV drip to rehydrate from my crying jags. We have the water births (where the doula climbs in the tub—in jeans—to support the mother for the final pushes). We have the at-risk births. The footage of a baby climbing up a mother's belly for her first feeding. Help me.

By Day Three it's obvious who has had a baby and who has not. The Have-Nots' general consensus: they would like to birth outside, preferably in a field of wildflowers, but ideally a water birth. With all their friends gathered round. A woodwind, fiddle, or Dobro guitar is ideal, but not required. Kind of like a picnic, but where the main attraction isn't the barbecue or canoe paddle, but watching a pregnant woman drop a newborn into a shallow, inflatable tub. And I must confess, despite my own lack of batik and a circle skirt, I'm right in there with my fellow Have-Nots. Bring out the gingham and let's go.

As a point of contrast, see the ideal birth of the Haves:

"If I have another baby, next time I would like to be a *smidge* closer to the hospital or, better yet, *in* the hospital rather than at home. Driving in the back of the station wagon with my midwife holding the IV bag while my husband raced us to the hospital for fear of an emergency cesarean was . . . not so ideal."

So much for the Woodstock-Meets-Rawhide-Ranch Fantasy of the Have-Nots. Shot down before we had a shot.

One certificate, five thousand slide shows, and two thousand relaxation positions later, I attend my first birth. And it is beautiful. Well, beautiful and educational. While the doula and the husband stay at the Head (yes, the mother gets a tad deconstructed), I take up prime real estate in the Action Zone, the Vagina. It's an eyeful. We have, as a group, gotten to ten centimeters and 100 percent effaced. It's showtime.

I've never seen genital warts before, nor was I prepared when I packed my little bag of snacks and left home hours ago. There is a Gore-Tex patch on the outbreak in hopes of containing them for the delivery. I've never seen mushroom-style hemorrhoids either—like giant cauliflower florets coming out of her rectum.

Keep it together, Megan. Focus on the baby. Stop looking at that patch. What's up with that patch? Does it really keep the warts in their own little area? Did the pregnancy cause the cauliflower florets or were they preexisting?

Now doesn't seem like the right time for a question-and-answer period.

How gross. How gross. NO, MEGAN!! The body is BEAUTIFUL. All bodies are BEAUTIFUL. I'm going to be sick. God, I should have brought something more than those measly carrot sticks. I ate my last one hours ago.

Focus on the baby, Megan. The baby. The baby. That's right. Oh, God, the head.

While the head of the baby crowns, the Head of said Mother passes beyond red. Her veins pop out. If this volume of pushing doesn't bring out a third cauliflower floret, I don't know what will.

Oh, God. Here it comes. Come on. You can do it, big gal. Oh, God, this is unbelievable. Head, then shoulders, a subtle slippery twist of the baby's shoulders by the midwife to ease her out, and that's it.

I hear that first cry. The rubbery little cherub is perfect. Like a real-life baby doll taking her breath for the first time. In this little hospital room, in this big hospital, in this medium-sized city, a life has just begun. I laugh and wipe my eyes at the same time. And while Mother receives her little girl to nestle—but oh, wait, here comes the afterbirth.

Holy Mother of God, the afterbirth. Oh, my God. It's alive. It's a disgusting, juicy, blood-rich blob. Oh, God. I can't look. I can't stop looking.

They carry the afterbirth over to a tray and spread it out like bloody pie dough. Transfixed, my nausea rises. *Must not look at placenta. Sweet Jesus, that's a placenta.*

As Baby Girl nestles in Mother's arms, Mother and Father are bewitched, enamored, consumed. Little do they know that down at the Action Zone, a conversation is taking place between nurse and midwife. They contemplate what to do about a not-so-typical tear. I look down. What appears to be a miniature umbilical cord hangs out of Mother's Vagina. Despite her bliss, something not small appears ripped and hangs out. The nurse looks at the tear and then back up at the midwife.

"Um . . . [*big pause*] what should I call . . . this?"

"Well . . . [*another big pause*] . . ." The midwife appears to be thinking. "Why don't you call it . . ."

My friend Sandy (a divorce attorney) thinks one reason second marriages sometimes fare better than firsts is that often the second husband doesn't see his wife's vagina blown apart. She thinks Vagina Rupture Viewing more than figuratively ruptures a bit of the mystique. While the midwife mulls how to describe the train wreck of an apparently-never-seen-before tear, I look back down at it. I can't *not* look. My curiosity overrides my stomach's wishes. Then over to the placenta. Then back at the tear—a bodily fluid and tissue Ping-Pong match.

I need to sit down. Why isn't there a chair in here? Where have all the chairs gone? Jesus, why isn't there a chair around when you need one?

The midwife's bark strikes me out of my chair search.

"Call it a tear of the fourth layer of the labia." *Did she say "Fourth Layer of the Labia"? I didn't know there were four layers.* The midwife takes out needle and thread and begins stitching. Mother all the while sees nothing, senses nothing.

Our Mother has one perfectly round, perfectly warm, perfectly pink little baby in her arms. A bomb could go off in this room and it would not shake her from her bliss. I walk to Mother and peer down at the baby. Mother looks up at me, smiling, and then her attention returns to the baby. I ask if I may touch the baby's head. It is soft and warm and perfect. I need to let them be now. I will exit without notice. I pack up my little rice bag and tennis balls and bow quietly out the door.

31

GET ROLFED

PURPOSE: Realign one's physical structure and, in so doing, realign one's emotional structure.

DURATION: Classically done in ten sessions to cover the entire body.

EQUIPMENT NEEDED: Massage table, willingness to stand and be stared at in your underpants. Trained Rolfer, ideally having completed the advanced training.

AGE: 30.

RELATIONSHIP STATUS: Really newly wedded.

COST: Something like $100 a session. You don't have to do all of them in a row, but it's recommended and I'm trying to swing it.

LOCATION: Downtown Bellingham, Washington.

Louise works on my ribs at the level of my diaphragm.

"You are tight here." She tries to—what feels like—put all her fingers, thumbs, and knuckles under my diaphragm.

"I'd like to be able to put half my fist up there, but I can't get in. You won't let me," Louise says.

The sensation shoots straight to my throat.

Boom. Pop. Wow. Out of nowhere, I start to sob.

"It feels scary to have you in there." I try to lock the crying down at my throat. But the more she goes into my diaphragm, the faster the tight feeling shoots up.

"Yeah, kinda locked up," she repeats. "The good news is that crying can loosen the diaphragm sometimes, as well as my hands. What's going on with you? Is there something you're particularly worried about?"

I scan my brain, my chest, my throat for an answer.

"Well," I say through my waterworks, "Tim and I just bought a house. I've never been so close to merging financially with someone. I'm scared. That's one."

"Ah, I see. What's scary about that?"

"I never saw my mom or dad handle money very well together. They eventually separated financially while married because they didn't trust that the other was looking out for them. And now, here I am with this scary house payment and new bills. We don't even have a shared bank account. I'm scared that if I do, right when I do, something bad will happen. I think merging itself scares me. My mom lost herself in my dad. I don't want to lose myself—personally or financially."

"Well, Megan," she says as she works on my weepy diaphragm. "I say go for it. You're married, after all. Take the risk. Trust yourself. Trust Tim. Taking the leap of faith is the only way to learn it can actually work out sometimes."

I'm a little uncomfortable with this piece of advice and her comfort dispensing it, but she's quite a bit older than I and seems pretty together. And why come to Rolfing if I'm not willing to try new patterns?

I cry some more. She presses up my diaphragm. I breathe a lot.

She starts moving down to my feet and then up to my head, where all sessions end. She calls it integrating the work.

And then it comes to me: *Come now, Megan, be brave. Trust Tim. Merge a little bit. Trust that taking a leap doesn't mean you'll get screwed.*

I'm not sure it's my voice. Might be Louise's.

I go home and make an announcement. "Okay. I want to plan and pay as a couple, a married couple, instead of being afraid of what might happen. I'll stop being so scared."

Tim seems touched. He pulls me down onto his lap on our kitchen bench and kisses my neck. I wonder if my risking merging financially will make merging physically (aka a baby) less scary for him too.

We go down to the bank a few days later and open a joint account. Both our names there on the paperwork. It feels good to leap. I'm not sure about the reality of a white picket fence. But I can start with a joint account.

32

EMBRACING THE BELOVED: RELATIONSHIP AS A PATH OF AWAKENING (REVISITED)

PURPOSE: Get closer to my beloved. My husband.

DURATION: I've been reading this book like others must read the Talmud. Daily and with reverence.

EQUIPMENT NEEDED: The book and the audiotapes both. I like the combo.

AGE: 30.

RELATIONSHIP STATUS: Not just newly wedded, but new homeowners.

EMPLOYMENT: Acupuncture student, boutique worker.

COST: $14.95.

LOCATION: Village Books (my New Age book selection spot), Bellingham, Washington.

I've been stressing over paint colors. I want to make our little house the cozi-est home either of us has ever had. I think that in the Northwest gray, yellow is the happiest of colors. I've become a maniacal Martha Stewart. I've built a tiny model out of paint-sample cards, with a roof and everything. Buttercream exterior with Elephant Gray around the windows, and a Perfect Red door. In feng shui, a red door is considered lucky, and I read that historically in America, a red door was a sign that a home was a safe stop for travelers. I love that. I can't wait to show Tim my model. It's far more fun than steaming off wallpaper and sponging thirty years of oil-heat residue off our walls. The previous own-ers were Catholic, and you could see the outline of the cross they'd hung over their bed. *Not* the confessional vibe I want for our bedroom. I'd scrubbed us clean. And if I do say, I picked amazing colors: an inviting red for our bedroom, that beautiful yellow repeated in our dining room. I didn't stress over our lack of furniture. I liked that we were starting with only the things we loved—the craftsman-style futon couch, the vintage bed frame that I'd stripped to perfec-tion, a cloisonné porcelain lamp I'd grown up with.

And so the night Tim was late to come home from that business trip, I didn't have just *Embracing the Beloved* on my mind, I had this idea of our red door of welcome that I couldn't wait to share.

Instead, a night has passed in nervous solitude and I have just picked him up from jail in his wedding suit. Red doors and Elephant Grays seem like the shallowest thoughts in the world. We had started driving south on I-5 to get his car. After he'd directed me to keep driving past the route home, I'd asked, "I thought it all happened right before our turnoff. Why are we heading way down here?"

There was that vast silence. My stomach dropped.

"Let's just wait to talk about it when we get home," he'd said.

Upon hearing those words, it was now as if I were driving the car somehow above and outside my body. And those silent words formed somewhere in my head. Maybe they were in my chest.

Oh. No.

That Stephen and Ondrea phrase kept surfacing.

The distance from your pain, your grief, your unattended wounds.

God, I feel sick.

Is the distance from your partner.

Where is Tim? He looks so vacant.

Whatever maintains that distance,

He's so still in the passenger seat, so stiff and upright.

Must be investigated with mercy and awareness.

I feel sick. Maybe I should pull over.

The mind creates the abyss.

Just keep it together. Keep it together. Just get this car home. Get you two home.

But the heart crosses it.

Focus on the road, Megan. Just focus on the road.

33

EMERGENCY COUNSELOR

PURPOSE: If ever there was a time to talk to a professional, surely this must be it. I'm triaging this thing as fast as I can.

DURATION: One hour.

EQUIPMENT NEEDED: A bit of a pushiness factor to get a same-day appointment.

AGE: Same as a few hours ago (on paper anyway).

RELATIONSHIP STATUS: Married and shocky.

COST: $65 (a sliding-scale student rate).

LOCATION: Fairhaven Neighborhood. (It's dense with therapists, and as mysterious geographic forces go, it's like the Bermuda Triangle of therapy. People can get lost for years here.)

Once home from jail, Tim leads me into our bedroom, has me sit down on the bed. He kneels down and says, "The woman didn't stumble."

"Okay . . ." I say slowly.

He takes a big breath and then says in one long delicate exhale, "I was arrested for soliciting a prostitute who was an undercover cop, and I . . . "

I swallow. Silence.

"What?"

He says it again. "I was arrested for soliciting—meaning talking to—a prostitute who was an undercover cop, and I was . . ."

He said more.

But I was no longer hearing like a regular person. And I wasn't sure he was even speaking in full sentences anywhere beyond that.

I swallow. Silence.

"What?"

For me, those next few sentences—however I may remember them now—were not just literal fragments. It was less like language, more like a felt experience. As if, when he began speaking, I was looking at him through thick blurred glass. And upon the rest of all he may have said, I could only describe it like an enormous bird heading straight toward a window at full impact. And with that bird strike, the words—like shards of glass—went flying. A strange mosaic of letters and phrases suspended in the air.

"There are things . . .

                            I haven't . . . it hasn't

             Not easy . . .
             Perhaps I should have . . .

                             I couldn't.

          Never told . . .   *He . . .*
          Or maybe I could have d . . .
      hurt . . .

                   me . . ."

I saw a tattoo like that once. Two poems tattooed and intertwined, stanzas tumbling down a woman's shoulder. It felt like that.

While he continues to kneel before me, I try to take in these few facts and this suspended foreign collage of both his present and past. I imagined my own face of shock as a shard he too was having to endure from the other side of this mosaic.

A few days later, on my birthday—both of us in some strange alternate universe—he mentions something about phone sex, as if I'd heard it before. But I hadn't. Or couldn't. The body's good like that, preventing us from taking in too much when the system runs too hot.

"I'm so relieved," he says, starting to stand up. "It's like a big weight has been lifted."

Well, if there was any weight lifted, I'm pretty clear where it got put back down.

I crawl into the fetal position, put my hands between my knees, and try to slow this all down. But I can't. This problem feels larger than me. I need a map—not a manual or a set of instructions, but guidance that is sensory, holographic, and three-dimensional. This is a moment when it would have been useful if I believed in God. I could offer myself up to her/him/it. Just surrender to Jesus. Or whomever.

I crawl out of my fetal position and go in search of the phone. It's been four hours since I picked up Tim. I keep picturing his wedding suit with the jail as backdrop. He smelled funny when he got into the car. Not like the cigarettes of a bar, nor like sweat, but not like himself. He'd brought the jail home with him. Smell molecules from a cell.

Now, hours later, my only thought: we need to talk with a professional. I make sure that within the hour we are heading to an appointment. Tim looks awkward throughout the session. The emergency counselor asks whether this is the first time he's approached a prostitute.

"Yes," he says, wiping his tired eyes.

She is white-haired and round, and looks like she could be jolly. She doesn't look jolly now.

"Tim," she says somberly, "you're incredibly lucky to be caught your first time out. Usually, by the time an arrest happens, it's been going on a long time."

Lucky.

I never considered this lucky. I definitely need to rethink. Her version sounds better.

But this emergency counselor seems insufficient to the task. It's just triage—to stop the bleeding—not actual repair. I don't know what the task is yet, but I know we haven't touched it. Although she gave his stage a number: Stage Two. That sounds good. I have no idea under what label these stages are grouped. I'm just thankful for the tourniquet. Whatever this stage means, at least it's not Stage Three. Stage Two cancer is treatable. Stage Four, terminal.

We're both catatonic. If nothing else, I heard that stuff he said earlier. Something about last night's arrest, and those fragmented references to younger pain and difficulty. I start thinking about the Levine quote. Turns out I don't know the first thing about Tim's pain. They said the distance from your pain was the distance from your partner. Whether the Levines were talking about Tim's pain or my potential Grand Canyon distance from my own, I wasn't sure the *who* of it mattered.

34

DUGGAN/FRENCH APPROACH

PURPOSE: They call it a Somatic Pattern Recognition, a hands-on intervention of the body in which interrupted emotional processes can be completed and inner balance restored after traumatic experiences.

DURATION: One can treat DFA like an alternative to therapy with a weekly session. In this situation, it is a one-shot deal.

EQUIPMENT NEEDED: Two chairs for preliminary discussion, then a massage table.

AGE: Benjamin Button faceplants onto Dorian Gray's canvas.

RELATIONSHIP STATUS: Married. Still shocky.

COST: $80 to $100.

HUMILIATION FACTOR: Low. This place has a welcoming environment.

LOCATION: Mount Vernon, Washington.

I need to talk to someone before my head and heart explode. I need comfort and protection, and experience tells me this is not my parents' strong suit. I don't have a classic mother bear. No shotgun-toting dad. And today, of all days, I don't need Dad's speech about each of us pursuing our Highest Sense of Right. Plus, I want to honor Tim's privacy. I will keep Tim's secrets. It will mean years of occasional lectures from my father on my not-so-smooth marriage, and not entirely kind comments from Tim's mom. She will blame our silent problems on my California-ness, and all that touchy-feely stuff that comes with it.

"Megan," Dad will say. "Sometimes we need to love people even more to make a marriage work. It seems like you're withholding." *Okay, not to point fingers, but I'm pretty sure I'm the one on the receiving end of a Withhold here, and this isn't a simple roll off the roof.*

And really? Me, withholding? If I'm hiding anything, it's how hard I'm trying. I would carve out my lungs with a spoon if I thought it might help Tim. How much of Dad's speeches are for me, and how much are just old echoes meant for Mom?

My lips will seal and largely keep both our families out of our drama. So professional counsel it must be. Before picking Tim up at the jail, I had arranged a bodywork appointment for him that afternoon with a colleague at Louise the Rolfer's office. I thought he might need some kind of trauma release from a night in jail. But now I think maybe *I* should take the appointment. Tim keeps telling me how much lighter he feels for having told me.

I've never been to Annie Duggan before. I only know she's the *D* in DFA. I'm in shock. I know because I can't stop urinating and I have tons of energy, but I haven't eaten since yesterday. I have no hunger—more this weird feeling in my stomach, like nausea, but with something else too. Annie gets me on the table, her room bathed in soft light. She has a warm face, naturally blond curly hair, and a lilt of an English accent. She feels maternal.

Annie begins by rocking my body with her hands, swaying me back and forth in a circular rhythm. She talks to me in soft tones, asks a few practical questions:

Where is he now? How are you piecing all this together? What is Stage Two? Did he say what brought him to this place? Do you sense he survived something more than he can plainly say?

These questions, no different than what I'm swirling in myself. Nothing is particularly clear minus one or two things. She redirects. I'm thankful. I need to be pulled out. If only for an hour.

She asks me about what I feel. My head softens. Other than the distraction of tears draining into my ears, this feels like I've landed.

While I may be in my own state of high alert, she approaches the material, the facts of my marriage, neutrally and without drama. Her touch feels kind, and helps my body catch up with my brain. I may ask her if I can move in here—live right on this treatment table. She quietly visits each region with her palms—finding tight areas and then helping me breathe into them. The blessing and the curse: the more I feel my body, the more I feel.

And then she does it. She asks me the question that will haunt me. With her hand on my chest, still rocking me back and forth, she puts her other hand right in the center of my sternum and casually asks, "Is he the one?"

I bolt open my eyes, in shock at the question.

Are you even allowed to ask this sort of question in a session like this? Do I even believe there is a ONE? I'm terrified to be asked. But the question has presented itself. I will follow it out.

Annie gently continues to rock me back and forth. She asks again.

"Is he the *one*?"

With her hand still resting on my sternum, I hear myself saying one very clear, quiet "No."

Where did that come from? And what in the world am I going to do with that information? That can't be right. Is that right? I assume that's shock talk. Or, I guess when answering from deep in your body, there's no guarantee your mind will like it.

This stuff is dangerous. Not dangerous like never try it. But dangerous like don't underestimate what can happen between you and you when asked a hefty question. Because in truth, what's scary about your spouse getting arrested is that it throws you (at exceedingly high velocities) toward your own beliefs. As it turns out, I believe in love, family, and the sanctity of home. And this, well, what to do about *this*?

35

THERAPIST SHOPPING

PURPOSE: For Tim to get a deferred sentence, he must agree to two years of counseling. I con't need a judge to tell me that I need to talk to somebody. That's a no-brainer.

DURATION: A couple of weeks of comparison shopping.

EQUIPMENT NEEDED: Looking for a therapist midcrisis is like being asked to calmly search for a life raft while drowning.

AGE: 31. Just had a super festive birthday. I didn't have the heart to cancel Tim's pre-arrest planned surprise for me of a night in a hotel. So we cried into our wilted room-service Caesar salads while watching a poorly chosen romantic comedy. Hence the crying and self-pity.

EMPLOYMENT: Acupuncture student (for the next three years), gardener, a mishmash of retail jobs.

RELATIONSHIP STATUS: Drama central, but trying to find the positive. On the upside, I've never met so many therapists before.

COST: $100 for every sample therapist. I kicked off with three.

LOCATION: All over and beyond Bellingham. Casting a wide net.

I believe a therapeutic model is missing: one for the person who doesn't need rehab and isn't quite ready for the lockdown ward, yet needs something a tad stronger than a standard weekly fifty-minute session. Alternatively, for my current needs, I fear classical five-day-a-week analysis would be too much leisurely childhood reflection and too little on the *help me, it's urgent*. But make no mistake. I want therapy. I want a lot of it. *Right now.* And I don't have time to go shopping for a therapist, spill my guts, and then have her say while tapping her watch, "Our time is up. But I think this is a *wonderful* beginning. Let's pick up right here, next week."

Did you say next week? *Like next week, next week? Now, hold on there, partner, have you been listening to me? Looking at me? I'm dealing with some serious shit here. Can't you tell that these sweatpants have become my 24/7 outfit? Isn't it obvious that no, I'm not actually going for the messy look, but rather I can't see my way clear to brush my hair? That I have carry-on bags under my eyes, and a twisted sense of glee that soon I'll be able to shop in the juniors department?*

But I don't say this at any of the trial appointments. To my family and conditioning, every problem is a growth opportunity. Here's an example of Griswold-speak. Let's say I've lost my arm. It's been cut off and my artery is spurting all over the room. Instead of the obvious statement, such as "Help me! Help me!" or "Holy Mother of God, I've lost my arm!" I'd say something like, "I'm experiencing something that I choose to experience as discomfort. I know none of you is to blame, not even you there, the one with the ax. This is *my* reality. But until I'm able to magically transform my reality into *not* a bleeding arm, could one of you kind people get me a towel? And think of the unique opportunities I might come to enjoy with a new prosthetic."

"Turns out," I told Mom, "the arrest wasn't a misunderstanding. But Tim hasn't been able to share much beyond the fragments I just told you. And that's really scary. I think I'm in over my head, Mom."

She paused for a long time, as if gathering herself, and then proclaimed, "Megan, think of what a wonderful growth opportunity this will be! Think how much stronger you will get from this! Think of what a resource you can be for Tim."

Really? What?

This was not what I wanted to hear. I wanted to fall apart in her lap and have her say in soothing tones how sorry she was that this happened not just to Tim, but to me. Her daughter. I asked once for that (the lap, the cry, the words) a few months after the whole jail deal on a particularly low day, but Mom couldn't do it. She tried. We tried—attempted an awkward me-in-her-lap thing. But that wasn't how she/we were built. And hugging, no, still not her thing. I shrank from her lap, kicking myself.

36

THE THERAPIST OF CHOICE

PURPOSE: Tim getting to the bottom of Tim. Megan getting to the bottom of Megan. In the meantime, nobody's touching anybody's bottom—except for the hemorrhoid cushion on the therapist's chair touching his.

DURATION: One hour a week each.

EQUIPMENT NEEDED: PsyD. From what I can gather, one part narrative therapy, one part classical Freudian. Throw in a little Jung—and a God complex. Perfect.

AGE: Still 31.

RELATIONSHIP STATUS: Optimistic? Yeah, maybe optimistic. We have a plan now.

COST: $200 a week for both of us. We're living on one full-time salary and my part-time work while I'm in school. This stretches us. Also, I didn't know you had to pay for probation.

LOCATION: A weathered therapeutic office. No waiting room.

Tim has resisted finding and selecting a therapist. I forced myself to ask him to sleep at a friend's until he could make a choice. After two nights away, he came home having successfully confided in one old friend (what all he might have confided I don't know) and selected one new therapist named Don. I feel relief.

Don is interested in seeing us separately as individual clients—despite it being against standard therapeutic practice. I agree despite knowing this. Don seems to really like Tim. Don is short, bushy haired, with even bushier arms, and his office smells like Thai food. He looks a little like a round hobbit with a bit of Santa's eye twinkle. He sits on a doughnut-shaped piece of foam and talks about Tim during his sessions with me (in the raspiest voice in the world, eyes wide, with plenty of leaning forward out of his hemorrhoid chair for emphasis).

"You need to understand that *Tim* is the sort of person who can't be opened too quickly. If we go too quickly, we risk losing *Tim*. He will close up forever, never to be heard from again."

Suddenly there are three people in our marriage: Tim, Don, and me.

37

LYING ON TOP BREATHING EXERCISE

PURPOSE: Don has asked us to do an assignment. More Naked Belly Lying, less Naked Belly Laughing.

DURATION: Ten minutes, once a day for two weeks.

EQUIPMENT NEEDED: The absence of equipment. Full frontal. And dorsal.

AGE: 31 in 81-year-old saggy pink sweatpants.

RELATIONSHIP STATUS: In play, in a shaky sort of way.

COST: The exercise is free. The therapy session is $100.

LOCATION: Our bedroom.

When facing a breach in trust—no matter how many times Tim tells me that breach was an isolated incident—I still don't feel right inside. So I go to therapy and wait. Wait for that feeling—that pit-in-my-stomach feeling that something more is wrong—to go. And when it doesn't, I try to pay a professional to take that feeling away. And so now I follow the most recent instructions from Doughnut Seat Don: to lie down together in the dark, naked, on top of each other. Don insisted that the most important part is that there's no intent to be sexual. It's just to feel one another.

I hadn't been able to have sex with Tim since the arrest. As for the practical side of it all, he had neither offered nor agreed when I asked him to take an AIDS test or a sexually transmitted disease panel. For me, all at once it felt terrifyingly urgent to do and terrifyingly easier to just hang in suspension. Suspended in what, I still didn't know. I did ask him to get tested. I wanted him to go in hopes I wouldn't have to. He still hadn't.

Beyond the absence of sex, I hadn't been able to offer a kiss beyond a peck. Hugs were to supply one another apology and forgiveness, not the deep embrace of lovers. When he would reach across the bed in the night, gently touching my waist, I would simply start to weep, coiling more deeply into myself. I wasn't repulsed or repelled by the revelation of his attempt to pay to put his penis in a stranger's mouth. It felt more like disillusionment, a loss of my own innocence regarding what the world was really like—as if the light and love not only for my husband, but for life itself, had drained out of me. Bound within my tiny coil, I only felt the world as a painful place full of broken people, like my husband. And now I had officially joined their ranks. By getting married, I'd promised to show him all of me, the good and the bad. And I'd assumed that because he loved that about me, he had offered the same. My coil felt metallic and intractable. But I wanted to help us out of this steely, guarded, suffering hole. I didn't care how painful it was to try to open myself. I would try.

I climb on top of Tim and lie on him in the dark. I can feel his broad chest. I try to arrange myself. (It's hard to have above-average-sized breasts and lie straight on top of somebody. Don't let anyone tell you otherwise.) I try to nestle my head into his neck. He smells familiar, salty and warm. His body feels tight under mine. We are to breathe together and say nothing. But I feel stiff. He feels stiff. This isn't that intertwined mush pile of lovers. It's two people doing an assignment.

And then, as the moment lingers, another appears: our wedding vows and Neruda. The promises to not push, to stay open.

> . . . I love you because I know no other way
>
>> than this: where I does not exist, nor you,
>> so close that your hand on my chest is my hand,
>> so close that your eyes close as I fall asleep.

And now, back in our bedroom, I lie on his chest. His hand on my chest feels very much his hand. The eyes I close are very much my eyes. It's been ten minutes. To me we feel like two children, bumbling through something called a rupture. I feel a pressure behind my eyes. I look at Tim. I see an awkward smile by the light barely coming through the window. I roll off his chest to my side of the bed. He spoons me, but I can't feel it. I just don't feel it.

38

PSYCHIC READING

PURPOSE: To get a different point of view by paying someone to enter a trance state on your behalf. Looking for a larger perspective.

DURATION: Two hours.

EQUIPMENT NEEDED: Tape recorder (all psychics use one), massage table (optional).

AGE: 31.

RELATIONSHIP STATUS: Feels desperate to try a psychic. But that's what it's come to.

COST: $100.

LOCATION: 1970s tract home, Vancouver, British Columbia.

Trance: /trans/ *noun* 1. a half-conscious state, seemingly between
sleeping and waking, where the ability to function voluntarily
may be suspended. 2. spiritualism. a temporary state in which a
medium is controlled by an external intelligence and used as a
means of communication, as from the dead.

Let's call my first psychic Gardenia Mellon. Her *real* first name was a flower,
and her last, the name of a famous family (unrelated). So Gardenia Mellon gets
us in the neighborhood. And Gardenia has covered her bathroom with every
nutty psychic joke/otherworldly postcard ever printed. Lots of psychic inside
jokes tacked up on every corner, over plugs, the edges of the mirrors: "How
many psychics does it take to screw in a lightbulb? I don't know, but they do."
Like that.

She ushers me into her inner sanctum, replete with macramé, driftwood
sculptures, a few more joke posters, and brown leatherette furniture. She has
long hair that, to my eye, could use a trim. She has those oversized glasses à
la Sophia Loren, and she's dressed like it's 1975. I opt to withhold judgment,
as genius and talent come in all shapes, sizes, and apparently haircuts. She
leads me onto a massage table, turns on a tape recorder, and starts to speak
as if spirits are in the room. Her voice is rhythmic and breathy, like the little
psychic woman in *Poltergeist*. She starts talking to the/a great spirit and various
entities—some famous, some I've never heard of. I'm not totally tracking, but
I'm getting the high points.

"Great Spirit . . ." *Wait, am I supposed to close my eyes?* "Jesus-the-Christ-
Child . . . Let us . . ." *Why is she talking about Jesus? Wait . . . is she talking to Jesus?*
"Gather . . . Guides . . . Medicine Wheel . . ." *Medicine wheels and Jesus? When
did Jesus become Native American?* "Celestial Power . . . Teacher's Vision . . .
Many lights . . ." *Okay, got it. Look up.* "Other guides. Teacher's Wisdom . . ."
*Fair enough, wisdom. Okay, now One Great Spirit again. Share in the Circle, then
something more about light. Or light beams? Is she in a trance?*

Then it's like a caucus. She's in a full-on conversation with a panel of apparently skyward individuals. *Can I interrupt? Or, uh . . . is it okay to get up and go to
the bathroom? Or is more coming?*

Whatever it is we're doing on the table, it takes about an hour to do it. Then
she moves back to the couch. I watch from the massage table, trying to be an

open vessel or something. Now inviting me over, she holds a piece of paper with a list of people I want to know about, running her hands all over my list like it's a Ouija board. It appears she's lost voluntary control of her hands. They spasm all over my notebook paper. She comes out of wherever she's been and begins talking—rapid-fire, rocking back and forth. Then, suddenly, she stops with the rocking, comes out of her trance, and speaks, making odd hand gestures around her head.

"Maygone!" (Megan.) "This crisis within your husband is worse than you think. In fact, your husband's darkness is much darker than he's shared with you."

Oh, God, I think to myself. *Worse. Define* worse.

I arrive home from Gardenia's office. It's a Saturday and Tim is making lunch. I sit down at the kitchen bench with the view of our rainy Bellingham street. Our neighborhood had voted to not bury all the electrical and phone cables, so there was always a bit of this exposed mess of wires through the trees. Our neighborhood leaders thought it more organic to show the mess. A historical mess.

"Tim, do you promise that the arrest was the first time you ever approached a prostitute? First time you ever talked to one?"

"Yes."

"It's just that the psychic says it's way worse than you've shared. Or technically I think she said that your darkness is much darker than you've shared. Is that true?"

After a long pause, Tim looks away and says, "Yes, it's true."

"Worse how? How do you mean?"

'Well, I can't really say."

"Why not?"

"Don says it's none of your business."

"What? How is it none of my business?"

"Don says I need to learn how to have appropriate boundaries—not be so concerned about what everyone thinks of me. So I can't discuss it with you. I'm supposed to tell you that Don and I are handling it."

"Well, surely, I'm not *everyone*. This is just *us*."

When I tell Don, he said, "That boyyyyyy has got to learn to keep his big *trap* shut."

Therapists aren't supposed to get angry. *But nobody's perfect, right? We all have our moments, don't we? But still, how do I get closer to my husband? We need to know each other. The light* and *the dark.*

It wasn't just the arrest, or the prostitute-cop, or the phone sex. I sensed that a torment from Tim's past was occupying his present, and he wouldn't or couldn't (*is there a difference?*) let me in on. Bits here and there. My main clues—despite Don's restrictions (it must be said, I'm the most inexhaustible questioner a nonsharing person could dream up; just ask Renee)—but when I would (skillfully-nonskillfully-awkwardly-smoothly-curiously-selfishly-generously-impatiently-lovingly-brilliantly-idiotically-circularly-directly-indirectly-seriously-lightly) poke and prod about his formative years, he would brace, or go silent. I wanted more.

How is it that Don is the sole gatekeeper? Isn't there another option?

"That boyyyy needs to keep his big *trap* shut."

39

ULTRAMARATHON

PURPOSE: Subject to interpretation—testing physical stamina, or the surefire way to lead to the systematic breakdown of your body—a race to see which happens first. Also, bragging rights and vibrating pain head to toe.

DURATION: Depends on the runner as well as the gain and loss of elevation. Cutoff time is often thirty-six hours.

EQUIPMENT NEEDED: More than one pair of running shoes, caffeine, protein bars, sugar in various forms, small pack, headlamp, socks, water, and a possible screw loose.

AGE: 32. And still in those sexy saggy sweatpants.

RELATIONSHIP STATUS: If anybody you love or live with—or both—is planning to run an ultramarathon, I think you/they are in serious trouble. I know saying this will not make me popular with ultramarathoners. I don't care.

COST: Entrance fee to race. Varies.

LOCATION: Any path from point A to point B that clocks out at a hundred miles. In this case, through the Wasatch and Bear River Ranges from Utah to Idaho.

It's official. He's going to run the Bear 100. It's what he's about now—running long distances, rebuilding old cars, gathering old car parts in the garage, getting tattoos, and now this. Yes, he has a tattoo now. Came home with it one day. He didn't offer to show it right off the bat. I saw something through his shirt. A big black symbol right over his heart. I'm not going to say what exactly in case you run into him on the beach. Just trust me when I say it's not a love symbol a wife dreams of. A big black anything over the heart, there's just no getting around that. So yeah, I don't know what to say. I couldn't help but think of Hester Prynne, both in theme and location. Except he branded *himself*. What was he saying? Did *he* know?

Now to the race—a grueling hundred-mile trail through the Wasatch and Bear River mountain ranges with over twenty thousand feet of altitude gain. From Utah to Idaho. A complicated route, with plenty of ways to get lost.

Michelle and Scott have driven out from Wyoming to join us as he races. They are those kinds of friends that, with luck, you acquire maybe once in your life. We lived and worked together during our second year in Patagonia. She, my brunette-Washington-D.C.–raised-Irish-Catholic-meets-Puerto-Rico-just-shy-of-five-feet-resourceful-cartographic-flora-and-fauna-naturalist-who-can-hike-forever powerhouse. She, the missing friend when I camped with the Chilean soldiers. We've trudged and navigated our way through the primordial ooze near the Baker River, been caught in rock fall together, and no matter the hellish conditions, she's never without a perfect silk scarf tied about her neck—a pocket-sized bit of style. As a Sacred Heart–educated woman, she lives by their mission of service. We've gotten large trucks stuck (and unstuck) on mud-saturated barely drivable roads, hauled rocks from rivers to make impassable sections passable, hiked across whole mountain ranges in a day, not to mention gathered delicate elderberry branches to decorate our wedding tables. She and Scott sat at the front of our ceremony holding hands as they witnessed our vows. After the arrest, they drove out to be with us because they said that's what friends do when loved ones are in marital trouble. They helped us grocery shop, bought flowers for the house, did the little things you stop doing when you are in crisis.

Now we would be the crew while Tim runs a hundred miles through day and night. You can have a support person for fifty miles, so Scott will run the last half. Scott has a constitution born to run fifty miles in a blink—light and fast, and always positive. I've never seen him in a bad mood. He will be up almost the whole night while Tim runs the first half.

Tim is more muscle than Scott, who has leaner, natural-runner musculature. Both are tremendously strong, but Tim has the denser quadriceps built for power—with a VO2 max and aerobic capacity in the elite realm.

I have my own theories why he likes to run long distances. One: that he walks around fairly numb, struggling to feel. Perhaps in these long distances, he starts to feel more—the push, the pain, the sweat, the exertion. Or conversely, maybe he's in so much pain internally, he wants his external physical condition to match. Maybe he needs to feel more in control, to set a course and follow it out. Compared with other entrants who've trained all year, Tim will run this race off the couch. He possesses such inherent formidable strength.

The preparation busied us for a while: discussing the gear, the food, the plan. When I was a girl, setting up to play Barbie was way more fun than actually *playing* Barbie. By the time I had to enact conversations between Barbie and Ken, I was bored. Tim's strategizing seemed like that—how many calories and in what form, how much water, what to wear, when to change shoes, which headlamp, studying the route. He'd been defizzing Coke for weeks—wanting the sugar and caffeine, but no bubbles.

Michelle and I pack up our camp near Logan Canyon—heading for Fish Haven, Idaho. We will be at the end waiting for them. I wish he would ask more of me, but this I can do. Impatient, Michelle and I run the route backward in hopes of intersecting them at one of the few food and water stations. And suddenly we see Tim, with Scott at his side, talking him down the trail.

"Come on, buddy, you're doing great."

Tim barely looks up off the ground. He heads down the trail toward the water table. He barely runs.

"I need some watahhh," he says. He speaks like his brain has slowed, or perhaps the running has pounded his jaw, making talk difficult.

"I need watahhhhh."

He seems to have lost both fine and gross motor skills. This scares me. Scott stays at his side as Tim reaches for water. As one of the most physically formidable people I know, Tim can now barely walk or talk.

I choke up. He is struggling, and tired, and grasping. He can't clearly complete a sentence, let alone ask for what he needs. And I don't know how to interpret for him here, to give him what he needs. He just has to stumble, walk, limp, run this last mile of the race. And he wants to do it alone.

Michelle and I run back to the finish line. She thinks as he crosses we should whoop and cheer words of encouragement. I know these whoops won't matter. He will feel the forced enthusiasm and it won't translate into his muscles or heart. I let Michelle do the whooping. But I know he is unreachable.

He will cross alone—in seventh place—with less training than anyone with whom he spoke before the race. He will walk around in a daze until he gets his feet under him. And he will need nothing from me—no hug, no encouragement, no kiss. He will limp into the car and sleep. I will drive us home. That I can do. That he needs—to be driven home.

40

GOTTMAN DISTANCE AND ISOLATION TEST BY JOHN GOTTMAN

PURPOSE: An exam that attempts to definitively assess the likelihood of a lasting couplehood.

DURATION: Thirty to forty-five minutes.

EQUIPMENT NEEDED: Questionnaire, pen, paper and guts.

AGE: 32.2-ish.

RELATIONSHIP STATUS: Married. Tim's still very married to his work as am I to my training. It helps to concentrate on acupuncture school.

COST: Free. Got the book from the library. I can't remember which one. It was more academic than pop psychology.

LOCATION: Bellingham, Washington.

I've taken the test. I'm scared to death to read the results. The Gottmans (John and Julie) are the famous couples counselors/researchers (in our fair state, no less—I don't know why I haven't yet considered dragging Tim and me to them) who study, empirically, whether a couple will make it or not. Questions, on every front, conflict styles (ours very rational), makeup styles, communication habits. Verbal cues. They divide augmenting signs of trouble into stages they call the Four Horsemen of the Apocalypse. It doesn't sound good. I don't know how many horses we've got.

All told, the test arrives at this one issue: research supports that there is some definitive point in a couplehood where so much water has passed over the marital waterfall (the Cascade, they call it), that there's no crawling back up or out. The test flushes out what point in the Cascade each partner is at. Because beyond that point, if one person has gone over the Cascade, the relationship is deemed unsalvageable.

But among the hundreds of questions I answered, the one that won't leave me is whether I "have started to imagine/wish that my partner is dead or has been killed." According to the authors, this is a classic—not to mention common—response for "normal," "average" couples who, despite the existence of legal divorce, would rather the other person go ahead and die. Or at least get riddled with some fast-moving disease.

So yes, goddamn it, even though I have never uttered this aloud, the Gottmans (this therapeutic pairing is a second marriage, if you must know) have read my mind. And what's better (or worse) is that they're telling me that my *possible* imagining that my husband getting accidentally caught in the wood chipper or tripping an old land mine while touring Vietnam is totally normal and utterly healthy marital behavior. I can't decide if this should comfort me or prompt me to take a vow of singlehood for the rest of my life.

Maybe there should be a twenty-first-century update to the classic marital vows: "I promise if we hit on hard times that instead of imagining you caught in a vat of silicone that will suffocate you instantly, or being attacked by a pack of angry spotted hyenas, or trampled by a herd of bison, I will consider *divorcing* you instead. Because that's how much I love you." And now, you may kiss the bride.

The Gottmans assure me this is normal. This is marriage. And that even some of *those* couples actually make it. Is our species a wreck or what?

But to *our* tests, it appears Tim thinks we aren't over the falls yet. My results are more dog-paddling under Niagara.

41

GO TO CHURCH

PURPOSE: I fear that I'm either unraveling or not unraveling fast enough.

DURATION: Two hours or so.

EQUIPMENT NEEDED: Spiritual materials and a place of reverence.

AGE: 32 and change. No longer dressing as if in hospice. Giving this venue proper respect. In proper dress.

RELATIONSHIP STATUS: Inconclusive.

COST: Free.

LOCATION: Bellingham, Washington.

I find myself turning to the stories of Barry Lopez the way some turn to the Bible. His words soothe me in a way I don't fully understand. Perhaps it's like the way he describes how paying attention to the presence of birds can calm you. All I know is, when I open to a story, I find some sense of the divine. While Tim helped me find Lopez, Mom has taken the ball and run with it. She scours for fresh publications before they will find their way into his next collection. And then she gives them to me. At night, or in quieter moments at work, or after cleaning the house, I go in search of his pages.

His writing is changing. I suspect something big—something painful, or its opposite, something glorious—has happened to him. I bet it's both. It's not just that he's turning strongly toward fiction, but to topics of love and human connection more directly. A Native American in prison, teaching his fellow inmates to find their totem animals and guardian birds, to transform themselves and take flight, leaving the bars of the prison behind. A husband taking refuge with an order of monks after his wife leaves him for another man.

As a trio—Tim, Mom, and I—we've listened to him speak. But ages ago. Before *the trouble*. All three of us wanted to talk to him, like groupies. Among us, I'm the least shy, so I made it our business to. *Was he like a regular person? Had he ever read* People *magazine? Did he own a television? Had he ever wanted to have children?* The particular questions didn't matter. We all craved—for our own distinct reasons—to get up close. There was magic there. We each were sure of it.

I hear he's doing a reading tonight in Bellingham. Pure luck that I found out, given where my head's been. Tim and I go. And deep in the basement of Vintage Books, Lopez reads one I hadn't. *The Letters of Heaven.* About the discovery of a set of secret love letters between two seventeenth-century Peruvian saints, Rosa and Martín. In the letters, we learn it is through their deep yet brief physical passion that they find communion with all that is most holy. Their love calls forth the qualities in each of them that later will be deemed worthy of canonization. And because this violates all traditional thinking about God, it becomes a question of how to protect (and someday publish) them, without the hands of the church destroying them as blasphemy. As it is their love for each other that brings each of them not merely out of their own darkness and self-loathing but intensifies their light, as does their ability to attend to all forms of suffering in the most violent and impoverished corners of Lima. Rosa turns her parents' house into a refuge for abused prostitutes. Martín develops the ability to talk to animals.

The Letters have got me. As we listen, I want to reach out and hold Tim's hand, but I find myself shy, not wanting to disturb his own listening. He's riveted.

As we walk to the car, I take his hand. I feel the sweet awkwardness of a first date. I recall an idea Tim returns to every now and again. He's always wanted to visit the Wenatchee River during the salmon's return. Not to just watch them at the river's edge, like we've done in the past, but to swim upstream with them, as they fight their way back from the wide dark oceans to the headwaters of their birth, where they will spawn and then die. If we rent wetsuits, he says, we can stay even longer.

I want to join him with the salmon. To find communion there.

42

SELF-PORTRAIT

PURPOSE: Doughnut Seat Don has asked me to do more homework—to draw a picture of myself. I don't just draw one. I draw six.

DURATION: Three hours of drawing. One hour (and a standard session charge) to have him analyze.

EQUIPMENT NEEDED: I dig up some colored pencils and an old sketchpad. I take these requests seriously.

AGE: 32.5.

RELATIONSHIP STATUS: Is it preaching to the choir to point out that Don's statements are a *teensy* violation of confidentiality when he reveals his opinions about Tim based on information Tim gives him privately (and vice versa about me)?

COST: $100.

HUMILIATION FACTOR: Medium. If someone put me in a trance today to recall that session's actual emotion—underneath, I'm pissed.

LOCATION: Same ratty office.

I bring in all six self-portraits. Actually, I think it might have been four, but six sounds more true in terms of my work on the damn things. And if you saw how truly elaborate rendering number four was, you'd give me triple credit. So calling it six really underestimates my efforts. Don focuses first on renderings one, two, and three. He likes to point out how stiff he finds the sketches of my body and face. I stand with my hands at my sides looking straight forward, like a soldier.

"Megan, you notice how *tight* you are here?" He says that like he's tasted a rotten olive and is spitting it out. He looks disgusted.

"Well," I say, "I think that must have something to do with the fact that I'm relying on some fourth-grade art skills. This is how I learned to draw people."

"Oh, no, I see much more. I think this *tightness* in your neck and shoulder area represents your tightness for life—your sense of control." He's grimacing up his face now, between bouts of really wide eyes.

"But I . . . well, okay, yes, I'm tight, those look *tight.*"

"And the neck, let's focus on the neck. Recall your mother . . ." (I had dragged my mother to Don once. She was repelled, didn't trust him or his condescension one bit.)

"Your mother had a big scarf around her neck. I've found women who wear *ssscarves* around their necks to be *represssssssssed sexually.*" He nods sternly. He says the words *scarves* and *repressed* like you might say the word *snakes* with a slow hiss, like you hope to creep someone out.

Don moves on to the fourth rendering. In this one I drew myself in the shape of a circle, and from that circle I have all the people who have meaningfully come into my life as other circles around me. I have color-coded them by categories they represent: a sense of family even if not in my family, a sense of humor, a spirit that enhances my own. Sometimes I color-coded for a person who, when I'm around them, I feel smaller inside. Within each circle is a word or phrase that reminds me of what I've learned with this person.

Don looks at the picture like he's never seen anything like it in his life (and not in a good way). He squints like it's terribly hard to read. For the record, the thing wasn't hard to read. I have that clean, block-style printing of an architect.

Don likes to stress he's not an ordinary therapist. He says this in a way that implies he is special or more advanced. I'm starting to wonder if he's unordinary in the same way freak lightning storms and getting your hand caught in the wood chipper are not ordinary.

"You have spent *a lot* of time on this." He squints and puckers again.

"Yes."

"Lots of *conneeeections* here . . . to *ooootheeeers* . . . yet you're connected with just these *gosssssamer* threads." He says it all as if English is not my mother tongue.

But I have no words. I signed on to the Don program. I will get something out of this, if it kills me.

43

VIPASSANA MEDITATION RETREAT

PURPOSE: A 2,500-year-old Buddhist tradition to cultivate a more mindful life, to explore the nature of consciousness and the human condition—to increase compassion, wisdom, joy, and integrity. One concentrates on the breath to calm and focus the mind. While Buddhist psychology provides guidance, it is a nonsectarian practice that can combine with any discipline or religious ilk. Plus, it's a week of silence. I'm tired of talking.

DURATION: Retreats in the United States last anywhere from a weekend to five to ten days or longer.

EQUIPMENT NEEDED: *Zafu, zabuton,* and blanket to wrap in when cold.

AGE: 32.5.

RELATIONSHIP STATUS: It's repetitive to say it's still rocky, but uh, it's still rocky. This all would go faster in the movies.

COST: Pay what you can. Buddhists call this *dana* (the Pali/ Sanskrit word for *generosity*).

LOCATION: Hunting lodge, Turpin Meadows, Jackson, Wyoming.

I've had so many people who didn't know what this was about come and say, "What the hell is this? I came here for bliss. I was gonna get really good feelings and love everybody. I thought it was about bliss." And I tell them, "Oh, yeah, that's what it's about. Just not now. Just not now."

—*John Travis*

Holy cow. I must be desperate. I recall before Tim's arrest telling Denise that my chances of doing a silent Vipassana meditation retreat were as likely as requesting that she lodge bamboo shoots under my fingernails. I mull this with Coco on the phone while she shops at Whole Foods a few states over.

"You're insane not to grab at the chance. He's one of Jack Kornfield's colleagues. You know, *Jack Kornfield*. Mr. *A Path with Heart* Kornfield. We *love* that book."

I hear scratchy phone and wind noise on her end.

"What are you *doing*?" I ask, laughing. "You're sure making a racket."

"Sorry," Coco says. "Just unlocking my bike."

Yes, Coco still bikes. For groceries. Nearly totally blind but insists she has enough peripheral vision to get there.

"Got it." I say. Classic Coco. Post-ride, she'll be cooking some completely organic and eye doctor–approved dish within the hour.

So here I am. In the heart of the Northern Rockies. About to start this retreat. Why is it that because *he* got arrested, I feel the answer to *our* problems will come if *I* meditate? I've taken a week off work and driven alone to the middle of Wyoming, and now I sit cross-legged in a hunting lodge staring up at a moose head, waiting for the other meditators. The irony of this setting is not lost on me, nor on our teacher John. We will take a vow of *ahimsa* (aka not to kill) in a room full of shot-dead animals staring at us. We finished our vegetarian meal and, like an addict going cold turkey, I'm jonesing for one last conversation.

My roommate just lost her boyfriend to a whitewater boating accident. He drowned. She can't stop crying, so our conversation was not particularly jolly. The only person I know is Denise. She's visiting friends in the dining hall. So here I sit.

As we gather in the classic introductory circle common to every healing art group known to man, I can tell instantly that I will love John Travis. After a lifetime of watching people hero-worship—from the Maharishi to EST to Lawrence—I'm immediately repulsed by any teacher who has even a sliver of a proud peacock puffed up by his or her spiritual superiority. I want to stick out my tongue and cross my eyes at people like that. John makes me want to do no such thing. More than anything, he comes off as shy and modest.

The first night is a little awkward. My grief-stricken roommate was crying so hard that the staff gave her a private room, and I got moved in with Denise. But halfway through the night I notice Denise is no longer in her bed. I mean, where do you go in the middle of the night, in the middle of the woods, in the middle of Wyoming? Is there some secret Vipassana love affair she began between orientation and lights out? The awkward thing is, I can't ask what the trouble is, you know, 'cause of the silent bit. I learn later she smelled gas and worried there was a toxic leak in our room. I'm touched she left me there to gas myself into oblivion alone. Off to a good start.

With morning still in darkness, I stir to the steady clang of the waking bell. I peek out the window and see the bell ringer walking softly through the property, making sure every cabin can hear it. I could get into this. I crawl out of bed, put on my sweatpants and pile jacket. A quick wash of my face and I'm out the door, headlamping to the meditation hall. Candles lit, I sit down on my *zafu* and wrap myself in my blanket. I close my eyes and begin to follow my breath as John instructs. An inhale. Another exhale. How lovely. So gentle.

Instructions over. Total silence. As in total. Suddenly this retreat business seems like a bad idea. *Sheesh, how does anybody get comfortable? I want to fidget, but if I move I'll make distracting noises. Plus, novices move more. I don't want to look like a novice. Maybe I'll do a slow-mo, totally silent fidget. Ow, my back hurts. Ow, wow, wow. Honestly, how can my back hurt already? I'm three minutes into a ten-hour day of this. Did I change my phone message? Crap. What about the Visa bill? What's today? I wish Tim had wanted to join. And Mom, oh . . . I should have never encouraged the move. Too isolated. Idiot. I'm an idiot. Maybe I should run a marathon. Stop moping and pound this out of me. Hooker shmooker. Buck up, wuss. Maybe after a marathon I could get those $150 jeans from Les Amis. It's a lot. But they're very nice jeans. And with the employee discount . . . Seriously, did I pay my card?*

Torture. Unabating. But I'm strapped in. I don't even have my own car.

Sit, walk. Sit, walk. Sit, walk, eat. Sit, walk . . . The idea: if I sit with myself long enough, I'll boil some of this crap out of me. But nobody told me what it would feel like to bring myself to a boil. Those bamboo shoots aren't sounding so bad right now. Another hour, but this time slow, measured steps of walking meditation, eyes gazing down and out—a small back-and-forth—like a very slow dog run. To call this peaceful would be inaccurate. Calling it a retreat is a misnomer. They should call meditation retreats what they really are: an assault. A meditation assault. A full-body, full-mind assault.

Welcome to the rest of the week. With the gentle clang of the bell, another sit ends and we slowly migrate to the dining hall—like slow-motion zombies in bad sweat suits and Smartwool socks. It's so serious, it's comedy. At lunch, I chew slower than I knew possible. I pay attention to the food on my plate like it's a fascinating light show. It's the most activity I'll see for some time.

But by day four, something odd happens. During a meal break, I walk along the river's edge. A few moose graze beyond me in the willow. So majestic. And who knew their knee joints bent that funny way? It must help them get through the thick snow. I keep walking and then—I start to giggle. I even want to skip, and I do a little. I'm pretty sure none of the precepts forbid skipping, but somehow it feels wrong.

"What *was* that?" I ask John during one of the two short private check-ins. I describe my high-giggling-skipping venture through the willow.

"Joy," he says.

"Pardon?" This doesn't compute.

"Maybe it's joy. You know—*joy*."

"Joy?" This never occurred to me. I'm a little disturbed that I treat this innocent word like he's speaking in tongues.

"You mean joy for, like, no reason?" I sound like I'm learning impaired. This is pretty basic stuff.

"Yes. Joy for no reason."

It's just, I think I forgot.

Well, I mean *really*. If I had known that suffering in total silence with an aching back and a mind running totally amok would lead to unprompted joy, I might have signed up sooner. I remember the pleasure of a good grade, my first paycheck, time spent with a good friend, performing in a play, being in the mountains. But not joy for no reason.

44

SALSA LESSONS

PURPOSE: To learn something new together. I love to dance. He hates it but is willing. It might be a hobby we can share.

DURATION: Ten weeks.

EQUIPMENT NEEDED: You can do salsa in any sort of getup. The music feels rather essential, though.

AGE: 32-ish with fourth-grade cotillion awkwardness.

RELATIONSHIP STATUS: I love my classmates in acupuncture school. Two years to go. There's such a sense of community, especially with Coco. Did I mention? She's taken up watercoloring.

COST: $30 per person for a ten-week series.

LOCATION: Bell Tower Community Center, Bellingham, Washington.

My sex drive has disappeared. I still can't seem to limp myself over to Tim's side of the bed. But I remember I love to dance, and we did meet in South America, after all. We climb the steps of the community center. Louisa and Jorge are dressed to the nines with matching microphone headsets at the front of the room. We slip in the back and start to follow along. Tim is next to me— awkward and shy but trying to pretend it's no big deal. Louisa wears a short skirt, heels, acrylic nails, and too much eye shadow. Jorge's collar is open to show his chest hair. Louisa and Jorge show what it's supposed to look like eventually. It is sexy: he, a little bit bossy; she, responsive. I find it kind of hot. They command the soggy Northwesterners into a circle. Women facing out. Men facing in. I practice the beginning moves with Tim the first five minutes. He has trouble creating a strong frame to hold me, struggles with the steps and hunches his shoulders apologetically as he pivots side to side. I struggle not to lead, because the steps come easily to me. Then Louisa commands the men to take leave of their women and change partners. Tim leaves me and begins circulating from woman to woman in a counterclockwise direction. I partner with a bantamweight Asian man with thick calves who can't look or dance straight at me, angling his hips away.

Jorge calls out to switch, and a man with a puka-shell necklace grabs me. I haven't seen puka shells since seventh grade and wonder at what possessed him to put them on tonight. He acts as though he believes himself to be very handsome as he pushes me about. The next guy has bad breath. I'm crushed there's not a kind, anonymous way to tell a stranger they might want to consider mints. I go through twelve men like this, thankful to see Tim again. I like the way he smells, the way his hands feel holding mine. Later that week, I ask him if we can practice. We try the moves but, really, only the initial one. Tim grows tired of it.

I stop bringing up the idea of practice. Sometimes I listen to salsa music in my car. I wonder if Louisa and Jorge have hot salsa sex or if they broke up ages ago and barely muster the energy to teach once a week without killing each other. I hope it's the former. I want to believe that the connection I saw on the dance floor lives between them when she's in sweatpants, not a skirt, and when neither of them is wearing matching headsets.

45

FAMILY RETREAT

PURPOSE: I told my mom I wanted to retreat. I really just wanted her.

DURATION: I wasn't sure.

EQUIPMENT NEEDED: Sheets, a set of towels. A warm bed. My mother's things around me. To watch a movie. To talk about houses or her chickens. And my marriage.

AGE: Almost 33.

RELATIONSHIP STATUS: Vulnerable. The kind I don't want to show just anyone.

LOCATION: River Bank Farm, Whidbey Island, Washington.

For a stretch after Tim's arrest, I tried bolting from Bellingham and living in Mom's old barn that she someday hoped to convert to livable space. It was presently full of rusty twin beds and my childhood brass one, a dormered attic with old armoires, and bat droppings. I wanted to take refuge there. Take refuge with the bats.

It didn't last long—like, part of a week.

"You're not dealing, Megan. You're hiding. I love you, but go work on what you need to with Tim," Mom said. The irony was, my mother was the beyond welcoming parent that all my childhood adult friends still understandably sought out to talk to because she was such a good listener. More challenging to listen, I suppose, when it hits closer and harder to home.

"Is there something wrong with retreating for a spell, Mom? I don't get it."

"Megan, you are the stronger one. Tim doesn't have the skills you have. Or the understanding you do. You're so good with people."

"But I've lost myself, Mom. I don't know what I'm doing this for. Or for whom."

"Megan, I need to support you the best way I can, and I don't think that means helping you hide."

I was too tired to push back. No matter how much we could connect through a book, a design, or a tiny object we'd found on a walk, I sensed that something in my mother's wounding made it impossible for her to see mine. I went home. I wasn't so much banished as embarrassed. I put the would-be retreat idea out of my mind. Closed it like one of those old armoires.

46

STICK THERAPY WITH JOHN TRAVIS

PURPOSE: Not even conventionally unconventional. This will take some explaining.

DURATION: One-hour intervals over a series of days.

EQUIPMENT NEEDED: The obvious: sticks. And no room for shame.

AGE: 33.

RELATIONSHIP STATUS: Tim and I still cling to each other like we can't decide if the other is a life raft or the one in need of rescue, but neither of us seems to be able to make a move—neither closer together nor farther apart.

COST: That Pali/Sanskrit word again: *dana*. Pay what you can.

HUMILIATION FACTOR: High. But surmountable. You can get over the mortification between you and *you* if the motivation is high enough.

LOCATION: Safari International Gros Ventre Wilderness area, Jackson, Wyoming.

The darkness in you cannot stay, it's going to be pulled out. It's not about the belief systems of the mind and who you think you are and what's right or wrong or what's good or bad. It's something much bigger. It's a setup to draw these things out. This is not a bad thing. The process is to turn you inside out so your mind is clear and your heart is open. And that takes a certain energy to distill some of the misbeliefs. They really can't stand up to this. So you are not wrong. You are just in a process.

—*John Travis*

God. I'm back. Back to Vipassana. I've asked Tim to come here with me, to meditate, to sit and just be. I'm waiting for clarity to replace the spinning we've been so spectacular at. But another rivaling fear mounts: that I could spin the rest of my life away.

By day four I notice that when I sit, I feel like the lower part of me is not connected to the upper part of me. And when I try to swallow, I start thinking a lot about swallowing and then start to panic that I've forgotten how to swallow and will never swallow again.

And hour after hour sitting in the hall, I find myself growing to hate this one guy across from me, this bearded, John-Lennon-glasses-wearing guy. He can sit and sit and sit and never move a millimeter. I take to opening my eyes to sneak peeks at him. *What a fake. What a snob. What an ass. Trying to look all together. How dare he. Well, screw him. How could I be more of a junk show than that bespectacled bozo?* I decided that he thought his patchouli-burning-simple-living-eating-steel-cut-oats-in-his-cabin-off-the-grid-spending-days-reading-the-Upanishads-or-Pema-Chödrön-wearing-those-goddamn-spectacles-in-front-of-his-wood-burning-stove-just-having-spent-the-morning-rescuing-wayward-falcons led to his calmness. And I didn't like it. Now, mind you, I didn't share the details of all this with John. I knew it was—let's just say—not my most evolved set of thoughts. But between my split feeling and the swallowing, I thought I should talk to John Travis in the one of two short private meetings where we could talk.

"It feels like my heart has disconnected from the lower part of me. Like I'm split. Literally. Right at the diaphragm. Like my stomach is severed from my heart."

John listens, then looks at me, and appears to take a long moment to think.

Then out of nowhere, as if it's the most logical thing to say when you are in the middle of a silent mediation retreat he says: "I want you to hike up into the Gros Ventre, gather a pile of sticks, and sit next to it. Sit and wait for that blocked feeling to come. And when it does, take one stick in your hand, raise it over your head, and throw the stick to the ground. And if there is a sound, make the sound. Then repeat."

I try to ignore the ridicule I give myself for needing some *special* activity. I take my marching orders and hustle up the ridge to get as far away from the hall as possible, what with that suggestion that I make noise and all. I go with an enormous pile of baseball bat–sized sticks.

I kneel down. Stick in hand, I close my eyes. I guess you can be embarrassed with only yourself watching because I am embarrassed with only myself watching. I wait for that tightness under my sternum. Yup, there it is.

And with the imagined posture of a medieval knight, I raise my sword (okay, stick) into the air.

Grab stick.

Grip. Lift. Tighten. Throw. Grunt.

Grip. Lift. Tighten. Throw. Grunt. Breathe.

Grip. Lift. Tighten. Throw. Grunt.

Grip. Lift. Tighten. Throw. Grunt. Next stick.

I spend less than a minute with each stick before they're too broken to hit anything further. The drier, thicker ones explode apart. The thinner ones feel like I'm whipping someone. I'm about thirty sticks and fifteen minutes into kneeling mode. My hands are starting to hurt a bit.

I feel a need to get up, to move around. I grab the more clublike sticks and look to see what I can hit, jump on. I continue on with the most batlike stick I can find and head out swinging and screaming. I picture people in my life I've never felt safe enough to get mad at and I yell. I yell for every moment I behaved when I didn't want to, tried to be rational when it was challenging, find the positive in some awful moment. I yell like it's my first and last chance on Earth to let the full chamber pot fly.

"Fuck you, you big fat fuck!!!" This is the angriest thing I can think to say. "You motherfucker. I'm going to smash your head off!!! Fuck. Fuck. Fuck. Fuck. You motherfucker. That's right!!! Take this, you big, fat motherfucking fuckface, fuckhead, asswipe, dickhole, shithead!!!" And smash, I slam the big stick into a tree. I jump up and down on a pile of branches. I yell every asinine, immature thing I ever wanted to say and didn't.

"FUCK **ALL OF YOU**!!!! MOTHERFUCKERS!!!! FUCK-FUCK-FUCK-FUCK-**FUCK**!!!! FUCK-YOU-CACK-FACE FUCK BUTT!!! FART-ASS-FUCK!!! FUCK YOU, YOU BIG FAT FUCKHEAD!!! FUUUUUUUUUUUCK!!

I hope to go until I pass out. I decide that's my new goal. I look like some jujitsu sword fighter having a psychotic break. *What kind of freak show is this?* I kick trees now. My hands start to bleed, but I don't care (I might be grabbing the stick a tad heavily). *I'm gonna smash that dead idiot tree to bits. Kill it. Kill that dead fuck of a tree.* Every few minutes I drop to my knees, take a breath, and sit totally calm to see if I'm done with whatever I think I'm doing. Finally, in about an hour, I declare the exercise complete. Not to mention, I'm beat.

I stare down at my bloodied hands, strangely admiring my handiwork. I've exceeded my own expectations. I'm such an overachiever. Plus, this is maybe the first real fight of my whole life. And nobody was hurt or even mad at me. In fact, I feel different. I feel happy, *really* happy. I decide I want to skip. I do a check around the area—always the good camper—to ensure I haven't left anything behind or made any kind of mess. All looks good. So I head out on my skip down the slope.

Yippee! I'm so happy to be alive! Life is beautiful! I love these little tuffets of sage! I love that mountain over there! I love the world and all its people! I even love myself! I love my life! I'm so lucky to be here! I feel the wind on my face and it feels gooooooood!

I run smack-dab into Tim in the middle of his walking meditation. I startle him.

I imagine I look like some sweaty cartoon character coming to a crashing halt. But I can't say anything—that goddamn vow of silence is nothing if not inconvenient. I want to laugh with that crazed joy that brought me down the hill. I try to have a mind meld with Tim about what has happened. The sticks. The smashing. The elation. And with his slight smile, I'm guessing he can imagine I'm up to something potentially ridiculous. We've been together for ten years, after all. I want to spill my beans and talk about the joy that seems to come after getting good and angry. I wonder who all he'd smash sticks for. He never lets himself get angry either. We have that in common. He, so earnestly walking back and forth, gazing down as instructed, looks like a man doing pen-ance. Like me, locked up in shame. Yet I felt like I'd just busted open one of the locks. All the trying we'd been doing. And for what? For whom? Like strangers paddling parallel upstream, yet on opposite sides of a river. Why is there no word for that? One simple word for being on opposite sides of the same river.

I smile awkwardly back at him and head to the hall, sending love all over him in my mind. After the next sit, the uncomfortable split sensation between my heart and belly has vanished. In its place, a squall of tears begin. I approach John that evening. He looked in my eyes, studying them.

I don't know what he saw. But the next day he sent me up to that ridge again. And with each sit, the cloudburst kept on. It went on for two days. I had no idea anymore why I was crying. I just cried. Through the breakfast breaks, lunch breaks, bathroom breaks, dinner breaks. And even with eyes closed with each sit, as I continued to weep after everyone left the room, Tim sat with me. Across that river.

47

BUILD A DREAM HOUSE

PURPOSE: Enact a, you know, dream.

DURATION: A while.

EQUIPMENT NEEDED: Both practical and conceptual.

AGE: 33.

RELATIONSHIP STATUS: Blah, blah, yeah.

COST: Depends on how far you take the dream.

LOCATION: Whidbey Island, Washington.

Mom's farm was a magical fifty acres: split-rail fencing, an original Victorian-ish farmhouse in need of improvements with an old barn right next to it. The place, all Douglas firs, fruit trees, open pastures, and a small heard of Scottish Highland cattle grazing through the rolling topography with a view of the water and the Olympic Peninsula. A home straight out of one of her storybooks.

What she wanted was to convert the bat-friendly cedar barn that lived be-tween the chicken coop and the cowshed into livable—sharable—space.

"If I could do anything," Mom said to the young architects at our first meeting, "I would create a refuge for women going through a difficult time or transition."

Oh, the irony.

". . . Maybe even add a tree house for a woman writer to retreat to."

The irony now multiplying.

It's funny, the blind spots we have. That's what I kept thinking. I wondered what mine were. I suspected one wasn't a blind spot so much as an all-too-comfortable pattern. In the face of a need of mine not met in a primary relation-ship, I compensated by meeting the other's need as if it were my own so I could experience a need fulfilled, stealing the nourishment that was not mine. What I dreamed about—my true house of belonging—included a mother or, better still, a *family* who could perceive the support I needed, a close-in someone or someones who had my back, who worried for the outcome of my life and spirits as much as or more than Tim's. But I had built and been taught to build my per-sonality around being (and looking) self-sufficient and impervious to difficulty (even when I wasn't)—so this was a tall order. Asking for support (and, worse still, asking for it and not getting it) felt as exposing and shameful as stumbling out of the ocean naked and menstruating—swimsuit around my head, blinding me like a game of piñata, dragging my broken surfboard through a pack of pro surfers and *Sports Illustrated* supermodels on their lunch break.

As for my need with my family, I could have used unsolicited, loving con-tact and reassurance from a tribe deeply protective of me for no other reason than I was a part of it. I'm not sure the gesture mattered: perhaps directive counsel and concern, or being taken to lunch, or being asked if I had consid-ered starting fresh, or if there was anything that would help ease my pain. My mother and father could give a mighty fine pep talk about being your own resource. Not as good a talk when resourced out.

Knowing those months ago how badly my request to retreat to her farm had gone, I would never point out the tragicomic overlap between what I'd asked for and the dream she wanted to offer other women. For my ego/heart/pride/dignity/vulnerability-preserving mechanism, it was easier to take all my metaphorical toys and go home. My pattern in full play here: I would offer her what I desperately wanted. A fresh start. A safe harbor. I would design her an inspired refuge. A home in a wild place like she'd already imagined in Wyoming. I had the skills. She taught me some of them.

Reclaimed wood, thick walls, clean lines would meet rustic worn-out cedar. The beaten-down exterior coming inside. We would design it. I would design it. I mean we/I would design it. Wait, *who* are we talking about again?

48

COUPLES COUNSELOR

PURPOSE: We've never gone to an actual couples counselor. I think it's about time. Don doesn't count.

DURATION: An hour and a half.

EQUIPMENT NEEDED: The quintessential therapeutic couch and corresponding chairs.

AGE: 33? I'm losing track.

RELATIONSHIP STATUS: Two-plus years since the arrest.

COST: $150. She charges more than Don. At least she has a PhD.

LOCATION: Fairhaven, Bellingham. Back to the Bermuda Triangle.

I feel like I'm not so much in a marriage as standing in a pile of rubble. I've spent two years digging and still know next to nothing—not much closer to understanding Tim than the day after the arrest. And even after all my (I should say *our*) work, the dust hadn't cleared. So today, another random office, another couch with pillows. Another professional face.

And right now I'm pissed. I know *pissed* is an ugly word, but *angry* sounds too mature. Not that I'm showing it on my face. Because for some jackass reason, I somehow think not being pissed makes this all better. Or maybe I think it makes *me* better. At this point, I would rather go purchase a pair of frivolous, oh-so-non-Northwest-y-politically-incorrect-overpriced-glittery-platform-clown shoes than sit on this couch with Tim while staring across at this new *sympathetic* soggy therapist: this dull-preppy-short-haired-floral-scarf–wearing-sensible-shoe-donning-PhD-carrying-boring-tight-assed Northwesterner with her 1980s gray walls, dusty rose pillows, and bad aqua art. This woman wants to put *Tim* at ease. Call it the Intrigue Factor. Even to the most seasoned professional, it seems once you say the word *hooker*, they all get a little titillated. So I just listen and wonder if she'll get one crumble of a new nibble out of him. Something that I don't already know. Some fresh material that will put this all in place, instead of this version of our life that I can't quite swallow anymore. I sit rather dumb and numb on the couch, watching Tim while he wipes his eyes and pushes his white-blond mop of hair up his forehead with an open palm as if he's just been awakened from a deep sleep. A gesture he likes to toss out when he wants to express bewilderment. As if it's all so eye-blurrying to him, so *outside* of him, this trouble of ours, this trouble of his. This trouble of mine. I've started to think he messes with his hair like this anytime things even get even a *tiny* bit closer to some missing truth. I can practically taste it. This way that nothing quite adds up and I'm supposed to pretend it does. As if what he's doing right now isn't this ridiculous performance. Pretending like his hands weren't at the wheel of his very own car, talking about this crash like someone else had ripped the wheel from him, launching this massive car into a wall, and he, a mere passenger. Like it happened *to* him, not *by* him. Or like someone swerved into his lane. Bollocks. He's the driver. *He's* the crasher. And like those stupid old cars he's rebuilding, this fucker is broken.

This is what I know: he got arrested for solicitation. I had grilled him ad nauseam on the arrest and his habits leading up to it. Phone sex and this one incident, he said. Although today I learn that the undercover cop wore a short skirt and, in Tim's words, "she was very wrinkly, weathered, and unattractive." I know I didn't enjoy hearing that detail. But I also know it is better and simultaneously horrific to *know* this detail—one of the few specific pieces of information I have. It helps me try to imagine what that night had been like. I know he approached her in his car, asked her how much for a blow job, and got scared and drove away. But then in his rearview mirror he saw her hands cross above her head to signal a police car. Then he saw the lights in his rearview mirror. Somehow those specifics feel essential—impossible for me to get more out of him, but essential nonetheless.

Our couples counselor takes the lead. Tim tells her that the night he was busted was the first time, and that his acting out was limited to phone sex.

"No, I don't know how much I spent on the phone calls." *(Yeah, right.)*

"I throw away the credit card statements." *(How convenient.)*

He had a separate credit card. And I didn't ask for duplicates. It didn't occur to me to insist. (I'm a real genius.) I saw only one statement and that one call alone had cost us $70. And I could assume there'd been a lot of calls. Years and years of calls. He told me he couldn't remember how many. Not even roughly. Just "a lot." "A lot" is not a very satisfying answer. (To put it mildly.)

So now, with Ms. Uptight-Northwesterner (did I mention I've begun to hate the Northwest and all its people?), here we were, another $150 down the drain, to hear what I'd already heard.

I'm starting to feel that all Tim's many kindnesses and compassionate acts—a thoughtful present for me an unrelenting dedication to his work, a call, a favor, a promise, of time, of labor, an above-and-beyond gesture for colleagues and friends alike, the literal and figurative distance he would go for so many, even his willing tone with this therapist—are all a shield. And it angers me. I want to rip it down so he will know that without any of his protections I will still be here. Waiting.

But maybe waiting is *my* protection.

Perhaps I use his wall to protect myself—to keep *me* safe. That Tower of Babel (another image of a wall, thank you very much) I have not the foggiest idea how to climb. If I could climb it and reach him, I told myself I would say:

Come here. I will hold all of you. Again and again. Bridge the distance between us. And then, please hold all of me right back.

What I want us to ask in this session with Ms. Hideous-Throat-Choking-Scarf, are the hard questions like: *Where do we go from here? Are you done? Are we done?* I want to not just fill in the gaps, but to *close* our gap. *If we can't close the gap, am I done?*

But we don't ask these. *Why?* Maybe if we really start talking we won't like what the other has to say. If it's too much to utter, is it too much to hear? What is actually holding us together? *Love? Guilt? Fear? Familiarity? Compassion?*

I am recalling our engagement party in his hometown. And the guest list his mother made without ever consulting him. Tim wouldn't object to certain guests, despite later telling me he had reasons for not wanting them to be invited. This confused me: the incredibly clear-line-drawing man, mixed with the Tim who couldn't speak up.

This is what I have come to know as the frighteningly passive part of Tim. The Tim—not just the Tim as a child, but the adult Tim—once told me of a time, a few years before we met, where he could not tell a trucker at a Shell station outside a national park to not enter the one-person bathroom that Tim occupied. The Tim that allowed that trucker to enter because Tim couldn't say no, either because Tim had forgotten to lock the door or because that lock was broken. The Tim who could not tell this trucker to stop using the urinal right next to Tim, as Tim used the toilet. This was not a bathroom with stalls.

But why couldn't he say, "Excuse me, sir, you'll have to wait. I'm using the bathroom, and it's built for one"? Who can't tell a sweaty trucker to buzz off? Who lets said trucker tell lewd jokes like, "What do you call twelve women upside down in a box"?

This is the Tim that makes me want to weep. The Tim I could believe would late one night offer a helpless stumbling woman—not a prostitute—the use of his cell phone. And while on the one hand it could make me weep, I also now want to shake him.

"Wake up, man! Wake up!" If nothing else, I am awake. Or part of me is stirring to rise.

Somewhere in the core of me I can feel that core of Tim. I can picture Tim's lack of self-protective instincts, how that lack would make it possible for less-kind people to not look after him, or worse still, harm him. What about those people who Tim was particularly relieved didn't come to that party years ago? Or the friend who married us whose adoration of Tim always made me a little

uncomfortable? Of those who had taught him to erect a shelter, to navigate a
route, why did one name make him clam up, but not others?

What other than the love of the mountains would motivate Tim to choose
to spend the bulk of his adult life in such tents—on a glacier somewhere or
hunkered down when the weather blew in? The same question could be asked
of me—the draw to such temporary shelter. The comfort, I suppose, is knowing
that the shelter is *yours* to control and the only dangers are natural ones. We
had fallen in love in such a shelter, after all—the tent in which we courted each
other across Patagonia—perfect just for two. Both of us, in our own way, hun-
kering down, hunkered down from some kind of storm—stormy upbringings
and too much trying-to-do-the-right-thing.

I am wondering if it is this passive part, this quiet tent-dwelling, natural-
history-loving, earnestly outdoor-instructing part of him that drew Tim to me.
I, who can say no *just* a smidge better than he can. Just barely. A girl-woman
who herself hasn't found her own voice when it really matters, who knows how
to swallow her words like she's doing now on this therapy couch. A woman who
is also looking for shelter from her own interior. A woman who, too, has forgotten what it was to say boo.

Outside the walls of any therapy office, we could still sometimes laugh together,
enjoy each other's company, fix a meal, plan a trip. But it doesn't feel like marriage,
more like roommates or brother and sister. I reflect on our days in Patagonia and
wish we could go back: camp out on a glacier, watch a bergschrund calve off, cozy
under the covers of our tent, reading a really bad spy novel while waiting for the
rain to let up. Where the hole in me would be filled up by the goodness of him.
Where the hole in him would be filled by the love I gave or the stories I told. And
somehow we could come out of that tent together and into the light as fully adult
selves ready to take on the world. Regular lives immersed in our full, strong, true
love, with work where we thrived, and reveled in stomach-tiring laughs. And,
hopefully, a baby or two. A family, not of our imagined orphan selves, but something we made from the best in him and the best in me.

Don't we have enough love and skill to get us back? Create some new version of us?

Tim tells this new professional that he wants to rebuild. But we can't agree on what rebuilding looks like. We need more than an hour and a half. I still think we have some rubble to clear out before putting in a new foundation. Tim doesn't seem to see the rubble, insisting nothing more remains to get to. He assures me that the problem has been handled, but he won't share how he's kept himself from having phone sex, or honestly any of it, because those topics are off-limits. And I'm tired of fighting Don and Tim for details to put it together. My sense: some of the puzzle pieces aren't even in the box. And worse still, I feel like I am suffering with the consequence of whatever he is still attempting to endure from long ago. The missing pieces. Mere bystander or unwelcome witness to his deepest shame without the invitation to be of comfort. However difficult things might get, I do not believe in the nobility of healing alone. I only see it as a path—for one or both of us—to further isolation. Or perhaps I'm wrong and certain histories are too difficult to be laid bare, no matter how much you love the bearer.

I leave this new office with no new information other than the detail about the cop and her wrinkles. Tim tells me I choose to be stuck. I think that's what you call a stalemate. Ms. Uptight-Northwesty says we should come back for another session. They always want you to come back for another session.

49

RAISE A FIELD MOUSE AS YOUR OWN

PURPOSE: Focus on something tiny, fragile, and alive. Help it grow.

DURATION: Many months.

EQUIPMENT NEEDED: Baby formula, an eyedropper, and a pocket big enough to hold a mouse.

AGE: 33.9.

EMPLOYMENT/RELATIONSHIP STATUS: I'm going to do my clinical training in Colorado.

COST: Small quantities of milk.

LOCATION: Bellingham, Washington, and Louisville, Colorado.

We've been storing the old convertible Tim got arrested in inside my mother's tractor shed. Turns out a baby deer mouse has been abandoned by his mama in the trunk. We might be able to save him (or is it a her?). We take the mouse out of the trunk and back home. Together we go to the pet store to get the proper equipment: eyedropper, formula, milk. We train him to take the dropper. He guzzles the milk throughout each day, grabbing the dropper greedily with his paws. He is small enough to curl up inside my belly button. We take pictures. We take him to the beach, where we practice kitesurfing at the shore. Mouse (we call him Mouse—or sometimes Hanta, after that mouse virus going around) rides around in Tim's shirt pocket or sleeps in my belly button. Sometimes we both are too enthusiastic in feeding and the milk covers him, a thick coating. He loses some of his fur because of this. We start to call him Patches and hope it grows back.

We don't exactly decide to separate as a couple, but we decide I will do my acupuncture clinical year in Colorado. The clinic is far superior, and perhaps we just need an undefined break. Together we drive Mouse across the country to settle me in Boulder. Mouse lives in a giant purple Tupperware that is too big for him. He's not big enough to jump out of it yet.

Mid–road trip, the three of us stop at Michelle and Scott's in Wyoming. Michelle thinks we (or just I) may have finally gone insane. She tries to pretend we're not hauling this little guy around. She doesn't use the term *little guy*. She prefers the term *rodent*.

In their guest room, I spend another sleep crying in the night. We had decided that Mouse, as a native Northwesterner, would return with Tim. But at the eleventh hour, as I braced for my heart-shattering good-bye to Tim, he tells me I can keep Mouse. Mouse and I move into the basement of my friends' house in Boulder. They tolerate Mouse because they know that maternal love must go somewhere.

As the months apart from Tim pass, Mouse gets too big for his Tupperware and begins jumping out of his house. I train him to jump into my hands, but I know he wants to jump beyond my hands. Flying home for a visit, I smuggle Mouse in a handkerchief, loosely tied with a rubber band, back to the Northwest, where he belongs. Tim and I both love him. That was never the question. Maybe we should have named him What Could Have Been. But that's a little long.

Tim gives Mouse his own room—the room that was once my office, but I don't live there anymore. Eventually the two of us agree to let Mouse free in the basement so he can he find his way to the outside.

I haven't found my way out yet, but I can imagine it.

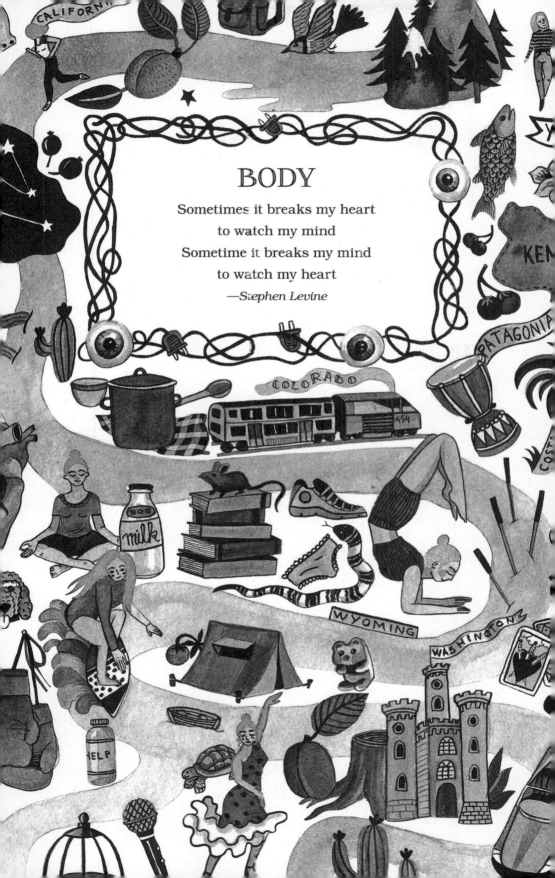

BODY

Sometimes it breaks my heart
to watch my mind
Sometime it breaks my mind
to watch my heart

—Stephen Levine

50

TAROT CARDS

PURPOSE: Is it cheating/amoral to ask a psychic for the skinny on your husband's sex life? It feels like cheating, but I think I'll behave more intelligently if I know the truth. With our new agreement that we can date other people, I don't really know what's up for Tim in that department. I wanna know, but I don't wanna know. You know?

DURATION: One hour.

EQUIPMENT NEEDED: Tarot is a pack of fifteenth-century game cards, commonly numbering seventy-eight, each to reflect different archetypes and meanings.

AGE: 34.

RELATIONSHIP STATUS: As for my own dating, I'm too busy with work and not ready. Still don't know if I feel done. I called Tim in the middle of a date last week. He answered. Nightmare.

EMPLOYMENT: Clinical intern.

COST: $100.

HUMILIATION FACTOR: Not so much humiliating as cringe-inducing.

LOCATION: Boulder, Colorado (via phone to Alexa, third-generation psychic, in La Conner, Washington).

Alexa Robbins is the polar—as in polar—opposite of Gardenia Mellon. Whereas Gardenia seemed one part lunatic (with, yes, arguably, a psychic gift), walking around with a really bad hairdo and oversized lenses, Alexa is the smartest girlfriend you've never had. Like a best friend (reasonable, rational, well educated) with a bonus akin to a magic crystal ball. What could be better?

With her recorder turned on, the call begins. Alexa shuffles the cards. My take on psychics: The natural ones find a tool to help sort the information they get. Alexa is quite visual and seems to use tarot the way visual artists use watercolor or charcoal. From the deck, she pulls a standard cross—a ten-card formation to interpret an overall picture of me. She looks at the cross. There's a happy little card with cherub children with pretty gold cups. That looks promising. But it's rather overshadowed by an impressive array of violent dark swords jabbing all over my spread. One giant sword stabbing straight through a heart, even. Brilliant. Then Alexa pulls the cards on Tim. It goes something like this.

Alexa: Oh . . . oh . . . Megan.
   Me: What is it?
Alexa: Well, first, Tim is seeing someone.
   Me: Just one? I was hoping it was still more than one person.
Alexa: Well, hmmm. I'm just getting the one person.
   Me: So he's dating one woman? What's going on?
Alexa: Well, it's very . . .
   Me: Very what?
Alexa: Very . . . well, I hate to say this but . . .

Having Alexa on the phone is like having a sympathetic friend with better eyesight who got a view of a really bad car crash, and her instinct is to avert her eyes. But she proceeds, almost forcing herself to look.

   Me: Okay, well, go on . . .
Alexa: It's very—how can I say? Very sexual. Like, very.
   Me: So you're getting visions of them having sex all over the place or . . . ?

Alexa: Yeah, something like that. I'm so sorry. He's really into it. I don't
         know what you were hoping for, but his attention is elsewhere.
         This one's got him. It's very sexual. Eye-popping.
  Me: Christ.

I ask her for any more details. I don't need the porn images that already
flash through my head. I need to hear how hopeless it is. I want to meet reality
wherever it is. In my gut, I know it's over. Over *over*. But I want to hear it from
somewhere other than inside my own body.

She shares what she sees as positive. At the very least, it eliminates some
options. This way, I didn't really have to choose. Or maybe I already did and
this is the result. Or maybe I took the wimp route, and he relieved me of that
last choice. It explains his distance on the phone. His heart resides elsewhere.

I take some deep breaths as my head spins. Alexa senses I'm trying to keep
myself together. (What is she, like, psychic?) I've cried dramatically enough for
a lifetime, so now I only do that when absolutely necessary. I ask a few more
questions. I get psychic-greedy at the end of the call, trying to cram in last-
ditch questions: Is he in love? (Not love yet, exactly, she says, but wildly hypno-
tized.) Which is worse? Will it last? (It's going to have him for a while. That's
all she can feel. The pull.) Is there anyone for me? (No. Not now, she says.) Of
course not, I think with irritation.

51

LOVING-KINDNESS MEDITATION PRACTICE (CLASSIC METTA PRACTICE)

PURPOSE: To practice love without attachment in the Buddhist tradition.

DURATION: Traditionally forty-five minutes, but any length of time, really. A few moments to a few hours at a time. Depends on the practice.

EQUIPMENT NEEDED: As a concentration practice, just the classic phrases.

AGE: 34.

RELATIONSHIP STATUS: Loss and loneliness. Trying to keep in perspective. I may be losing a husband, but Coco is still losing more vision. There are millions of men in the world, but we get only two eyeballs, tops.

COST: Free.

LOCATION: I do this to and from the Louisville clinic a lot these days.

A pearl goes up for auction
No one has enough,
So the pearl buys itself

—Rumi

Known as the sweet lubricant that softens the heart, it is said that doing Metta while falling asleep leads to beautiful dreams, making it also an antidote to both nightmares and insomnia. The practice begins by silently uttering four classic phrases: first to oneself, then someone you love deeply, then someone you feel neutrally about, then a difficult person, then all beings. The classic phrases: May I be happy. May I be peaceful May I be safe. May I be free.

John Travis had taught me that I might feel silly at first saying such nice things to myself, but that despite our cynicism, there's some part of each of us that could use hearing these words. Sometimes I jog, repeating: Happy. Peaceful. Safe. Free. In lieu of *Sincerely*, I like to sign my letters with *Metta* when I am feeling particularly Metta-groovy.

52

GET DUMPED BY THERAPIST
OR DUMP THERAPIST
(YOU CAN'T REMEMBER WHICH)

PURPOSE: In the best of therapeutic relationships, the professional partnership eventually comes to a gradual, well-considered end. In the worst of relationships, it goes something like this.

DURATION: Something like a half hour.

EQUIPMENT NEEDED: Phone, and steely insides, mixed with mushy ones.

AGE: 34.

RELATIONSHIP STATUS: Christ, I feel alone. I wish it were something that a good basket of chips and guac could soothe. It ain't.

COST: It costs $100 for a therapeutic breakup by phone. It's a billable hour.

HUMILIATION FACTOR: Pretty impressive.

LOCATION: Lander, Wyoming.

I hang up. I've abandoned Kleenex and gone straight to my sweatshirt's ratty sleeve to mop up. I think I got dumped. Or maybe I did the dumping. I've never been good at letting go. And yet, suddenly, I'm doing it. The Era of Don is done.

It started harmlessly enough. When I moved to Colorado, I'd been therapy-free for more than six months. Instead, clinical work became my ally. But with no patients scheduled for the weekend, and after the Tarot Fun, I headed to the safest place I knew: 801 South 3rd, Lander, Wyoming. After the five-hour drive, I sit in Michelle and Scott's living room in their Barcelona chair, surrounded in earth tones, a Chilean rug, Bolivian tapestry pillows, and red douppioni silk curtains Michelle made herself.

While I'm grateful for Michelle and Scott's sacred space, I don't want to obligate them to a world-class processing session. They've gone above and beyond so many times. I call Don. We haven't spoken since I left Bellingham, but he was Tim's and my therapist, after all. I summarize. New woman. Tim moving on. My grief pours into the room, like I lost an organ, like a liver or my spleen, or my right arm.

"I think it's really over. Tim's in love."

"Megan, to be this upset seems deeply . . . You should be seeing me or someone multiple times a week. This is not a sign of health."

"But I . . . I know it wasn't the best relationship. But it was *mine*. And all the dreams that came with it, gone. Can't you see that? I'm sad. I think that's normal. I've been holding it together at work, but . . ."

"Megan, this is excessive. You should . . . This is a sign of your deep, deep, pro—" Suddenly, without validation from anyone, I know it's understandable to feel sad. Especially now.

"All right. Well, good-bye, Don. I wish you the best." I don't mean the last part, but the politeness taught by Mom runs deep, even here. I try to find the gracious part. It's pretty soulless.

For the violations in confidentiality, I will file a report with the state. I keep the report neutral and factual, but inside, it took a lot to keep from boiling over. Once I started to ask around, I learned this wasn't the first time a group (an unusually large web of friends and couples) had run into Don's bleeding confidentiality and clients who felt manipulated. However, to get a license *fully* revoked, it appears you need to be more like Hannibal Lecter, rather than merely unethical and incompetent. The complaint application: a tome of every misstep I had witnessed with Don. I had interviewed friends who were therapists or had therapists in their families, and discussed Don's breaches. Don, unbeknownst to me, would eventually see not just Tim, but Tim's new girlfriend, Vee, as well as one of Vee's siblings. The web, out of hand. With that last phone call, I could see Don much more clearly, and feel a duty to protect other potentially vulnerable clients. He actually wanted to keep me stuck. I think he liked me there. He liked Tim there too.

The state opened an investigation and they put him on probation.

Tim would eventually file a report too. As would Vee. A Cascade effect not in a marriage, but in counseling. Apparently, we'd all reached some sort of breaking point independently. I didn't read their reports but knew what I saw: a therapist fascinated by a case, not interested in helping two people—separately and as a couple—try to put themselves back together, which was what we had asked for. He actually sounded surprised when he once mentioned seeing us holding hands at the grocery store. The first time he realized we might love each other and want to share our lives, not some pathological narrative of abandonment and repression in his mind as the only elements that had brought us together. Well, screw him and his stinky pink office, his ratty couch, and his mad-scientist desk.

Of course, we loved each other. That was never the question.

53

TWO THERAPISTS SIMULTANEOUSLY

PURPOSE: Why have one when you can have *two*?

DURATION: The intro interview calls are quick. The in-person is a standard session.

EQUIPMENT NEEDED: One therapist is more pillows and art supplies. The other more PowerPoint.

AGE: 34.

RELATIONSHIP STATUS: When your husband has a girlfriend, that feels pretty single.

EMPLOYMENT: Clinic girl. I'm still packing in the hours in record-breaking time.

COST: $80 a session. Tim and I still share expenses, but I'll need a loan if we divorce. This is why those geniuses invented credit cards.

HUMILIATION FACTOR: Moderate to high. Feels unnatural to two-time.

LOCATION: Niwot, Colorado.

At this point, I don't give a rat's ass if it's not kosher to see more than one thera-pist at a time. I need a longer courtship. After the Don debacle, I now refuse to rush into a full commitment, therapeutic or otherwise. I also wonder how Tim's life might have unfolded had Don never laid his words on him. In my gut, I sensed this wasn't the first time Tim had been harmed by someone he trusted. But if I'm honest, the same could also be said of me here, as well.

I get the number for Therapist No. 1 through Coco—a guy named Majie. Doesn't that mean *magic* in French? I read about Therapist No. 2 in Boulder's holistic magazine, called *Nexus. Nexus* guy wants me to plan for being on my own and my new acupuncture practice. Seems useful. He also asks that I do that exercise where you write all those letters to people in your life—to *get it out,* whatever *it* is—but never send them. Sure, I'll write some letters. Kinda bugs me that I won't be sending any, but okay.

Majie feels right. He practices a therapy called Hakomi, which was founded in Boulder: a body-centered, experiential somatic psychotherapy. I tell each fel-low the same story on meeting, but when I talk to Majie, I can actually feel my-self more. How weird is that? He feels like both mirror and lamp—I feel myself both reflected and more illuminated. And he has me slow down. Not talk so much. We start with what it's like to be in the room, just as we are.

We do things like talk from my throat, to feel what that tight place has to say. That place that hates to utter a word or complain. Sometimes he asks me to talk to pillows. It's mostly how it sounds. Except the pillows represent different parts of myself. Each pillow gets a chair, and we have a conversation, except I have it between me (the Head Pillow) and all the other pillows: the enduring pillow, the critical pillow, the sad pillow, the younger pillow. It's like lining up the seven dwarfs, if the dwarfs looked like square feather bolsters. But Snow White's dwarfs had better names. I have Throaty, the Judge, the Particularly Mean Judge, the Collapsed Voice, Wisest Megan, the Angry Buzzard (she's the most reluctant), Christina Aguilera, and the Delusional Megan who begins all sentences with "If Only I . . ."

The point: a couple of pillows say some stuff I've never heard before. It's like an employee meeting—I'm the boss with a couple of disgruntled employees. A few have some ideas worthy of a suggestion box. I'm taking it all under advise-ment. Because that's the kind of manager I am. I don't want anybody quitting on my watch. Although I might have to do a few layoffs. A couple of these guys are a waste of my time.

54

EYE MOVEMENT DESENSITIZATION AND REPROGRAMMING (EMDR)

PURPOSE: To resolve symptoms from disturbing and unresolved experiences. A structure of alternating left-right stimulation (eye movement, hand/leg tapping, or bilateral tones or vibrations). Oversimply put: this allows the brain to release chemicals like acetylcholine to move incompletely processed memories from the right brain into long-term storage on the left.

DURATION: Less than an hour a session. Can be done repeatedly or as a one-off.

EQUIPMENT NEEDED: Headset, vibrating paddles.

AGE: 34.

EMPLOYMENT: Clinical intern (still).

COST: $80.

HUMILIATION FACTOR: All these wires make me feel a little like a rat.

LOCATION: Niwot, Colorado.

It's been two months, and this time with Majie is changing me. The focus is finally heading in the right direction—not between me and a husband or me and a complex, metaphysically overwrought family. I was left with yours truly. Plain old me, for-better-or-worse me.

Majie thinks we need to do a little EMDR—something to do with how much I report this can't-sit-still feeling. It's a nearly constant and not very comfortable buzzing sensation up and down my spine. I've had it since Tim's arrest. My stomach is routinely jumpy. I can no longer comfort-eat. Instead I feed on nervous energy as though I'm still in a high state of alert.

Part of EMDR means working with old traumatic memories. They don't slap some equipment onto a Vietnam vet and let his eyes zigzag back and forth for a few minutes and send him packing. It's gentle. It doesn't really matter what memory you start with because once you conjure a troubling memory, your brain takes it and runs where it needs—an elaborate dot-to-dot game through your head.

Headphones on. They connect to two flat plastic objects that look like skipping stones.

"Hold one in each hand. Let's do a sound check to confirm the left headphone makes a sound while the left paddle vibrates." Majie smiles, his large French-blue eyes crinkling around their edges. We begin.

Beep-to-the-*left.*

Beep-to-the-*right.*

"It feels like electric Ping-Pong inside my head. Does it really come down to needing to be physically rewired? The contraption seems so . . ."

"Concentrate on the sound. See if we should speed up or slow down."

I feel like Frankenstein. Or like I hold the means to blast off into space with controls in each hand. Now, a few beeps later, it's a different kind of Ping-Pong—flashing movie scenes from my life—a veritable Baskin-Robbins of familial and relational memories.

My dad (all 220 pounds of him) pinning me down in a wrestling match, not letting me up, in a way that scared me: "This will teach you that men are stronger than women"; the moment I took Tim's call from jail; the impact to my ribs and skull and shaking eyeballs when that horse threw us, slamming us into that Patagonian earth: the sensation of cracked ribs, the pain of an inhale; my sister and I in that bizarre fistfight in her car, the rage in our punches; the humiliation at five of pacing outside a neighbor's backyard, dying to be invited to the birthday party of a much elder kid; my father telling me I can't talk to him on the phone alone; not able to tell him how this hurts in a way that impacts him; hearing Tim say that, unlike me, Vee really understands him; my grandmother Deany's bluish corpse and bad makeup in her open casket; a shaming from a professor after a Yale economics exam; utter fear at thirteen after some older boys told each other I was the dumb-as-a-stump girl they said would be a *good fuck*; my mother telling me of her childhood neglect, alone in that room she always describes; a twisted clothesline of snapshots through my body and brain.

Physically, I can boil it down to some trembling, the occasional moan, and a little clammy sweat for good measure, all the while aware something deep is transpiring. Majie and I take brief breaks between sets. We do a little Chinese torture test to bring up the initial memory of Tim's phone call from jail, to see if the disturbing event has lessened. I rate it on a scale of one to ten. And now the memory pain has dropped from a high of seven to a one.

After slowly opening my eyes, I stand up to stretch. My bare feet feel strange and more sensitive to the subtleties of the carpet under me. The vibration up and down my spine has departed.

55

BOUNDARY EXERCISE

PURPOSE: To discover your limits. Majie thinks I need help in this department.

DURATION: Twenty minutes of a sixty-minute session.

EQUIPMENT NEEDED: One other person, preferably with limbs.

AGE: 34.

RELATIONSHIP STATUS: I might be open to a date. With whom, I have no idea. I join Coco on her weekend hikes in the red rocks of Fort Collins. She's thinking of joining Toastmasters. I'm willing to bet soon she'll be Toastmasters president.

EMPLOYMENT: Clinic and a growing business plan. Nice to know my work time is spent in a white coat and that my private time is spent making sure men dressed in similar white garments don't come for me.

COST: $80.

LOCATION: Niwot, Colorado.

So here we are. Magic Magie and I. He wants to see if we can learn a little something about my boundaries. Majie gets up from his chair at the window and stands at one end of the room near the door. Granted, it's a small room, but the other side of it, nonetheless. I stand across from him with the window to my left near the wall, where the pillows and art supplies—and bataka bat (the big padded stick you pound things with)—live.

"I want you to tell me if you are comfortable with me at this distance, and if it's okay for me to step closer." Hakomi therapy is particular about contact, minimizing touch between client and therapist, to maintain professionalism and, yes, healthy boundaries.

"Yes, good," I say. "You can step toward me."

Majie takes another step. "How's this?" We stand four feet apart.

"That's okay, you can step toward me. I'm good."

He steps again. We stand arm's-length apart.

"Now," he says, "I'm going to put my hands over your head. Tell me when it no longer feels comfortable." He reaches his hands up and sort of arcs them like Chewbacca surrendering. Then his hands and arms slowly inch toward me.

"You still okay?" he asks.

"Yep, you haven't gotten there yet. This feels comfortable."

Majie looks slightly alarmed, as now his hands rest squarely on my head. We look at each other and laugh. Jury's in. I have no boundary.

The following week I tell Majie, "Tim came to visit. We can't seem to cut the cord. He's still seeing this Vee woman. I guess her name is Vee."

"And how'd that feel?" he asks gently.

"Well, I'm watching my jealous part make an appearance. I don't think I've felt jealousy before. Of course, she's younger. Must they always go younger? Apparently she is ultra-petite, with a fierce blond bob, and a graceful tattoo across her diminutive clavicle, and quadriceps born to run a thousand miles across the Kalahari Desert barefoot. When not running she prefers steel-toed boots, the kind smokejumpers wear. You know what a fire whirl is, Majie? They are like flaming white hot tornadoes of fire and power. I keep picturing her like a sexy hot fire whirl. And she sounds cool in a tough way that neither Tim nor I have ever been. They met in a bowling alley. I had no idea he was a bowler. He asked her for a light. Apparently, he smokes for real now too. He smokes and he bowls. And is looking into a motorcycle."

"Um-hmm." Majie sits with me in my irritation, waiting for me to settle.

"But, Majie, I don't want to smoke and I don't want a tattoo. The fierce blond bob sounds nice. But if Tim needs to go sexy biker or whatever, I'm not sure I'm the one to go there with him. It's not me."

"How'd the visit go?"

"I've missed him. Regardless of everything, he's my fellow traveler, my touchstone. We talked about his job, my patients, his running, the old car he'll take a hundred years to rebuild. Then we tried kissing. It had a certain sweetness. He wanted to be intimate but not wear protection. He said, 'Come on, it's fine . . .' as we rolled around. That startled me out of the sweet part. I said, 'No.' I don't think I've ever done that before, and I pushed back, but he kept pushing with more 'Come ons . . .' all very unlike him. I said, 'I'm sorry, but I'm not going to have sex with you without a condom. I assume you have slept with this person Vee, and I don't know her sexual history. I don't want to expose myself to anyone else.' And he said, 'I've told you a thousand times. You can trust me. I was never with anyone else. I'm safe. And Megan, it's different with her. I can really be myself with her.'" *I think of Alexa's reading about how sexual it all is.*

"I was like, 'So what part of you couldn't you *possibly* show me? How much more understanding can one woman show? What is it? Do you fuck her upside down in a box? Hog-tie each other? What is it? I mean, who in the *world* is this *you* that you can't show me? Name *one* time I've shown a lack of kindness or been cruel about *any* of this *ever*. Really, can you tell me?'"

"And when you said you don't want sex when he's with another?" Majie asks.

"To say such a straight no and lose it? I've never been that clear before, but man, my rage. Then I asked, 'Have you always worn a condom with her? There are things you can get even with a condom, you know. There's no way I can do this, in these circumstances. I don't know what understanding you have with her. In a way, it's none of my business, but God forbid she or I got pregnant. Let's keep this simple. One sexual partner, even if it's not me, while we're still married seems more . . . clear or something. I can't get into it. I love you, but this doesn't feel safe. I know what you've told me, that it was only that *one* conversation with the undercover cop, but, well, this just doesn't feel okay. I'm trying here. I know you're a great person, but I have this feeling . . .'

"'You have this feeling,' he'd said, not totally without mimicry. And I said, 'For today, all I can tell you is I can't. Does Vee know about the arrest?' And he said in his politer version, 'Don't you ever give it a rest? It's not her concern and it's not yours that it's not hers.'

"And I said, 'So much for your really being yourself with her.'

Tim sighed. 'Here we go again. You can't let it go. I promise you, I've never been with a . . .'"

Majie interrupts my retelling. "You know what I hear, amid all that?" Majie smiled like a warm, kind Buddha.

"What?" I asked, still irritated at myself.

"I think you found a boundary."

"Well, I don't like it."

56

M&M PARTS WORK

PURPOSE: I call it Internal Family Systems therapy meets Mars candy. IFS uses one's imagination to identify parts of oneself. Apparently, one of my internal parts looks like actual candy. While corny, this is my chocolatey middle, I guess.

DURATION: This is our first meeting with the M&M, but we will work with him/her regularly.

EQUIPMENT NEEDED: My mind's eye; Majie's safe, warm room; and his two comfortable chairs.

AGE: 34.

RELATIONSHIP STATUS: My sister is getting married. I love her fiancé, Rich. He's kind and charismatic. In a sweet way, he's like a taller, larger-eyed, fiery version of Dad. I'm so happy. I want somebody in this crew to have a successful go.

COST: $80.

HUMILIATION FACTOR: Majie and I kind of get a kick out of the M&M image, but I'm a little embarrassed to share it with you, dear reader.

LOCATION: Niwot, Colorado, on Majie's cul-de-sac, a charming modern cottage.

Everyone carries a shadow, and the less it is embodied in the individual's conscious life, the blacker and denser it is.

—Carl Jung

Ever play with an inflatable ring in the pool as a kid? Ever try to push one of those things down and keep it submerged at the bottom? It's nearly impossible, creating the idea that the object under the water is enormous. But let it come up to the surface, and it's obviously a tiny, harmless, inflatable horse or duck. I think that's what I've done internally. There are aspects of myself that I'm not giving enough airtime.

With Majie and I each in our own chair, he asks me to close my eyes, get very quiet, and see what physical or emotional sensation I first run into. Right now it's a sad part. "Imagine this part in your mind's eye. What does it look like?" Majie asks.

"Um. It sits on this couch, but its legs are so small, they can't touch the ground so they dangle. You know those walking M&Ms in commercials? It's like that, but clear. It's on this couch, by itself, looking out the window at these big, beautiful trees. The problem is, it's so collapsed. It doesn't know why it's deflated, but it feels like it could cry forever."

"And if this part spoke right now, what would it say?" Majie asks.

"Honestly? It would say, 'I'm really sad. And I don't know why. I feel little and dark and like nobody knows I'm here. And I don't have any words. All I can do is cry and that's not okay. So I don't. So I sit here, and feel stupid.'"

I (Megan) feel ridiculous talking like an M&M, but it knows exactly what it wants to say.

"Do you think if we gave this part some room, would it like to cry?"

I nod.

"Can you let it do what it wants?" he asks.

"Maybe."

"And if this part lived somewhere in your body, where does it live?"

"Probably my throat. I feel tight there. I want to relax it. But this thing grips tightly. Majie, I think this is kind of silly."

"And this part that thinks it's silly, Megan, what should we call it?"

I know this name well. "The judgmental part."

"I would like to ask the judgmental part to step back for a minute. Do you still have contact with the M&M?"

"Mm-hmm."

"Would it be okay with the M&M part if it cries if it wants to?"

"Yeah, okay." So I relax my throat and feel a wave of grief rolling in. It feels older than the hills.

"What's happening now? How do you feel toward this M&M?" Majie asks.

I perk up. "I feel, um, sort of soft toward it. Looks pretty cute sitting all by itself on that couch. I mean, it's sweet the way its feet don't touch the floor or anything. He looks like he's waiting around—for something good to happen. He's kind of cute." With my eyes still closed, I smile.

"And how do you feel about his being this sad?"

"It kind of makes sense. I mean, it looks really little on that couch. And those trees outside look so big. I think it's scared and I understand. I mean, it doesn't know any better."

I've reached some sort of ground floor. I don't think there's anything scarier underneath. And apparently, I'm not sad to the core. It's just a part—not scary at all. I always pictured that if I ever completely let go, I would blubber forever. Turns out, my imagined M&M was like that inflatable ring. Once on the surface, it didn't feel so overwhelming.

Now, the fact that my shadow comes in the form of a candy designed for the trenches of World War II—well, nobody's perfect. Although, maybe a candy with a history like that *is* perfect.

57

LEARN TO SURF

PURPOSE: Surfing is a surface water sport in which a person moves along the face of a breaking wave. Water or no, I'm too uptight. Something about water loosening my tight places feels right.

DURATION: Seven days.

EQUIPMENT NEEDED: Borrowed board, rash guard, swimsuit. Decent first-aid kit.

AGE: 34. I've packed a lot into these last months.

RELATIONSHIP STATUS: Had an actual date. A taxidermist-furniture-maker guy I met in the Fort Collins Whole Foods protein-bar aisle. I'd abandoned Coco in produce, overinspecting melons. Never met a taxidermist before, let alone a smokin' hot one. Maybe I'll see him again after my pro surf tour.

EMPLOYMENT: Clinical intern (still . . . but the end is near!).

COST: Around $800, if memory serves. Includes breakfast (which I make big enough to count as lunch), lessons, lodging, and equipment.

LOCATION: Nosara, Costa Rica.

I've just logged 1,500 clinical intern hours in record time and have been going to Majie for four months. Too bad I can't get frequent-flier miles for either. I haven't seen Tim in what feels like ages. The last *official* thing we did together was attend my sister's wedding at Mom's farm. What a strange last event to share. But I need to look forward—not back. I intend to celebrate crossing the acupuncture finish line.

What do I imagine would feel fun, even if I do it alone? Hands down, it's surf camp. I grew up in the perfect place for it but was too busy acting as some part-time, underage, unlicensed, self-elected mediator during dinners out with my parents at California Pizza Kitchen instead of getting properly barreled at El Morro Beach. More often than not, I'd find myself between my parents, trying to decipher the language of their discontent—one attenuated, nameless, faceless unspoken argument. Such nonargument-arguments usually resulted with Mom in tears (but trying to hide them), followed by Dad's subsequent grumbling sounds, and finally punctuated with my pathetic search for my most recent philosophical analogy, in hopes such orations (and they were like orations, said too frequently, all in one breath) would narrow the chasm between them. A cherry on top of the dessert that we were always too tense to order.

Now, most important about this camp, I'll meet new friends, have big group meals—all social, all the time. The classic family meal without the dysfunction. Easy talk in the presence of hot food. Exactly what I love about wilderness trips—minus the mountains, minus Tim. The package, including all meals with the other campers, seems overpriced, but it's worth it. I loved camp as a kid. I'm semipanicked about the alone time, so I pack my duffel with twelve books so when I'm not surfing or socializing, I'll read.

I arrive at the small lush airstrip of Nosara. Tyler, the camp leader, picks me up. Classic surfer type: blond, lean, big chest (that for some unexplained reason is never hairy), with a confidence in movement, a fluidity as if still moving through water, even when on dry land. Tyler helps carry my stuff to the purple camp Jeep and throws it casually in back. I can't wait to meet my surf buds.

"So are we headed to meet up with the other campers, or do we not get together till dinner?"

"Um," Tyler pauses. "Well . . ."

Oh, no. In my experience, big pauses mean trouble. I look down at my hands, as if I'm contemplating a manicure, while I await his reply. I'm nervous about meeting everybody.

"You are kind of the only camper."

Silence.

Are you kidding? I am the whole *camp? Jesus. Of course. I can't believe I flew all the way down here to eat alone again.* But I pretend like it's no big deal. As we drive down the dirt road past underfed cows and rubber trees, all I can think about is what I shelled out for these big *group* meals. If it's just me, I'd rather have a street taco. Plus, does that mean I'd be paying Tyler to eat alone with me? Like some sort of surf escort? Not only is this overpriced, it's humiliating.

I'm embarrassed to ask, but my pocketbook urges. I muster the guts to ask before camp actually starts. Tyler helps me take my stuff to my room.

"Uh, Tyler . . . about those big group dinners . . . could I, um . . . downgrade from the deluxe package?"

God, this is embarrassing. I hate that I'm nickel-and-diming him. But I will not rent a dinner companion. But I'm also freaking out about spending all day alone with myself without work. And surfing with the "group" only happens twice a day. *That's right, I'll read those books.*

After the awkward but successful group-meal downgrade discussion in the motel courtyard, I unpack my gear. My room is simple: two twin beds and 1970s orange-and-blue bedspreads. Tyler pops his head back into my room and asks, "You wanna go snorkeling?"

There is only one answer to this question. Ever.

"Yes."

I now ride behind Tyler on a red ATV headed for some secret snorkeling spot. We arrive at a small, gorgeous beach. He hands me some fins and a mask and we scramble onto some rocks out on a point. The tide is high. He calls me out farther on the rocks. We stand over a big hole—the kind of blowhole you see in Hawaii, but without the blow part.

"You a strong swimmer?" Tyler asks.

I nod. (I'm thinking, *Define* strong, *would you?*)

"Awesome. We have to time this right with the swell. Now . . . jump! *Jump now!*"

Now? I don't have time to ask. Tyler's gone. As in Gone-In-*Gone.* I have no choice. I jump. The swell takes me, its massive surge slamming me against the rock-walled edges.

Sweet Jesus. That was the safety briefing? The "you a strong swimmer?" bit?

My entire body slams into the rock again. I know a hematoma-inducing slam when I feel one. I don't mean bruise. I mean Hematoma with a capital *H*.

But by day three of two lessons a day, and five of my twelve books in, and one totally seductive hematoma later, my paddle feels stronger. I'm confident. Aside from the little mishap with the stingray two days ago—the gash in my foot from stepping on his tail is healing nicely, and the shooting foot-to-groin pain from his venom has subsided—besides that, things are going really well. And soaking my foot in a bucket of scalding hot water to address the pain was tremendous fun. It forced me to meet my motel neighbor, Haduwig. She's a grumpy German looking for solitude from her life as a sous chef on a cruise ship. She helps me refill the scalding bucket, as it's hard to walk (it's more of a dragging technique, really) with one leg in a bucket of hot (now warm) water. And from the look of Haduwig's stack of spy novels, she's blowing through more books per day than I am (and I've read five of my twelve). *Is it just me, or are we in a book club?*

And surely, the odds of encountering *another* lethal black sea snake like the one I saw the day after Sergeant Stingray, certainly the chances of *that* must be minuscule. But I understand they're short on antivenom in town, so fingers crossed. Tyler says you'd be dead before you'd get to town anyway.

Despite my encounters with stingray-this and deadly-that, the good news: Tyler thinks I'm ready to paddle to the outside, beyond the whitewash waves you learn on, which today are bigger than I've seen it here. *But I can do this. I will do this.* So I'm paddling out, paddling out, getting absolutely nowhere. The waves surround me, repeatedly launching my monstrous board into the air. I'm getting hammered.

In the distance I hear, "Megaaan!" "Megaaan!" It's Tyler. *What in the world does he want? Can't he see I'm busy getting beaten senseless in some cruel oceanic spin cycle?* I ignore him. I've got work to do.

"Megaaan!"

Dude, shut up. Seriously, can't he see I'm working? I'm busy paddling.

But he won't stop. "Megaaaaaan!"

Lest I get in trouble, I turn my board around, catch some white wash, and reluctantly head in. I scramble to my feet, dragging my behemoth board to him. He looks irritated.

"Megan, you were stuck in something we call an impact zone—where multiple waves from different directions all crash together. You were in the center of it. But you were so busy fighting it, you couldn't see it. You're one stubborn chick. When you find yourself struggling that hard, you know you are in one. Don't stay in an impact zone. Ever. Paddling harder is not the answer."

I drop my board and sit down on the sand. "Impact zone?"

"Yes. Often it's best to head in, stand on the shore, so you can look back out and get a better view, find a smooth line to the outside. Look right now. That passage ten feet over? The water is much calmer there."

"Oh, God." Nobody ever told me about an impact zone, let alone that I could opt out.

"You mean I'm not supposed to get sucked down, chewed up, and spit out with my swimsuit on backward?"

Tyler shakes his head. "It doesn't have to be that difficult. With practice, you can exit those clusters in one swift stroke, and eventually avoid the trouble entirely. Don't worry. Today was your first time in those conditions."

"Well, Tyler," I say, looking out at the water, shaking my head. "I didn't know I had a choice. When I look at the bigger picture of li—"

"Look, I don't know about all that. Grab your board and get out there. Stay to the right this time."

I grab my longboard and put it over my head. The thing is unwieldy. I can't wait to be skilled enough to ride a shortboard that I can tuck coolly under my arm. But that's not happening anytime soon. I start to paddle out again. I'd always thought giving up the struggle would mean I was a quitter. Or would it? I mean, just because I'm capable of treading water to the point of near drowning doesn't mean it's a good idea. Maybe sometimes sitting on the shore with a mango iced tea is the bravest choice you can make.

MADNESS

As the light increases we see ourselves to be worse than we thought. We are amazed at our former blindness as we see issuing forth from the depths of our heart a whole swarm of shameful feelings—like filthy reptiles crawling from a hidden cave. We never could have believed that we have harbored such things and we stand aghast as we watch them gradually appear. But while our faults diminish, the light by which we see them waxes brighter. And we are filled with horror. Bear in mind for your comfort, that we only perceive our malady when the cure begins.

—*Monk Frances Finolan, 1651*

58

QIGONG

PURPOSE: To literally cultivate life energy.

DURATION: As long or short as you like. A martial-healing art, mixed with Chinese medicine and philosophy. Picture less martial, more healing. And a little less flowy-looking than tai chi.

EQUIPMENT NEEDED: Just you.

AGE: 34.

RELATIONSHIP STATUS: *Must* I tell you everything? Jeez.

EMPLOYMENT: Clinic work. National board exam impending.

COST: Drop-in for $10.

HUMILIATION FACTOR: Zip.

LOCATION: Fort Collins and Estes Park, Colorado.

"Don't I know you?" I'd heard from behind me there in Whole Foods a few weeks ago.

I just had abandoned Coco, who almost exclusively shops the healthier outer ring of any grocery store, in produce. I had headed straight to the most processed (I like to think of it as the most eating-efficient) middle, taking seriously my decision between a regular Power Bar and the more cakelike Lemon Luna.

This has got to be a line. Who would I possibly know in Fort Collins? A friend had recently told me that some men's magazine rated Whole Foods the number one pickup spot in the nation. *It must be true.*

I turn around. The face in front of me now is not the kind one forgets. He had the most vivid green eyes I'd ever seen. And I *had* seen them before. *I guess it's not a line then.* His hair, a dirty blond, was tied neatly in a low ponytail at the nape of his neck. He was in Carhartts, boots, a light flannel—the whole artisan-on-a-break nine yards.

We stare, heads cocked. I don't want to admit I recognize him. I'd feel cooler if I didn't. My mouth starts talking anyway.

"I think we both were in my friend Coco's qigong class that I crashed a few months ago. The one with that guy visiting from France or something."

While waiting to enter that class, I had started warming up just outside, under a tree. And there, Mr. Green Eyes had kneeled to essentially tease me about why I was doing sweaty push-ups in the grass *before* qigong. Let's call him Laird.

"You might want to think about not trying so hard." Laird whispered down at my face, mid-push-up. "This isn't *CrossFit*, you know," he'd said with a bit of a smoky voice and a twinkle in his eye, his hands gently resting in the grass.

"Just trying to get stronger," I'd said back, but kind of splatted onto my face midsentence. He'd then leaned down—rather closely for a stranger—and looked into my eyes. We laughed for a second. I shook my head in giggly embarrassment. As he stood back up, his hand lightly grazed my shoulder. He smiled again and headed into class. That was it.

And now this, a whirlwind conversation. We covered: exercise; Earthships (he lives in one); furniture (he made some); and taxidermy (he literally stuffed some). The last two made his living.

I never thought I could get hot for a guy who knew how to stuff a dead animal: a bird, a mountain lion, apparently even a fish. But there you are. An exchange of numbers ensued over some talk of acupuncture, and a shoulder complaint. I'd send him to Coco. If it came to it, I'd rather *date* him than *treat* him. And couldn't do both.

The Whole Foods run-in was followed by a spectacular dog walk up Horse-tooth on a perfect sunny day, with an ideal bask on a large red rock overlook-ing the reservoir, and chemistry-snapping-pulling-out-all-the-stops date-talk: family, favorite animals, little kids, personal stories, and how in the *world* one falls in love with taxidermy. A few dates later (after some kind of Estes-Park-Earthship-share-your-favorite-hot-sandwich potluck with a bunch of his cool artisan-type neighbors) came our sparks-flying first kiss—a kiss so potent, I told him I might have immaculately conceived. And now, it's like I've been drugged. And studying for the national acupuncture board exams while falling in . . . you know . . . love . . . isn't easy.

Straight after my library closes in the evenings, I head to his small Earth-ship near Estes Park, greeted by the aroma of whatever he's got cooking for us on the stovetop. Roasted poblano peppers with Auricchio provolone on a toasted baguette. Caesar salad with capers, grilled organic chicken, and dress-ing from scratch. He smelled a bit like the gorgeous olive oil he cooked with.

"Do you want mushrooms or tomatoes in your frittata this morning?" he asked, walking back from the kitchen to his bedroom with a cup of coffee for me.

I was still cozied under his red flannel duvet, watching the sunrise through the ponderosa pines out his windows, his beloved Bernese mountain dog, Taraco, curled at my feet. *Taraco* was short for *Prince Ruspoli's Taraco*, a rare Ethiopian bird that was discovered by an Italian aristocrat but was trampled by elephants before the bird's history was properly identified. To me, the bird name better suited Laird. When turned toward the light, the bird was said to glow with crimson. And the *Prince* part fit this slow old-world elegance Laird carried as he moved amid his home and workspaces. And with this slow gracefulness, I imagined, Laird was someone who *could* be trampled by elephants.

"It all sounds delicious." I wasn't hungry yet. Too many butterflies.

He kissed me on the head after placing the coffee beside me, Bach playing from the kitchen. This was becoming a routine. I hadn't slept at my own place in days.

"Shall we swim before or after breakfast?" It wasn't a matter of *if* we would skinny dip, but when, as we had done every morning since I started camping out here. Plenty of morning romance, before I headed to the library at nine. He snuggled back under the covers, his fairer skin a pleasing contrast to my more olive tones. His work-callused hands found my hips, turned me over, and kissed me. Now neither of us could be bothered with coffee.

I had been transported to an easygoing planet I'd never been to. The food, the pace, the romance, the setting: the small garden, not to mention the turkey he was raising for Thanksgiving (he only taxidermied the wild kind); the pool he and a neighbor shared; his meticulous workshop of well-loved tools and minimalist Rocky-Mountain-meets-Bauhaus pieces within.

Magic. Cozy nights snuggling with him on his favorite Le Corbusier lounge chair. And mornings after, you know, the groovy-sleepy-intimate stuff, the pre-breakfast skinny, the egg frittatas; I felt as lit up as that mountain sun screaming in his windows.

Nobody had made me an egg frittata before. Nobody had whispered to me in such sweet tones before. Nobody had tried to slow me down before, or gotten romantic with me so slowly before. While I didn't know him deeply yet, I liked his day-to-day relaxed vibe I was learning from him. Like molasses. Molasses that was also good at day-to-day routine.

Before he headed to his workshop and I to my books, we hopped in the shower. I had picked some music we could lather up to.

"We may have to do something about your musical tastes," he said with a grin, kissing my shoulders. (I had selected a little Shakira. He preferred Glenn Gould.)

Laird says, "I can imagine telling our children, 'Come on, kids, let Mama listen to her music.'"

"Our . . . chil—" My stomach flipped. I was smiling.

"Yeah, I've been imagining you pregnant . . ." He rubbed my belly in wide slow circles as he whispered in my ear. *God, I loved those words. Dangerous words. Early-to-arrive words.*

"Let Mama listen to her music." He nuzzled down into my neck. I got chills down my sides. This was some shower.

"Let Mama listen."

Nobody had rubbed my belly, or held me like this, or called me the future mother of his children. I felt overloaded with joy. New territory.

Depending on how you looked at it, I was either in heaven or in real trouble.

59

MAGIC PHONE SESSION

PURPOSE: In lieu of being local with your therapist, this is the next best thing. What you lose in proximity you gain in familiarity. Is it as good as in person? No.

DURATION: One hour.

EQUIPMENT NEEDED: The usual with phone sessions—phones.

AGE: 34.

RELATIONSHIP STATUS: After seven months together in Estes and Fort Collins, Laird is moving with me back to Bellingham, where I'll open my practice. Doesn't feel like a full romantic leap; feels like a halfsie.

EMPLOYMENT: Proudly opening my acupuncture doors in the cutest little office.

COST: $80.

LOCATION: Bellingham, Washington (me); Niwot, Colorado (Majie). Renee's pregnant and near now. She wants to live on Whidbey Island near Mom too. Fingers crossed someone in this group ekes out normal.

We take our time as the session begins. I relax in my chair. Majie in his—a couple of states over. We breathe. Like always, we start with the level of sensation. Before my final move in a few weeks, I was in Washington for the birth of my niece.

"I'm so happy. Renee had her baby girl. Her name is Kelsey, like Kesela, Deany's guardian angel. Renee was induced. Dad flew in for the birth too, which was good, but left before the baby came. I was relieved Renee missed the part where Dad asked the nurse for her best estimate of the baby's arrival. He said if Renee timed it right, he and Margie could still catch the four o'clock instead of the seven. The nurse explained that birth didn't work like that. I pretended he hadn't asked birth itself to accommodate his flight plans. The doula part of my brain came back. My sister only wanted her husband, Rich, in the room, so I spent Renee's entire labor just outside the door with my ear to the ground. I guess some things never change. I gave Mom blow-by-blow updates as she sat cross-legged next to me. Renee was so brave, as the birth stuff scares her."

And then I say, trying to slow down my thoughts, "In other news, I saw Tim yesterday. We filed the divorce papers. I'm buying the house from him—meaning I'll assume more of our credit card debt in exchange for some equity. I got to see how he's had the house without me, Majie. It was weird. Not to mention, Laird and I arrived with our new dog, Isabelle, we just adopted. And somehow next, Tim is taking what feels like a Christmas photo of Laird, Taraco, Isabelle, and me, kneeling in Tim's and my yard. *What* am I *doing*?"

"Go slowly," he says. Sometimes I ramp up so fast, I prevent myself from feeling. I take a breath. I feel that tightness in my throat.

"I saw a picture of him on the fridge that he told me Vee took. He obviously likes it—it's on the fridge. Maybe it was a Halloween photograph. But somehow, I'm guessing not. He's wearing a dress, a bowler hat, and high heels, lipstick, and posing rather seriously. But more than the heels or the lipstick, I see . . ."

"What?" Majie asks neutrally.

"Fear. I would know that look in his eyes anywhere. I think I get it. To me it looks like Tim is trying to express something that seems essential but that also scares him and makes him feel vulnerable. And if I were the one taking the photograph, I couldn't have laughed that vulnerability or fear off. I would have felt it as my own. In this one photograph, I had a better sense why he chose Vee. I imagine she can see it as cool and fun—a gesture meant to break down social taboos. I bet she can support him in a way I couldn't. If Tim needed to dress up with heels, I wouldn't have been laid-back about it. I would have worried if he was comfortable. I would have wanted to know the why of it, and as much of the story of the outfit as I could get out of him. If he needed to break out, it certainly wouldn't have been easy to do with my putting him under a microscope."

"Aside from him, what's happening inside you?"

"I feel flat. A little bewildered. Maybe *bewildered* is a cop-out." I pause. "Tim said he could be himself with her. Maybe for him, the outfit was more of the darkness he said was there, but Don told him not to talk about. Maybe that's what Tim meant. I always prided myself on trying to not be judgmental. But . . ."

"What?"

"A letter showed up at the house from Private Encounters. They offered Tim 'the same great services he used to enjoy,' but at new reduced rates. For such a loyal and long-standing customer, they said they could offer $2.99 a minute instead of $3.99. They wanted him to know the virtual chat room was even more affordable. I guess it's a group discount." I start to choke back.

"What's happening now?" Majie asks softly.

"I still wonder, how do you know when you gave enough?"

"Let's slow down here. Do you feel your feet on the floor? Feel your feet and speak from that place." His voice always has the most soothing tone, almost like a coo.

Arggggh. It was so much easier to spin and babble.

Okay. *Big breath. Feet on floor.*

"I think that the problem isn't about heels and lipstick. It's not even about him, not even a little bit. Not what he did or didn't do. It's about this: in my life—well beyond this relationship, as in *well* beyond—I rely too much on external validation to confirm what I know in my gut and minimize my own pain in the process, getting lost in other people's. The point is, the person I promised to be with *forever* didn't trust me with his goddamn shadow, pain, darkness, whatever, and I didn't listen to that sufficiently when I felt it in my bones. I mean, maybe I couldn't have been there in the exact way he needed, but does that mean he—or any significant person in my life—has my support to hurt and lie and hide? Why do I behave as if other people's pain—say, Tim's secrets, or Renee's fear of using her full voice, or Mom's unrealized potential, or Dad's narcissistic wounding from *his* father—is all somehow harder than my own? Why do I think that hiding secrets is more painful than being hidden from? In my practice of compassion, I've pretended that secrecy doesn't injure as much it actually does. How do I get rid of that lie I've told myself? Why in the world do I think stomaching duplicity or half-truths is something one must do to be a good partner? Honestly, none of the whys matter. It's *how* do I do it differently going forward? How much stomaching is okay? Because we all have light and dark. *All of us.* The truth is, I picked *such* a *good* man to marry. And I *also* picked *such* a liar-hider. Both are true. We all have goodness. We all hide. And I'm *terrified* I'll never have a strong enough radar to know what balance in those two sides of us is acceptable."

60

THE ENNEAGRAM CLASS

PURPOSE: The Enneagram of Personality is a psycho-spiritual typology intended to help people develop their "true essence." Each personality type (one to nine) expresses a distinctive pattern of thinking and emotions.

DURATION: Ten-week class. One week for each type, plus a bonus.

EQUIPMENT NEEDED: An Enneagram book, an organized group, and snacks.

AGE: 34.

RELATIONSHIP STATUS: My Bauhaus-loving-boyfriend Laird and I are settling into Bellingham, but a lot of it feels more complicated than a frittata and a swim.

COST: Can't remember. Affordable.

HUMILIATION FACTOR: I invited Tim and Vee to the class so Tim could be on the "One" panel. Why am I *still* trying to figure that guy out?

LOCATION: Columbia neighborhood, Bellingham, Washington.

A panel shows up each week for workshop participants to interview. First week it's a panel of Twos (as nurturers, they're the friendliest kickoff, putting everyone at ease). We talk to each panel about what it's like to be *them*. Next it's Threes and so on. I plan to figure out everyone in my constellation. And as cocktail party games go, it's not half bad. Right up there with diagnosing people's Five Element Causal Factor. Our Enneagram book gives us some examples to help with the mapping. I add in my friends and family. My new baby niece, Kelsey, is too tiny for me to figure out just yet. But, oh, her time is coming.

1. **The Perfectionist:** Celine Dion, Mahatma Gandhi, Hillary Clinton, Jimmy Swaggart (a pathological One on a downward slide), Pope John Paul II, and Tim

2. **The Helper:** Doris Day, Coco, Barry Manilow, and Mother Teresa (Who doesn't want to be like Mother Teresa? I secretly want to be a Two.)

3. **The Achiever:** Madonna, Dick Clark, Michael Jordan, Oprah, Tom Cruise, and the United States (Apparently, you can type a whole country.)

4. **The Individualist:** Martha Graham, Ingmar Bergman, Joni Mitchell, Edgar Allan Poe, my mom, and me (Can go dark. And they fancy themselves particularly unique, arty.)

5. **The Investigator:** Albert Einstein, Friedrich Nietzsche, and Jodie Foster (*Obviously. Nietzsche and Jodie are veritable twins.*)

6. **The Loyalist:** Malcolm X, Tom Hanks, George W. Bush, Princess Diana, and my sister (Good in corporations and the military. Renee would make a good officer.)

7. **The Enthusiast:** JFK, Robin Williams, Mozart, and Regis Philbin (Again, Regis and Mozart, a no-brainer . . . nearly interchangeable. Regis. Mozart. Regis. Mozart . . .)

8. **The Challenger:** Fidel Castro, FDR, Donald Trump, John Wayne, Courtney Love, and my father. (Yet, come to think of it, maybe my sister is more of an Eight. Man, she can be solid when she speaks up. Where she used to go quiet, now she can go stern and strong.)

9. **The Peacemaker:** Walt Disney, the Dalai Lama, Joseph Campbell, Keanu Reeves, and My Bauhaus-Taxidermy-Lover

I'm gonna *love* this class. That is one cuckoo-for-Cocoa-Puffs-crazy list. It makes no sense and tons of sense all at the same time. Possibly my favorite combination, let me see . . . Tim's One, I bet, liked my messier expressive Four. That must run deep with him. He's picked another Four, Vee. But with the One's strict rules—when especially rigid, rules practically *no one* can live by— Ones can develop what they call a sexual trapdoor, a hidden life. *Hmmm.* And I'd say Renee's Eight is a more accommodating Eight than Dad's. Regardless, matching Eights like Renee and Dad command the front seat while irritatingly arty-emotional-life-is-a-poem twin Fours like Mom and me talk romance in the back seat. And my Nine, my frittata-preparing-conflict-avoidant-mellow-let's-all-go-eeeeeasy Laird . . . no wonder I have to practically lob a grenade to get him out of the tub. No surprise he can't stand that I don't enjoy spending an entire afternoon savoring the hint of rose petals with leather notes within a single sip of Barolo, or worse still, deconstructing the ingredients to the best fish sandwich in Bellingham.

I can't *wait* to tackle the Instinctual Subtypes: Sexual (prioritizing one-to-one dynamics and intimate relations), Social (prioritizing one's place and purpose in community), and Self-Preservationist (governing our material need for security, food, shelter, family group). I bet Renee and Mom are Self-Pres (they both need to be at the airport twelve hours early, and let's not forget Mom's Armageddon stash of peanut butter). Dad is . . . probably Social, definitely not Self-Pres . . . Mr. I-Don't-Believe-in-Savings-Accounts-but-Let's-Save-the-World-with-Fuel-Made-from-Cheddar-Cheese. I'm certain Michelle is Social (she runs nearly every nonprofit in Lander and accumulates so little garbage, she and Scott share a trash can with five other families). Coco, Self-Pres. Although maybe I think Coco is Self-Pres because I didn't know her before her vision loss, which would make anyone more careful. She's worried one eyeball is going to start shooting off somewhere, like Mad-Eye Moody. So far, they're both tracking fine. Okay . . . and Tim . . . Social? (I try to protect his work identity on the page, so you wouldn't know much, sorry about that, but his true passion is supporting underserved causes); and me, yeah, I'm a Sexual Subtype through and through. Self-Pres, no way. I have asthma and absolutely no idea where my inhaler is right now.

61

PHONE SESSION WITH MAJIE II

PURPOSE: I have a new kinda-sorta therapist/bodyworker named Cornelia, but she's opinionated in a way that feels too absolute. So I call Magic Majie sometimes instead.

DURATION: One hour. Not every week, though.

EQUIPMENT NEEDED: I have these sessions in my office waiting room between patients.

AGE: 35.

RELATIONSHIP STATUS: Sometimes it feels like with Laird and Taraco, we are a family, especially now with our brown Portuguese Wonder Dog, Isabelle, and her ever-present stuffed cow or froggy in her mouth. Perhaps we're a foursome with twelve legs.

EMPLOYMENT: My own practice in Bellingham, a year in. I miss the clinic and working with Coco. We're on the phone together when we aren't needling people.

COST: As ever, $80.

HUMILIATION FACTOR: Absolutely zero. It's positively soulful to talk to Majie. I miss his softness, smarts, and French accent.

LOCATION: Fairhaven, Bellingham.

Perhaps he knew, as I did not, that the Earth was made round, so we would not see too far down the road.

—*Karen Blixen*

"Maybe moving back wasn't so great an idea."

"How do you mean?"

"Well, the plan looked so good on paper. This new man, his picking up and leaving Estes Park, moving to Bellingham with me, so romantic. Getting my own practice going. Being nearer to my mother to look out for her. Tim and I coming full circle, now in close proximity. But Majie, as for keeping it together, I'm a bit of junk show."

"How so?"

"I think I was starting to get it together in Colorado, starting to feel safe to look at my darkest parts, the unresolved parts. Maybe I got cocky and thought I could leave the stability I'd created: the clinic, the sun, our work together. Now I'm far from all that, taking on my trickiest stuff: new business owner, first business loan, new relationship, new dog parent, new divorced status, covering a mortgage solo. Plus, I think I've always had this romantic notion that I would magically thrive professionally once I was solid with my true love. Obviously, that was delusional. So, all this new, all in a city I think I've always hated. I associate it with every bad moment in my life. Hanging gray isn't exactly a color you want around when you're feeling gray on the inside. Yet here I am."

"What's the junk show part?"

"I'm overwhelmed. Work, love, family—it's all right here, asking me to be more competent. A huge part of me wants to only watch movies and eat gummy bears. I don't know if I'm ready for another big relationship. And, turns out I'm not that prepared to live so close to Tim. Don't know how to transition into being friends officially. Are we *supposed* to be? I think I've gone overboard, wanting to be too cool, too together, when the truth is, the whole thing is pitifully sad. The man I grew up with is no longer in my life like before. And heck if I know whether to commit deeply to Laird. By the way, I might be trying to turn my Walking Talking Valium into someone he's not, someone ambitious—maybe that's a separate session. I'm taking all the risk in our conjoined live/work/acupuncture/furniture ventures. I can't float both rents much longer. And he has no plan how to pay me back. Without my having wanted him to jump into such a large multi-use space concept—no matter how cool it is—I don't think he would've. Despite what he says to the contrary, I think he'd be plenty happy working in someone else's carpentry workshop, with his own day-in, day-out rhythms that don't involve business and marketing plans or late-night work sessions. He's more about kicking off the Carhartts, hand squeezing a margarita, and heading on to a very leisurely bath. I'm *fucked*. And I think something's wrong with my mother. Not just her profound disappointment about Tim's and my divorce. She's been canceling social plans and struggles for words sometimes, which isn't like her. Renee and I are taking her to a neurologist. Ever since she rolled her SUV, she hasn't been herself. Maybe it's the stress of moving alone to a large farm at sixty-five? Also, Cornelia, the counselor here, she's starting to remind me of Don, and not in a good way. And the buzzing up and down my spine is back. It might be the worst it's been. Yet I'm unwilling to let go of any of these commitments, which may be the cause."

"Let's settle for a moment and breathe."

I slow down. I feel my chest rise and fall and, underneath the buzzing, I feel that grief. And I don't want to feel any more grief.

62

FAMILY SYSTEMS THEORY
MEETS SCARY DIAGNOSIS

PURPOSE: Family Systems is a theory introduced by Dr. Murray Bowen suggesting that individuals cannot be understood in isolation, but as a part of an emotional unit.

DURATION: Unknown.

EQUIPMENT NEEDED: Two definitive texts on this combo-platter matter: *The Family Crucible* by Augustus Napier and Carl Whitaker and *The 36-Hour Day* by Nancy Mace and Peter Rabins.

AGE: 35. But feeling Mom's additional 38 almost as if my own.

RELATIONSHIP STATUS: It's official. My mother has Alzheimer's. We just came from the Memory Clinic at the University of Washington.

COST: Medicare.

LOCATION: Whidbey Island, Washington.

Here's the truth. Or *a* truth. I'm ashamed to admit it because it sounds righteous, but my mother's pain is a map I have navigated my life by. I'm an expert in my mother's pain. She didn't mean it to turn out this way. Of that I am sure. She loves me fiercely, in all the ways she could. I don't question that for a minute. What she doesn't know—not consciously, anyway—is how well I have studied the landscape of her interior, a compass to map the world by.

I searched for all the ways to help. I was aware of the job early. If my mother got a mantra, I got a mantra. If my mother studied Transactional Analysis, I studied it too. If my mom did EST, I did EST. If my mom did a seminar, I did a seminar. She never pushed. Never forced. She always let me decide. But what she didn't know was that I was hers, utterly. And that you take the help that comes your way, whatever form that takes. You take it. Especially if you're desperate. I knew I was being asked, in some unspoken way, to help put the broken pieces of her disjointed, painful life together, to help try to make her whole. And if she had known she was in some way asking me to do this, it would have killed her.

Sometimes people experience so much pain—it's just too much for one person to hold. So someone else helps you hold it. That's what I did—what I do. I have held her pain. And the worst part is, even that hasn't been enough. She still has to hold plenty on her own. But if you are really good at holding it—in this case, for somebody else, holding their pain—they don't even notice you're carrying it. So then they don't have to feel bad about it. And that's a good thing, because if they knew, you'd only be adding to it. You don't want them to feel bad about your carrying some of their load. Ever. Carry it long enough, and suddenly one day it's yours. It's hard to even separate: what was originally hers, what was mine. What was hers that became mine.

I don't know exactly what happened or when it began, but I suspect it started early. Her first memory is of neglect, alone in a room, sitting in a chair with no parental contact. No memory of a hug, a kiss, a pat. She's told me this more times than I care to remember. Because you can't blow something like that off when someone—anyone—tells you a memory like that.

In her, I'm an expert—I know when exactly she is going to cry. What she is going to say. How she will welcome a group. When she will retreat into her room. Why she won't ask for help. How to sometimes help her anyway. How she likes to decorate a table. Where she would put an extra chair in a living room. How it's easier for her to love animals than people. Why she always makes sure if she arranges figures on display that they have some sort of a relationship. Two china dolls would be facing each other, never turned away. That's the kind of contact she could handle.

I know that she will always feed a man before she feeds a woman. Why she loved my husband and my marriage perhaps more than I did. She couldn't see that I was starving because she was sure she was hungrier. Why she couldn't give me sympathy when Tim got arrested. That she would worry about Tim more than she worried about me. Because she recognized my strength and knew what I could handle, because I could handle her, carry her, and not even make it look like I was carrying her. That she wouldn't need to protect me, because she believed I would always protect myself. That she couldn't be kind to me in places where she wasn't kind to herself. That it wasn't easy for her to hug, and she felt bad about it. That she's always liked to say she didn't have any belief in her role as the birther of me, the creator of me. That she couldn't understand why a child wouldn't like hearing that.

I know what it means when she starts wiggling her finger when she chokes up. She wants to show you the interior but not open the door. Just a peek at the enormous despair right behind those pocket doors. That she didn't see that I came from her. That she was neglected in that room. That she was swept off her feet when she met my father. That if she ever needed to articulate something serious, I would find the words. I would help map the world for her. When she built her barn on Whidbey, I gave the architects the words she would have used to describe her aesthetic. When she had the accident and needed trauma work, I found the person who could work the territory. Then I described the territory. Down to the smallest detail.

The practitioner thought I was a clinician. I told them every unspoken need I knew, every family pattern I had witnessed in her, patterns in her language. Which yes really meant yes, and which yes meant go no further. How to approach her body. How not to touch her, and what touch she wouldn't reject. The things about herself she most hated but would never say. Her biggest fears. I gave the words for what she would wish if she could start all over.

That she wanted me to fly, but couldn't let go of my wings. That she wanted to talk about why I couldn't fly, while holding on to my wings. That she would be happy for me if I broke away, and yet she would feel abandoned. That she would tell me she felt I hadn't stuck by and weep the kind of tears that take a lifetime to build. I felt like I'd betrayed her. I didn't stick by her side and translate for her indefinitely. Now, I lapse in and out of it, trying to hold on to something for myself. I am guilty and proud in the same moment.

And now she's leaving me. And she's not leaving me in an easy way. Her words are failing. And I was born to help find her words. I will fail here. I can't help her map the world any longer, to travel out of her pain and into the light. People wonder why I am a late bloomer. That is where I spent my time. My interior was mapping a way out for her. That was the idea, that to map a way out for her would lead to a map for a way out for me. To crawl out from under her pain. From under my pain. From under my pain, over her pain. An ambitious plan.

This, though, is a force I cannot fight. Her brain is losing words and memory, and with those memories, she is leaving me too. Bits of her flicker and fade out. Flare up again and she is back. But it is a dying fire. There is not enough wood in her to reignite. But I try.

And still I fail her. The instant I see her, like in the car today, driving home from the diagnosis. The moment she got that diagnosis, her pain filled me, vibrated me. From the too-solitary childhood, to the haunting ulcerative colitis of her young womanhood. To her ever-devolving marriage with my father. To each time she needed something for which she couldn't ask for help. Because that would mean she needed somebody. And my mother made it her business to never need anybody, and because of that she couldn't have needed anybody more.

My mother was a bright, burning flame that got part of her snuffed out early. And she asked me not just to carry on the flame, but to ignite hers through my intelligence, my ability to sense people and what she needed. So in the end, she gave me something. Once you become a good cartographer, you can map just about anybody.

My tender heart is a big, broad landscape. Within that landscape is the route to the heart of another woman, who is thirty-eight years older than I am, who will die before I will, who wanted to be loved as badly as I do, but who will not get to revel in the basket of love that I will get to feel in my lifetime. I know that she was gifted and talented and beautiful beyond what she ever imagined. And I know she saw some of that in me. I fear she will die lonely, and riddled with grief, or in wordless silence, but will try to rally and find that spirit in her that hasn't fully died. That spirit that grabbed on to me and said: *Take this. Run with this. Help me. Help me and then fly.* She just didn't know how big what she was asking was. The help-me part just took a lot longer, longer than she knew, longer than I knew. She will die before my job is done.

63

IN THE BARDOS

PURPOSE: While the Bardos (meaning an "in-between state of awareness") most often describe three specific stages in Buddhist philosophy that one passes through after death, a metaphorical Bardo can represent a time when one's typical life is suspended, as in the face of illness.

DURATION: Teachings suggest one can pass through a Bardo in a split second, or take up to forty-nine days to go through the last three.

EQUIPMENT NEEDED: Ideally, relative comfort with uncomfortable states of mind.

AGE: 35.

RELATIONSHIP STATUS: Super pumped that I just pulled the Tower Card from my tarot deck. The image of two people jumping out of a flaming castle with their hair on fire looks extremely positive. A round for the house on me! Top shelf. Only the good stuff.

COST: Usually it requires death. It appears I've lucked out.

HUMILIATION FACTOR: Fair to middling.

LOCATION: I think I'm currently in the third Bardo, where a feeling of stupidity is the natural outcome of a limited point of view.

I've heard it described that the Achilles' heel of consciousness is that we forget. I couldn't agree more. I've started to wonder if my consciousness needs support hose. You know those really strong grandma ones? *Those. Those hose.*

Given that 80 percent of the brain's function isn't even understood, who am *I* to say that my most essential thoughts haven't started to pool—potentially drowning in cerebrospinal fluid or conversing with each other down at my ankles? Maybe with special pantyhose I can keep all my best knowing *right at the top* instead of feeling as if it's wandered off. Gone missing. Fallen and can't get up.

My love affair with Laird is slipping sideways. He feels distant.

I overheard my ankles talking. They say we've been here before.

64

ATTEND A READING

PURPOSE: I want to listen to an articulate person talk about love. Not the way it's been pulverized by advertisers and shallow tales. But the true give-and-take deep abiding kind.

DURATION: An evening. But a certain residue can remain.

EQUIPMENT NEEDED: Ears.

AGE: 35.

RELATIONSHIP STATUS: I think I'm trying to turn Laird into someone he's not; i.e., someone ambitious.

COST: Free.

HUMILIATION FACTOR: It's more of a vulnerability factor. And it's high.

LOCATION: Village Books, Fairhaven, Washington.

When I found out Barry Lopez was reading, I couldn't call Tim fast enough, suggesting I get tickets for him and Vee. I ask Laird as well, dying for him to be dying to come like I am, like Tim will be, but he declines. I arrive early. Saving seats for the three of us. As they descend the stairs into the cavernous basement, I wave them down like I'm trying to hail a cab in a deluge. Vee is so petite, I feel like an ogre waving down a fairy princess and her prince. If ogres took cabs.

Lopez greets a packed house. The last time Tim and I were both in this room, we were husband and wife. Now we're . . . what? Survivors? Fellow travelers? Friends? A shared memory? The walking wounded, each with opposing (or mirror image?) limps?

Lopez begins reading "Traveling with Bo Ling," a piece I haven't. It's a love story between a North Vietnamese woman named Bo Ling and a bitter Vietnam veteran named Harvey Flemming. They meet and fall in love in Santa Cruz, decades after the war—both blind from different traumatic injuries. He loses his eyesight (and his genitals) from the shards of a grenade. She loses her sight when her first husband throws lye in her eyes for looking at another man. They marry. After a few years, Bo Ling asks that they revisit Vietnam—the location of their mutual loss of innocence: she as a survivor of war and abuse, and he as a former enemy soldier in her homeland. Through their shared sightless return, the bitterness begins to wash out of him. While it's literally the blind leading the blind, he credits Bo Ling with opening his eyes, leading him out of his darkness and back into light. He continues to shed himself of his anger enough to find an expression of artistry with his hands—the delicate tradition of origami. Their travels continue to other countries—bridging the gap between what they survived and the very full possibility of what they can still become.

I feel this urge to reach out to Tim. I know it is inappropriate, and so I sit with myself, emotion welling up in me for all that may never be said. I have no such experience with a man, nor acknowledgment of the lengths to which I went to get us there. I think of Laird and all I wish for us now: the thoughtful meals, our dogs, the slow living, old Alan Watts recordings in the background at breakfast, the sweet melancholy of the Goldberg Variations. And then as my yearning spirals, I no longer am sure of the face I attach to such desires.

The story ends with Bo Ling suggesting they adopt a baby, and Bo Ling assuring her beloved that with the tincture of time, he will have shed sufficient anger to make room in his heart for a child.

To wash out the anger, she says, fall in love. Be in love with a peach, she says, its summer juice running down your bare chest. Be in love with the sound of your brother's truck as it pulls up to the curb on a summer night with supper just ready on the table. Be in love with me, she says . . . Reengage your innocence here, in the Dresden of my face.

By this point, internally, I'm toast. Mushy, super soggy toast. As people begin to queue for book signing, I rise, feign a smile at Tim and Vee, and head to purchase more books for signing. But really, it's to gather myself, to take a break from this strange threesome. Once sufficiently regrouped, I join the queue. As I wait for my turn with Lopez, I see Tim and Vee well behind me. I know that Tim places as much meaning on talking to Lopez as I do. What I'm struck by is how Lopez takes genuine, nonrushed time with each person. No one is forgotten.

When my turn comes, I hand him a stack of books. One for Laird, and, of course, one for my mother. I ask for him to inscribe those, too shy to ask him to sign my own. He takes the third book.

"And what is *your* name?" he asks.

"Megan," I say quietly.

And then I find myself speaking. "I've been trying to be someone's Bo Ling. And I don't think it's working out. His name is Laird. He's . . . that other book you have there . . ."

He smiles at me with sorrow at his edges.

"Yes," he says, nodding directly. He returns his attention to writing in the third book.

I look up at the ceiling, using my sleeve to manage the mascara situation I've created. He looks back up at me. We settle onto one another's eyes for a second longer. It's always those last held seconds that seem to mean the most.

"Thank you," I say, smiling while biting my lip in apology for . . . I suppose . . . my vulnerability.

I go in search of a chair. From there I can see the backs of Tim and Vee. She adjusts his hair with a gesture of the lovers that they are. I imagine her as Tim's Bo Ling. I tip my head back to catch the water in my eyes like a saucer might catch a spill from a teacup.

I open my book to the title page. And in a script of thick black cursive, I read what he's written:

Megan—
not to forget,
unknown to each
other, still we
are holding each
other in the
storm—

Ooooooooooooooh. It hits right at the center of me.

I jump up and head to Tim, rushing like a little girl might, to show her parents what she made at school. But unlike a proud schoolgirl, my melancholy comes too.

"Look what he wrote in my book . . ." I say. But as I look at them while I speak, I know it's a moment neither Tim, nor I—nor the three of us—can linger in together. It's out of step. Out of place. Out of time. He smiles meekly, with a kind but conflicted expression. I take my book back, closing it under my arm. I redirect, looking down at Vee's strong black boots and then back up. Another gathering.

"What story in the collection spoke to you two most?" I ask. I'm interested, but mostly I just want out of the tension that's gripping my throat like a vise.

"'Mortise and Tenon.' I want to talk to him about 'Mortise and Tenon,'" Tim says.

I know the story well.

A mortise and tenon describes a simple joint in two parts made by wood-workers for thousands of years. The mortise hole and the tenon tongue are carved to fit tightly together so that the mortise can support the shoulders of the tenon's rail. The masculine and feminine joined at ninety degrees. "Mortise and Tenon" the *story* follows a season with a highly skilled itinerant furniture maker. We meet him in Bangalore, as he never chooses to settle in one place—not because he doesn't love companionship, but because he does not believe himself capable of the kind of reciprocity such intimacy requires. Staying with any one person means he would "have to fake the life unfolding in his blindspot."

Our woodworker has a haunt. Sexually abused as a child by the betraying hands of a doctor, he—up until this point—considers the fallout of those events no more severe than walking with a light limp. But through violent circumstances in Bangalore, he comes to realize that his old wounds were far more extensive than he'd always told himself. And without dismantling his coping strategy—to keep those he most cared for at arm's length—his itinerant life would remain driven by the compulsion to isolate rather than choose a life fully realized.

To what extent and specifically how did Tim relate to the woodworker? And which struggle within the character—I'm aching to know—compels Tim to speak to Lopez? I can't imagine wanting to know anything more. I think I've had a case of what researchers call *cognitive dread*, the phenomenon describing how most people would prefer to experience pain immediately—even higher levels of it—rather than sit and wait for it. I think of it more like the waiting-for-multiple-shoes-to-drop condition. It's not just a curiosity but a deep haunt of mine about his oldest, deepest haunts. I think back to a time when I asked Tim when or what prompted his increasing use of sex on the phone.

He said, *"It seemed to really increase when I began my relationship with you. The closer we got, the more it grew."*

What did that mean? Had our bond somehow brought him too close to an earlier wound? And did that pain or memory—living in close proximity to our intimacy—manifest as phone sex and an arrest? Does knowing more of his particulars even matter? I stand in this cavernous, familiar place and I wonder. I wonder whether the death of our relationship came not from *what* was withheld, but merely from the *withholding*: the fatigue, the disillusionment, and perhaps just an unrecoverable distance. That bloody Cascade. I don't know. And certainly Tim isn't telling me. Perhaps he will tell Lopez. Find comfort there.

And so, now, here we are, with our haunts in a basement. I watch as Tim and Vee approach Lopez, the distance between us growing. I watch Tim lean down to speak in hushed tones with him. I tuck my books into my coat and head for the stairs. Out into the rain.

65

M&M PARTS WORK REVISITED
(SHOCK TALK)

PURPOSE: A way to talk about shock. While still in shock. Internal Family Systems Parts Work still makes it easier sometimes to tackle difficult topics.

DURATION: Acute stage, about four days.

EQUIPMENT NEEDED: Couch.

AGE: 35.

RELATIONSHIP STATUS: Can I just bow out of all this relationship stuff now?

COST: Hard to measure. But not cheap.

HUMILIATION FACTOR: It's not so much humiliation (well, kinda). More like disillusionment. (All over again, but maybe worse.)

LOCATION: Bellingham, Washington.

Hi. I don't know if you remember me. I'm pretty shy, and I mostly ever talked to Majie. But Megan told me she wrote about me. That's kinda embarrassing. 'Cause I'm the M&M. Remember all that stuff about Parts Work? I guess I'm more like a metaphor. I don't think of it like that, though. I think I'm just her most tender part. I take the hardest hits, as her most trusting part. Some people call that naïve. But I see it like her always-try-to-see-the-best-in-people nature. I like my part. Her no-matter-what-I-want-to-get-it-right parts. Well, turns out she kinda got it all wrong. But she kinda got it right too. It's confusing.

Here's what I know. I just got kicked. Or I should say we did. Hard. In the gut. It was a couple of days ago, but I've been curled up with her and Isabelle on this couch ever since. It's the only thing that helps. Megan loves this couch. All deep and flowery. She and Tim bought it together. That was a long time ago. But this couch is wide. Wider than most. And deep. Deeper than most. And warm. So we're staying put. And anyway, it's the weekend.

Megan's been helping Tim house-hunt, encouraging him to buy. After an afternoon of house-hunting, Tim was dropping Megan off at her singing lesson, and I don't know why then, but suddenly she blurted out some questions. It's not like it was the first time for these. This is what I overheard.

Megan asked, "Tim, I know I've said this hundreds of times, but I always imagined this turnoff as the spot where it all happened, even though I know it took place much farther south. For some reason, I picture this spot. I always thought it an incredible coincidence that the first time you talked to a prostitute, you got arrested. Was that really true?"

And he hesitated. Then Megan asked, "What could possibly happen now? What are we going to do, get a *divorce*?"

Turning away, he took a big pause.

"No, it wasn't the first time," he said.

"Well, then, how many times were there?" Silence.

"Was it more than one?" Silence.

"Two?" Silence.

"More than two?"

"Yes, more than two."

So she's like, "Okay, three? Four?"

"Yes, more than four."

It was like pulling teeth. She got him to ten, yes, more than ten. Twenty, yes, more than that. Finally, after jumping past twenty to forty, then fifty, then fifty got to sixty. He paused and said, "I guess I'm comfortable with the number sixty."

Comfortable with the number sixty.

She learned later, he'd said it was more like a hundred. He said it started when he was in in grad school at Brown. Now I'm just a World War II candy, but even *I'd* like to know, *where had he found the time?* And if he was comfortable saying a hundred, I wondered if it was like cigarettes, and we should double the amount, make it two hundred.

Two hundred anonymous faces.
Two hundred motel rooms or back seats.
Two hundred different bodies.
Two hundred made-up stories.
Two hundred cash transactions.
Two hundred extra showers before he came home.

66

POST-TRAUMATIC STRESS RESPONSE

PURPOSE: This isn't so much a therapy I selected, but a therapeutically understood experience that selected *me*.

DURATION: Varies.

EQUIPMENT NEEDED: Case-by-case basis.

AGE: 35.

RELATIONSHIP STATUS: Who knows.

COST: Adrenaline and other chemicals. Large recruitment of the sympathetic nervous system.

HUMILIATION FACTOR: There's no time for that.

LOCATION: Practically any neighborhood north of Mount Vernon, Washington, and south of Vancouver, British Columbia. When trauma takes over it's hard to keep track.

I'm not one of those people who automatically believe things happen in twos or threes or whatever. But within a few weeks of the 101 announcement—after my prompting endless discussions about commitment and how to share the business loan—Laird had moved out. To complete my nauseating style, I should have purchased two cream velour slipper chairs for the bedroom and insist we drone on there. It was not just an all-too-Griswold-family-style thing, it also resembled my breakup with Tim, where I got to say I'm not *really* sure who did it. Both were at my pushing, but then I don't have to own that I started the process.

And so, I found myself staring at the television with a nightly dose of gummy bears. When Laird said there wasn't anybody else, I didn't believe him. This time, I listened to my gut. And instead of sitting on that couch thinking about Tim's hundred anything, or about my mother losing her mind, I snapped. All I could think about was confirming that Laird wasn't telling the truth.

What does snapping look like? Becoming possessed by one solitary thought to the exclusion of all else: upon rising, in the middle of treating a patient, while making marketing calls, while throwing the ball for Isabelle. Snapping looks like having this same thought while walking to buy gummy bears at the Haggen twenty-four-hour grocery store while driving by Laird's new borrowed apartment, while walking Isabelle through Whatcom Falls Park, while waking in the night, while driving by Laird's apartment just one more time, while attempting sleep again. Upon rising in the morning, upon eating breakfast. It was the worst kind of loneliness. A crazy loneliness. Day in, day out, just this one thought:

Is he lying too?
Is he lying too?
Is he lying too.
Ishelyingtoo. Ishelyingtoo.
Ishelyingtoo. Ishelyingtoo.
Bye-bye, Megan. Hello, Nutjob.

I was concerned that if, God forbid, Laird left town, I was just one jumbo box of Depends away from a nonstop cross-country drive in search of him. I think snapping is possible even with *normal* people, but it's not normal when it's happening.

So this is the part where I show you the very worst in me, the part you aren't supposed to show anybody, because then the jig is up, and you've shown that you're just a mess of tangled wires, currently without the orderly circuitry of a "sane" person.

But I have this theory that it's precisely the thing we like least about ourselves, the parts we struggle with the most, the parts we are most likely to hide, that are actually the parts that in some strange way most endear us to one another. Here goes.

67

FREEZE YOUR EGGS

PURPOSE: Get my head above water? Stop time. Stop time so I can get my head above water?

DURATION: The process takes about a month, Freezing appears to last potentially til the end of time.

EQUIPMENT NEEDED: A lot of hormonal drugs, self-administered shots.

AGE: 35. Which means my eggs are what? *Geriatric?* A mere 12,775 days old?

RELATIONSHIP STATUS: Sister-wise and fertility related, Renee had an easy time getting pregnant. Although she's not big on the details, or asking or answering personal questions. She's nesting, which is cool, though. Nesting with Kelsey and Rich. And starting to quilt.

COST: $10,000 (!!!). That's almost a dollar for every day these eggs have been sitting around inside me.

HUMILIATION FACTOR: Asking to borrow money to pay for it will be humiliating. I don't believe in borrowing money.

LOCATION: Boston, Massachusetts, and Pasadena, California.

I'm not doing so well. I'm still growing my practice, but half the time I'd like to crawl onto my acupuncture treatment table and have my clients stick one right between my eyes. I like to think I just rolled with the punches with Tim. But maybe I just kept rolling, and rolling, or spinning like a dreidel. Now I'm concerned my spinning is more like the going-down-the-drain sort of spinning: becoming a big-picture caretaker and advocate for my mother, spinning over this man/love/relationship stuff, being a successful business owner who looks to no one but herself.

Here's the one thing I know: whatever I'm in, it's going to take me longer to get out from under it than I would like to imagine. Longer than it would take a *normal* me or a *normal* person, whoever that is; longer than that *normal* nonblindsided woman would take to meet a nice man again, date, settle into a committed thing, consider marriage, or whatever feels right, and then have children together.

The spinning: why did I waste so many fertile years trying to save what I merely hoped I had with Tim? Am I just naïve enough to I think I can fix any relationship? What am I holding on to with Laird? Our Earthship-skinny-dip-two-dog-easy-livin' fantasy? Did I intuitively *know* about this hundred-hooker business? What do I know about Laird that I'm not acknowledging? How different is this from thinking I could fix my parents' marriage? What else have I gotten so categorically wrong?

For all this spiraling, somewhere in me I still believe that motherhood and a solid relationship are possible for me. That I can raise children with a deep love of my life. And I will protect that part of me while I try to weather and crawl out of this storm of disillusionment. Where the loss of my mother doesn't prevent me from becoming one. And with luck on my side (my mother had me older, and my sister got pregnant easily in her late thirties), maybe this could work.

So I'm taking some of my eggs out. I will offer them protection, from time. Maybe this way I can still bring even just one into the world. I can do that for me, for them, for the man I hope to meet who also dreams of a family.

Once I find the Extend Fertility clinic and begin the shots, I start talking to my eggs. This is what I tell them. Every day. Before I rise and before I go to sleep. With my hand on my belly.

Listen, guys—well, technically I think you are all ladies until the sperm comes along. So listen, little ones. I'm going to try to grow a bunch of you at once, as many as I healthily can, and then once you are all around the same size, a nice doctor is going to go in and take you out. He'll put you to rest for a little while, in something that looks like a nice propane tank, but it will be kind of cold, so I'll ask just the hardiest of you to come. Please, eggies, only come if you're up for an adventure. If, down the road, somebody wakes you, thaws you, rehydrates you, please know that something really good must have happened for me to feel it's the right time to bring you into the world. You'll have to trust me on this. Maybe you can think about my waking you like Sleeping Beauty out of her deep, beautiful sleep.

Yes, yes. Think like that. You are all sleeping little beauties. Just know, I suspect I may be going off the reservation for a while, and I would rather—if possible—shelter you. Why should you have to withstand the squall?

Turns out eleven eggs are up for the journey. They are sleeping deeply in Boston and Pasadena. Thank goodness. Cause a storm, it's a-comin'.

68

SPY ON YOUR EX

PURPOSE: A defining moment that tells you, in no uncertain terms, that your system's in trouble. It's said that when traumatized, the body can seek out what's familiar—repeat a pattern within a disturbing event. All I know is I'm a woman on a singular mission, and not a reasonable one.

DURATION: August, a week or so before my birthday, like the night of Tim's arrest.

EQUIPMENT NEEDED: A spymobile. Cell phone to give Coco the blow-by-blow.

AGE: Same.

RELATIONSHIP STATUS: I mean, with the above chapter heading, do I really have to spell it out?

COST: The price of gas.

HUMILIATION FACTOR: Fantastical. I hate telling you about it.

LOCATION: The Lettered Streets Neighborhood, Bellingham, Washington.

I am thirty-five years old and I am squatting in a bush. Not a small bush, but a rather large one. I have not lost my keys. I have not stumbled and landed here. I am not gardening. I am hiding.

It gets worse. I am thirty-five years old, hiding in a bush, and I am eavesdropping on my nonboyfriend boyfriend and his nongirlfriend girlfriend. For more than two years, he'd been my primary relationship—dogs, dinnertime, and morning coffee. And what with my pressing the issue of commitment, he left, but with equivocal words like "I love you, but I need to feel like I can freely choose you. Let's see if something naturally unfolds between us. There's nobody else."

And now I am the oh-so-uninvited guest, hiding across the street in some stranger's yard, straining my ears to listen to their dinner-party conversation. My heart is racing.

One minute I'm behaving like a young professional, albeit peppered with above-average breakup disappointment. And seemingly the next, I am Inspector Clouseau. Despite, I might add, Coco's sage advice every step of the way: *I wouldn't get out of the car if I were you* (as I get out of the car); *I wouldn't crawl into that bush* (as I drop to my hands and knees while still holding the phone); *Well, if you are going to do it, by all means turn off your phone because I can't ring you back to tell you to turn off your phone as he will hear the ring from the bush* (as I settle into my squat in the shrubbery). I had the literal voice of reason (hers) in my ear and proceeded anyway. And if I had my wits about me, the wisest me—floating omnisciently above my neighborhood antics—would be able to look down and see that Coco isn't just the voice of reason but a powerful sisterly force of unconditional kindness, forever offering me the rope to pull me out. She, the steady ground to pull me in. And yet I prefer to grasp at a phantom, a ghost, a shadow on the wall.

And so now, obstinately remaining in my bushlike cave, my body is crouched in a small ball, and I'm listening as though I'm receiving instructions for how to deactivate a nuclear bomb. This dinner with Miss Nobody Else is none of my business, nor is their conversation even all that interesting. In my imagination, they had been having a far more unbelievable, life-altering, mind-blowing experience than what I was hearing. If I could for a moment overlook the fact that my adrenaline is pumping about a million liters a minute, I am, frankly, a little bored.

In my own defense, spying was never my plan. I was just going to drive by. But one thing led to another, and the next thing I know I'm shimmying past some garbage cans, hoping I'll be mistaken for an extremely large, blond raccoon.

Maybe hearing the words *there's nobody else* led my entire system to blow a fuse. As of now, I am hostage to an entirely different set of thoughts. *Nobody else, my ass.* My husband's version of *nobody else* turned out to be a hundred or so somebody elses who, unbeknownst to me, had invaded my vagina by extension. I would not downplay that sinking feeling this time. And this time it wasn't a low-grade message. It was fully amplified.

Maybe this was my desperate attempt to stay connected to Laird. To feel like we were somehow still in a relationship. Also, if I knew where he was, I wouldn't have to confront my own isolation, struggling to accept that in the end, a maybe isn't a yes. The truth: I was thirty-five and I'd given and changed all that I could for someone who no longer wanted to be with me. And now I was alone.

Or maybe I was driven to know what sneaking, hiding, and feeling terrified of getting caught felt like. To be bad and dark and break the rules. Maybe I wanted to travel Tim's terrain and feel that place in me.

After a back-numbing hour on my knees, I hear some good-byes and the next thing I see is Laird leaving the house in his skateboard sneakers with his kick-a-stone-home gait. There's no lingering good-night kiss. He looks over in my general direction. Oh, God. Did he see me from the streetlight over this shrub? I stay a while longer and pray he doesn't take a wrong turn and stumble onto my car, with Isabelle's teddy-bear self sitting upright and shotgun, on active lookout for my sneaky return.

I crawl out. Was I a stalker? I race home to look up the definition of stalking. I ring up Coco to review various definitions. There is a website for everything, so there is a website for how to know if you are being stalked—or, conversely, if you are a stalker. It appears what I did would be more accurately described as *surveillance*, as I had no intent to harm, scare, or intimidate. I could live more comfortably with that—far less frightening than stalking. Surveillance sounds rather official, even downright responsible—the harmless gathering of information. Christ, surveillance is requisite in some of our finest institutions, the bedrock of our most heroic crime-solving and whistle-blowing—that which makes our great nation great. One could argue this is nothing short of goddamn patriotic.

But perhaps (and I can assure you, Coco concurs), if you have to split hairs to define whether your behavior is within legal limits, you're in some kind of trouble.

69

SEX TOYS

PURPOSE: An object used on the body, designed to produce pleasurable erotic stimulation. I'm pretty sure when Tim gave me these, it was to bring us closer together.

DURATION: While I've had them for years, I haven't used them in ages.

EQUIPMENT NEEDED: The obvious. Less obvious: trash can, trash bag, trash.

AGE: 35.

RELATIONSHIP STATUS: Does grasping count as a relationship?

COST: They were a gift (from Tim a million years ago) to salvage our sex life.

HUMILIATION FACTOR: Come on, now, take a guess.

LOCATION: My house in Bellingham, Washington.

I'm digging through my boyfriend's garbage. I mean my ex-boyfriend Laird's garbage. I mean, technically it is *my* garbage because it's *my* can in *my* house. But this is his garbage. Laird stayed here to dogsit Isabelle for me while I was out of town. And regarding this averagely intelligent, not hugely handsome, but kind of smoky, sort of lazy person with a quiet life—this guy, this *guy*—the first thing I want to do when I return is search for clues of his presence. I don't understand my own motivation. It doesn't seem right, yet knowing it doesn't seem right in no way prevents me from doing what I'm doing. He's not even all that interesting. And my head knows this, but my paws, they don't care. They *have* to dig.

And the scary thing is, in the whole wide scheme of the human spectrum, even with this, I would still be considered a highly functioning human. I'm one of the "together" ones. If that doesn't tell you how odd, how bumbling it feels to be a human, I don't know what will.

I can't seem to shake him. I don't know why I can't, but I can't. He keeps entering my thoughts, and I have no control over it. This troubles me—but the fact that I'm troubled over it also in no way curbs my enthusiasm to dig. This guy has gotten more of my brainpower (not that he asked for it) than my graduate degree, my acupuncture training, and the contents of my wardrobe all put together. And, like an archaeologist, I have this idea that I will know more about him, and somehow believe I will learn something of myself, if I dig through his layers of discarded waste.

So, trash can pulled out from under sink, hands in full excavation (aka pawing) mode, first I stumble onto, you know, just garbage—paper coffee filter with old grounds, a banana peel, some bits of a salad, the cellophane from some fancy cheese. And then a wine bottle. Now that's moderately interesting. Apparently, he drank a whole bottle of wine—either on his own, or with someone.

Maybe some clues are just under this yogurt container . . . and yep, yep, this is looking . . . what do we have . . . a condom.

A condom?

Okay, this refuse just got exponentially more interesting.

Are you kidding me? Are you kidding me? I pull the thing out of the trash— touching it with as little of my fingers' surface area as possible. I hold it up to the light to check for semen. I turn it this way, turn it that, nope. Nada. None that I can see. If only I had a microscope. Do I know anyone who owns a microscope? I mean how pricey can they be? Do they sell microscopes at Target?

Suddenly, nothing else I need to do with my day matters. I will get to the bottom of this. I lift the condom into a plastic bag. I'm a one-person forensic unit. Here is my exhibit A. To prove my *point*, whatever that may be. I'm sure my *point* will focus on some *fact*, with this trashy condom as evidence. My fact: I'm a way better human being. I'm kinder, more educated, more thoughtful, clearly a better investigator. Better dresser. Somehow I have this mistaken notion that finding this condom in my trash will in the long run make me feel better about myself. It's a lie one part of myself tries to tell some other part of myself.

The investigation must continue. I'm in my car. It's driving. My car is driving Isabelle and me to his studio. What's wrong with me that I can't *not* know what's been going on in my house when it comes to this guy? It's sick that finding this sort of object is now intensely interesting. It's like I *want* to find something this sordid, this private. This physical urge to cut through the veil between us. And somehow, with a condom sealed in a plastic bag (which I will tuck tidily in the bottom drawer of that Ikea dresser my mother *made* me buy at twenty-two), this will somehow make me feel oddly, twistedly closer.

I wait outside his new workspace.

"Hey," I say, feigning casual. "I've got to ask you something. And not here. In a more private place."

He looks startled to see me at his shop.

"Uh, okay, well, why don't you walk with me to my truck," he says.

We walk to his blue International Harvester Scout. We get in his blue International Harvester Scout. I waste no time with chitchat.

"Listen, I was taking out the trash . . ." (In my own defense, in a manner of speaking I *was* taking out the trash. Just with a little more attention to detail.)

I continue, "And I . . ." (Big pause to look at him. His eyes wide.) "And I found. . . . a condom. A used condom. And I have to . . . did you really have sex with someone in my house, in *our* old house?"

He turns away and looks a little odd. This really awkward smile, more like a grimace. I wait.

"Listen, Megan"—another big pause—"It's not what you think . . ."

What does he mean, *not what I* think? What else do you do with a condom? Hand puppet? Water-balloon fight seems too obscure. It's not even warm out.

He continues, "It's that I . . . well . . . I kind of . . . I kind of . . ."

I'm getting impatient. "You kind of . . ."

"I kind of took your dildo, and you know . . ."

The rest of the sentence is *placed it in my rectum/shoved it up my rectum*, but he can't utter the words.

And here's the clincher, folks. This is why I'm definitely out on a limb here, showing you my worst. My response is not "How dare you!" or "You did what?" or "I don't think they were made to . . ." Instead I turn this right into:

"Sweetheart—" (I may not have used the word *sweetheart*, but it sounds truer that way.) I say, "[Sweetheart], is this something *we* should have been doing? Something we needed to be doing?"

He says nothing. He blushes. I think for a minute. Is he making this *up*? *Is this really a preferable story in lieu of his possibly bringing a girl to the house?*

I focus on the technical aspects. I've lost my mind.

"So you—let me get this straight. You took my dildo and put it up your ass?" (I may not have used the word *ass*, you know, to be more sensitive. I may have opted for hand gestures.) "And part of your plan—to be thoughtful, I take it—was to put a condom on it? Do I have this right?"

"Look," he says, "must we go into this?"

"Well, it is *my* dildo." I had forgotten it was even in my drawer. I try to say this with extreme gentleness. *But, hello, uh, boundaries?*

"I mean should you maybe have started with something the size of that dildo?" *I know they sell these little pellet things . . .*

He wants to get off the topic. He asks me to lunch.

I may be irrationally obsessed, but I draw the line at discussing stolen dildos placed in nearby rectums over Laird's go-to hot pork sandwich at Coconut Kenny's. I decline lunch, but I'm still trying to understand.

"So, were you, I don't know . . . on your back? Or did you turn on your side? I mean, were you—successful?"

He shakes me off. "No, it wasn't really all that successful."

I'm trying to think how in the world this happens during a house-sitting gig. What is the thought process on this? I picture Laird sitting around my house thinking, "Hmmm. Nothing good on TV, no more wine. Let's see. It's too dark to take a walk. This book is boring. Maybe I'll . . . get Megan's big blue dildo and . . ."

I don't know how fruitful it will be, but I definitely know what topic I'm bringing to therapy. But I won't bring the right questions to the session. I'm not yet discerning enough to ask, "What am I doing rooting around in the trash to feel closer to another human being?"

70

THE NON-THERAPIST THERAPIST

PURPOSE: Cornelia is that non-therapist therapist I took to seeing once back in Bellingham. If Majie is a body-centered psychotherapist, Cornelia is a psychotherapy-focused bodyworker.

DURATION: Once a week. I think Tuesdays.

EQUIPMENT NEEDED: This is supposed to be bodywork with talk, but we rarely get on the table.

AGE: 35.

RELATIONSHIP STATUS: Super-Sexy-Stalking-Sorta-Stuff.

COST: $100 an hour (there's a pattern here—have you noticed?).

LOCATION: Bellingham, Washington.

I sit across from Cornelia, who looks like a little fireplug with Shirley Temple red hair. Like a cute curly topped tomato. I explain the other night's bush shenanigans: the shimmying past the garbage cans, the spiderwebs, the back-numbing hour on my knees. The stalking-versus-surveillance question, as well as digging through Laird's refuse. Like that.

"So, then I sort of crawled out and headed back to my car and . . ."

"Megan, this is stalking. You stalked." She talks to me in that voice you might use with mental patients, or to talk somebody down off a ledge. I know what I did is bat-guano bonkers, but she keeps talking like I don't.

"I'm going on vacation, so I'll make a deal with you. I'll give you my cell phone number if you go on antidepressants."

Huh?

"But I don't think I'm depr—" I defend myself.

"Well, I don't think you realize how crazy this behavior is."

First off, yes, I do. That's why I shared it. That scared me enough: I'm going to make sure that never happens again. And second, are even non-therapist therapists supposed to use the word crazy?

This feels like some weird professional coercion, taking medication in exchange for a personal number. Meek and muddled by recent events, I take the phone number of a doctor she likes. I make an appointment. What have I just agreed to? *I mean, what's so great about having her phone number again?*

71

SELECTIVE SEROTONIN REUPTAKE INHIBITOR (SSRI)

PURPOSE: Get on an antidepressant as some weird deal to get Fireplug's phone number.

DURATION: They say it takes six weeks to get to a therapeutic dose. People usually take them for months or years, but it varies.

EQUIPMENT NEEDED: A prescription. SSRIs are believed to increase the extracellular level of the neurotransmitter serotonin, inhibiting its reuptake into the presynaptic cell, increasing the level of serotonin available to bind to the postsynaptic receptor.

AGE: A few days later.

RELATIONSHIP STATUS: I talk to Coco on the phone a lot.

COST: $100 out of pocket. I only have crap catastrophic insurance. And this period, however catastrophic it might feel, doesn't qualify. Not to mention I haven't met my deductible.

LOCATION: South Bellingham, Washington. Some doctor I've never met before, some medical complex to which I've never been.

I just agreed to take an antidepressant on a whim suggested by an unlicensed therapist giving pharmaceutical advice. I think this doctor even deferred to me—let me diagnose myself. I read somewhere that Paxil was more about anxiousness. And I don't think I'm depressed, so that seems better. But what do I know? But I told Cornelia I'd do this, so I'll go with it. And this guy gives me the one I asked for. I'm pretty persuasive even when I don't know what I'm talking about. Lucky me.

And, because supposedly the drug won't show its effects for weeks, the doctor gives me a prescription of Xanax for the short term. *(Maybe this doctor isn't so bad after all.)* Cornelia gave me my first Xanax yesterday. I felt deliciously relaxed for four hours. So I'll start with the SSRI pills and shake this crazy. I'll drive east to Wyoming to climb the Grand—the grandest of the Tetons—for my summer vacation. Crazy or not, a time-out still seems prudent.

72

OLYMPIC THERAPY
(MY SICK IDEA OF A
MAJIE COMBO-PLATTER
VACATION)

PURPOSE: I'm ditching the Grand Teton climb due to my current cuckoo factor. Call it triage. Between the bush, the dildo, and these surges of anxiety, I need to nip this. Despite the breakup, I've asked Laird to join me after my Therapy Week with Majie for a couples intensive in Evergreen.

DURATION: Seven days.

EQUIPMENT NEEDED: It's a combo platter, really. A little acupuncture, a little EMDR . . .

AGE: Same-same.

RELATIONSHIP STATUS: Beelining it to my besties.

EMPLOYMENT: Young acupuncturist on summer vacation.

COST: My "business loan" is getting used again. Four sessions of three hours, with breaks.

LOCATION: Niwot (Majie's office), Fort Collins (Coco's house), and Longmont (acupuncturist's office), Colorado.

I hope to be successfully reprogrammed. I'm not sure what this means exactly, but it sounds right. When I was little, I never thought getting reprogrammed would be one of my life goals. But neither did I imagine I'd become Insane Scary Person taken to hiding in shrubs and digging in garbage. The unabating nausea only rises. I'm now losing a pound every two days, with wonderful burning pain under my sternum. This is stress on steroids, and I'm plagued by obsessive thoughts. Fantastic.

I've bailed on the Teton climb. I thought climbing the Grand in my state was as intelligent as heading into oncoming traffic. I head to Coco's instead, my de facto command central, to de-nutter myself. Coco greets me at her front door. Usually she would throw open her screen door with a sunburst of welcome, like "Ta-da!!" Instead, upon seeing the yellow, skinnier Nutjob, she pauses, trying to take in the hot mess before her.

"Uh . . . come on in." Her large, normally happy eyes squinch with concern. She lingers at the door to watch me sort of drag in. I can feel her eyes on my back. I think she's just put on her invisible clinical hat to inspect who (or what) I've dropped in her lap unasked.

"Can I get you some tea?' She shuffles about the kitchen and draws a glass of the nettle tea she's been brewing in the backyard. I can't be bothered with tea. The most obvious conclusion: I am simply going crazy. I want semi-easily amused, mostly collected Megan back. I have seven days. A tall order. Nutjob is really only capable of the following thoughts:

Where is he? I wonder what he is doing right now. Is he with her? I wonder what they're doing. I wonder if they're having sex right now. I wonder if he likes it. I wonder if he thinks of me. I wonder if he'll really come to the couples counseling here. I wonder what couples counseling will be like. I wonder what they're doing. I wonder if he is having fun without me. I wonder if they are having fun. What's he . . .

Blah. Blah. Blah. Nutjob was a real bore. Nutjob needed to be taken down. Iced. Eliminated. Taken out back and shot. Worse still, the Paxil wasn't cutting it. Nutjob was like a house on fire—a three-alarm fire. Unfortunately, those next days, Coco had to spend the bulk of the time she would have liked to spend with Megan with Nutjob instead. Megan and Nutjob would spend part

of the day in therapy, then come home to Coco's house—without Nutjob—
because Magic Majie time was effective. But somehow Nutjob would descend
upon everybody again. Nutjob didn't like to be alone. Ever. If Coco was in the
kitchen, Nutjob was in the kitchen. If Coco was at the computer, Nutjob would
pull up a chair. When Coco had to go to the bathroom, Nutjob would follow
her and sit on the tub. Nutjob continued:

Where is . . . ? I wonder what he . . . ? Is he with . . . ?

Should Laird arrive in four more days for the Passionate Marriage intensive
Megan had invited him to before departing (a last-ditch effort after sending
him a pizza and having sex with him, knowing he was also seeing Miss Nobody
Else), it would take a miracle to get Nutjob to calm the fuck down.

When she wasn't cyclically droning on about his physical whereabouts,
Nutjob spent a tremendous amount of time waxing rhapsodic about his penis.

*Coco, I don't think you understand. It's so beautiful! (Sob. Sob. Sob.) I
loooooooove it. So sexy. (Sob. Sob.) The way it curves to the right. Will I ever
see it again? Will I? Seriously, you don't understaaaaand! His peeeenisss!
(Nutjob dropping to the floor, knees to chest.) The way it banked toward his
leg! I loooooooove it! I miss it! (Now rolling, wailing, full-fetal.)*

Nutjob felt it absolutely necessary to craft the right e-mail to review logistics for
Laird's arrival: short, to the point, cool. A literal three-line e-mail, Nutjob chose
the words like it was an addendum to the Universal Declaration of Human
Rights. Nutjob roped Coco into reviewing it.

"Do you think I'm clinging with my use of the word *you* in that first sentence? Should I say: *Dear* _____ or *Hello* _____ or just *Hey*? Maybe I
should say Hey *there*. That's what he says." Nutjob needed to be sure they were
the right three sentences—the right comma placement, intimating the right
inflection. A misplaced dash could prove disastrous.

73

DEPOSSESSION
(THE DRAGONS TREATMENT)

PURPOSE: It's very hush-hush in the Five Element Acupuncture world. We're taught to do it prior to a standard treatment when signs indicate. Failing to do *Dragons* when needed can prevent treatment from proceeding successfully.

DURATION: It takes about an hour.

EQUIPMENT NEEDED: Seven needles along the Stomach Meridian (ankles, thighs, belly, and sternum). The pathway relates to the Earth Element: to the center, to digestion (physical and mental). It relates to the mother, to home, to getting grounded. Place needles. Open a window and wait.

AGE: Same-same-same. But 36 in about a week.

RELATIONSHIP STATUS: Not to be repetitive, but I'm not at my best.

COST: $65 (sliding scale if necessary). It's a generous clinic.

HUMILIATION FACTOR: Nada. I trust my acupuncturist and colleague Marie implicitly. Coco's advising too.

LOCATION: Longmont Alternative Health Care Clinic, Longmont, Colorado.

Possessed. Possessed. Possessed.

Holy smoke, Marie used the word *possessed*.

My big *vacation* in Colorado to de-stalkerize myself appears to involve four depossession treatments in a week. It doesn't feel so good to have your close friend and then two colleagues tell you they think you need to be depossessed. Not just once, but four times. Talk about the big guns. But neither does it feel good to come as close to loco as I care to touch.

The first time I heard of acupuncture depossession (aka Dragons), all I could picture was *The Exorcist* and Linda Blair's head spinning around and vomiting green. While I have seen dramatic responses to this treatment, I don't feel a need to believe one thing or another when I do it (or now, having received it). Do I go home to the family holiday party and share, over cocktails and olives (and a fair number of anti-doctor religious relatives), that I *occasionally* depossess people as part of my *job*? No, I do not. But I do perform the treatment and have witnessed unbelievable, difficult-to-explain results.

The way it's diagnosed: check the eyes. Ever look at someone and, no matter how hard you try, it's like you can't get in? Their eyes feel impenetrable? That's the look we check for, in a particular, close-up way. The seven points are the acupuncturist's best shot at bringing the person back to earth—no longer absent or preoccupied.

My initial experience with Dragons: my friend Delia's three-year-old son had stopped talking—virtually overnight—six months before she consulted me. During those months of silence, he was diagnosed with autism. I took my more conservative friends to lunch to pitch Five Element treatment. I wanted them to take him to one of my supervisors—bracing them for smelly herbs and unusual questions. (I never used the *P* word. What am I, crazy?) Based on the suddenness of her three-year-old's silence, I imagined my supervisor would do Dragons. Touch, let alone needles, agitated the toddler—so the acupuncturist (who was also a neurologist, which made my friends feel better) medically sedated him to receive the needles.

Because the boy was sedated with eyes closed, it was impossible to verify the treatment's success by evaluating that key change in the eyes. So the practitioner put in the extra needles (seven in each of the locations, forty-nine all told) to ensure that the locations had been hit properly. After the treatment, Delia took her sleeping babe home. That night the acupuncturist-neurologist dreamed that by morning, the boy awoke and crawled into Delia's lap and called her Mama for the first time in six months. And that is exactly how it happened. And Delia? Ecstatic. And her son never stopped talking or connecting again.

Now Marie, my acupuncturist, sticks those seven special needles in me. So open that mysterious window, bring on those Dragons, and bring back normal.

Medic!

74

PAROXETINE (AKA PAXIL)

PURPOSE: Used to treat major depression, anxiety, obsessive-compulsive and panic disorders, and social anxiety. The first antidepressant in the United States approved for panic attacks. Typically causes weight gain.

DURATION: Seven days, so far.

EQUIPMENT NEEDED: It comes in pill form.

AGE: 35.99 staring down 36. Impending spinsterdom lurking over the horizon.

RELATIONSHIP STATUS: Laird is coming for counseling in the Rockies. Hurry up and get normal!

EMPLOYMENT: An acupuncturist exploring Western medication while on vacation.

COST: $100 to get on it. Sweat equity to get off it.

HUMILIATION FACTOR: A delayed response.

LOCATION: Coco's guest room. One of the two most comforting houses on the planet.

Perfect. This is absolutely perfect. We have finally figured out why I'm having these surges of anxiety. The week's therapy, acupuncture, and Dragons have done a world of good, enough that I can separate my calm emotional state from the sudden surge of anxiety that occurs exactly twenty minutes after ingesting a Paxil. Marie, my acupuncturist, put it together. After all this, it appears I'm not actually crazy. The source of the week's insanity appears to be these big yellow pills. Every out-of-control symptom I have is listed in the *Physicians' Desk Reference*. I feel I must speak to the person in charge of pharmaceuticals in this country at once.

> Possible Paxil side effects: Anxiety; nervousness, restlessness, agitation, nausea, loss of appetite, anorexia, weight loss; talking, feeling, and acting with excitement and activity you cannot control, muscle pain or weakness, insomnia, trouble sleeping, unusual tiredness or weakness, dyspepsia, pain in the center of the chest or behind the sternum.

I have all of them. Coco and I go to the appropriate websites to learn how to get off the Paxil. We learn it is considered one of the more frightening antidepressants in terms of scary withdrawal symptoms. The highlights:

> Muscle cramps, loss of appetite, nausea, hypersensitivity to sounds and smells, concentration problems, profuse sweating, especially at night, intense insomnia, panic attacks—even if you've never had one before, intense fear of losing your sanity, feeling of shocks pulsing through your body, slurred speech, steady feeling of existing "outside reality as you know it," suicidal thoughts, extraordinarily vivid dreams/nightmares.

I call my doctor (I don't know if you can call someone *your* doctor after seeing him once for ten minutes but there you go) to get advice on how to go off it. I was convinced he was an eighty-year-old moron who only picked Paxil because he had a few free packages floating around in a drawer. I get no call back from him. Instead, some nurse with no expertise calls me back. So I intend to go it alone. At first I thought I would break one pill in half and step down that way; but mine are time-release, and I'm concerned that if I break one in half I'll feel the absence of the time-release coating. I fear with that, the anxiety surge will be even more immediate. So I decide to go cold turkey. Off the Paxil, as well as the Xanax that was helping me sleep in reaction to the Paxil.

I enter the guest room. At this point I'm only mildly concerned I will spontaneously go into cardiac arrest, one of the possible side effects of withdrawal from Paxil or Xanax—I can't remember which. I crawl into bed, say good night to Coco, and stick my MacBook earphones into my ears and wait for Larry David to help me to sleep. I start to get drowsy, turn away from Larry David, and roll onto my stomach. I think: *This can't be so bad.*

I'm on my belly for a few minutes and decide I should roll over. But what do I roll over upon but a big lump in my breast. *OH MY GOD. I think I just felt a lump in my breast. Wait. Is that a lump in my breast?* I take my little hand and get the nerve to feel around. *Oh my God, that's a lump in my breast. I am going to die. I can't believe it. I am going to die.* This thing is big and round and hard. *How could I not have felt this before?* It might not have helped that I'd lost about seven pounds in a week, so my breasts were simply that—breast tissue with no surrounding fat.

This is why Laird is coming out for couples counseling. He is intuitively coming so he can get back together with me so that I can die of breast cancer, like his mother did. I am thirty-six years old, or about to turn thirty-six the day we meet up. His mother died at thirty-six. *I will have gone through all this hogwash with Tim and Laird, only for this last guy to help me die. I—his nongirlfriend girlfriend—am in a relationship with him so he can heal from the loss of his mother, who died when he was twelve. Fuck off, Freud. And take your cockamamie female-hysteria misogyny with you.*

I start sweating. I am officially having a panic attack. It is unmistakable. *Why did I have to find this thing two days before my birthday? And even more upsetting: how is it I am learning I have* cancer *on the* one *night I'm trying to eliminate an* anxiety-provoking drug *from my system? I feel sick. I think I'm going to throw up.* I decide I need to wake up Coco. It's two in the morning, and if I wake her, I'll also wake her husband, Ross. She is the closest, least judgmental, most resourceful person I know, so I absolutely must wake her. I feel terrible about this, but I have no choice. I am dying. I have cancer. She knows about these things. She will inspect my lump.

I crawl out of bed (I'm too nauseated to walk) and into the hallway to knock on her bedroom door, still on all fours. I'm experiencing my first flop sweat. Coco can't come to the door soon enough. I'm too queasy to get up, so I wait. She comes out, finds me on the ground, and gently kneels down, placing her hand softly on my forehead the way one might delicately approach a small injured bird. Kindness in the middle of an imbecilic meltdown. She appears alarmed that I'm so flushed with sweat.

I try to look up at her as she strokes my face, but in the same breath I'm just trying not to throw up. At the moment, I'm a pretty big fan of staying as still as possible.

I summarize the situation efficiently, highlighting the most important points. I have found a lump and it appears to be cancer. I merely need a second opinion to confirm my diagnosis. No pressure, but everything hinges on her opinion.

In her gentlest soothing voice, sweetly rubbing my brow, she whispers, "Let's get you back to bed."

She helps me up and back to the bed, holding my sides, shuffling along with me in our mutual sweatpant pajamas. She retrieves a cool cloth for my forehead, kneeling next to me on the bed, wiping the washcloth in slow circles while making calming sounds.

Like a deer in headlights looking up at her, I ask her to feel my breast with her other hand. Not just once, but a hundred times. She feels it again and again. And again. I say: "Do you think it's cancer? Is that what cancer feels like?" She's had lumps in her breast.

"Does it feel like the benign ones you've had, or does it feel different?"

She says it's not cancer. But I am too smart for this. What else do you say to a dying woman? She says the lump is mobile and that this is a positive sign. Secretly, I know she is worried because despite its mobility, it is also incredibly hard, much harder than a normal squishy cyst. We play out this nonstop breast exam till dawn.

Given the previous night's discovery and shenanigans, the logical thing to do would be to go to a doctor and have my lump inspected. This would have been in keeping with my nature. I ascribe to the view that more information—good or bad—is always better than less. I prefer my bad news up front. Just rip the bandage right off, instead of a slow torturous tug. But with my current pharmacologically altered state and the upcoming couples counseling and birthday, I decide to take a revolutionary stance and embrace denial.

Well, I ignore it enough to avoid a doctor's appointment, ultrasound, and mammogram. But I continue my own personal physical exam at about five-second intervals for the next few weeks. My version of ignoring also includes the purchase and memorization of Dr. Christiane Northrup's definitive text, *Women's Bodies, Women's Wisdom.*

I memorize the section on lumps, compulsively palpating the sucker while driving with Coco and Ross to Wyoming, where we'll meet up with Laird and celebrate my birthday with Michelle and Scott. As we drive, Coco and Ross hold hands in the front, listening and giggling to David Sedaris's *Me Talk Pretty One Day.* While Coco gazes out over Wyoming's sage steppe, twirling her hair and appreciating nature, I'm busy in the back, medically fondling myself. I palpate my lump thoroughly in various positions in the back seat of Coco's SUV: lying down on my right side, lying down on my left, on my back, as well as my favorite position, looking wistfully out the window, contemplating all the things I will never do—bear children, rock on my front porch with Laird and our grandchildren.

By evening, I am preparing my eulogy and making a list of the music I would like played at my service. I stress in my notes the request to have a big campfire as well. (It is my favorite smell in all the world.) I also request Andrea Bocelli's classical hit "Time to Say Goodbye."

I decide to not tell Laird about my lump; I don't want him to stay with my lump and me out of sympathy. I'm not sure how I would arrange his not knowing about my lump if we fool around. It would be as easy to overlook as a boulder hidden between our mattress and box spring. But I will cross that bridge later. I decide to officially worry about my cancer *after* the couples counseling, where I'm certain we'll end up permanently broken up. I will have plenty of time to contemplate my impending lonely spinster death. I don't have time for cancer. The depossession hasn't entirely rid me of my focus:

I have a boyfriend to win back.

75

EMDR RESOURCE-BUILDING PROTOCOL

PURPOSE: Paxil-free in four days. That's roughly how long it takes to get out of the system and back to planet Earth. Instead of using EMDR to get rid of old traumas, we are using it to imprint new patterns.

DURATION: A few hours, over more than one session.

EQUIPMENT NEEDED: The old vibrating paddles and headphones are back.

AGE: Same damn week.

RELATIONSHIP STATUS: I've let my guard down here, been held here. Majie and Coco and Marie have seen my worst, and it didn't kill me. Sometimes you have to make a sense of family to learn what family can feel like. I wish I could return the favor immediately.

COST: $80.

HUMILIATION FACTOR: The idea of it is embarrassing. The actual doing is not.

LOCATION: Same home office of one Mr. Magic.

I can eat again (I go with a nice chicken dish); that burning epigastric pain has vanished. And my joints have stopped hurting. The spinning thoughts have departed, and my sleep is deep and normal. Majie and I created a whole new protocol of EMDR to help ensure that I would not act like a Stage-Five Clinger, even if this nuts couples counseling retreat went terribly.

We're using EMDR not to revisit old traumas but to do the opposite: we are running my brain through a rehearsal of sorts of how I'd like to behave, like an athlete coached to run through a perfect performance in her head. And somehow, the EMDR paddles and beeps act like a booster. After one particularly good session—playing out seeing Laird *without* my behaving like a lunatic— I leave knowing that enough anxiety has departed that I have picked the nervous callus on my thumb for the last time. With all this mental repetition, I feel like the Manchurian Candidate (but in a good way?).

Sure enough, when I see Laird, I am calm—so calm, he asks, "Are you on some sort of medication?"

"Nope," I reply serenely. Privately, I smile, knowing I'm Paxil-free. A week ago, Coco and I were in hysterics, rolling around on her living room carpet at the impossibility of my being back to myself when I saw him. But I'd done it. We'd done it. I felt calm, like I would be fine even if we didn't get back together. The only thing I hadn't gotten out of my system: my preference to win him back.

76

POST-PAXIL SKINNY

PURPOSE: This time, it's not so much purpose as an effect. But it totally counts as a modality as weight can be used in hopes of *transforming* oneself. Right/wrong. Good/bad. It's true.

DURATION: A week or so.

EQUIPMENT NEEDED: A scale. In my case, the one in Coco's bathroom.

AGE: Officially 36.

RELATIONSHIP STATUS: Limbo lower now.

COST: Free. Emotional drama has its own charge.

HUMILIATION FACTOR: Split down the middle between maniacally suddenly skinny pride and utter mortification. Pride at my skinny self and atrocious mortification at said pride. Mind you, I still plan on wielding my thin body at Laird. Like a knife. In brand-spankin'-new pencil jeans no less. Not to mention, it screams desperate (at best, dogged) to convince an old boyfriend who's sleeping with someone else to do marital counseling. And watch me do it anyway.

LOCATION: Evergreen, Colorado.

Skinniness has become my shield. Why have I been working so hard on incremental spiritual growth when I feel the way this unplanned plunge into skinniness makes my spirit soar? That crazy Paxil has caused massive weight loss, making me in one week the thinnest I've been since I was a ballet dancer on scholarship in high school. I now have six-pack abs, and my cheekbones are making a tremendous showing. Nothing like a week of burning sternal and epigastric pain and a near total inability to eat to put me one step closer to the supermodel version of myself. And I *love* it.

I'm well aware this may be *extremely* screwed up. So I *promise* I'll look into it, just *after* this Official-Last-Ditch Laird-effort. Because other than noting my current *Alice in Wonderland* Drink-Me-Shrink-Me self in the mirror, I'm pretty focused on the Win-Him-Back thing. That said, I find this crash course back into the world of skinny makes the world, for the moment anyway, seem like an entirely kinder place. If I told you it felt otherwise, I'd be lying.

Laird could leave me, Tim could shag a hundred to two hundred hookers, but there is no denying that my ass looks awesome. And I feel powerful. Even if I have my hands at the helm of the Skinny Ship and am steering that ship smack dab into a seawall, I feel *in charge*. Not to mention, in this state, I notice I give myself all sorts of nice compliments instead of circular cruel criticism. I've watched that criticism run inside my head for ages. Thank goodness there's not a stenographer in there. It'd be a boring read.

But back to the Win-Back-Laird part of this: I know that the woman, you know, *that* woman, that Laird has started dating (I also call her Miss Live-in-the-Now because I read in her qigong teacher bio that she teaches people to *live in the now*), I don't (just between you and me) find her all that compelling. She goes a little heavy on the prayer beads. And anyway, the only people I know who really *live in the now*—let alone teach it—are two-year-olds, a couple of monks, and an elder with Alzheimer's. But the point: Miss Live-in-the-Now not only taught people to *now-it-up*, but to do so with a far more generous ass and a tremendous amount of beadwork. Nothing wrong with a gorgeous round ass. But somehow I only adore them on *other* people. And in my Win-Back-Laird weekend, the virtual absence of my own ass shored me up. I seem to be wired (or trained) to feel so much bigger when I'm smaller. I feel emboldened by my own Alice-Drink-Me-Shrink-Me-but-in-jeans routine. It isn't so much that I think Laird will find me more attractive or not. The point is that right now, weighing *less*, *I* find myself *more*. Bigger. Stronger. More in control. Over myself. Over my own internal Little Miss Nutjob. Over the sense of failure I will feel if I can't make this man love me.

As if the size of my jeans can save me. As if those mean-spirited little fat cells aren't already stalking their way back to me since I went off the Paxil.

Can anyone say *sub-clinical eating disorder*?

77

PASSIONATE MARRIAGE

PURPOSE: The mother lode of couples counseling. This is where to go when the counselors no longer know what to do with you and the two of you don't know what to do with the two of you. Two-on-one counseling (just you, your spouse, and either the wife or the husband of this dynamic duo—Ruth Morehouse or David Schnarch).

DURATION: Four days.

EQUIPMENT NEEDED: Bring your preference (stay together, or break up, or on the fence). The *Passionate Marriage* peeps will disclose a belief in the learning that comes when couples stay together. The outcome is unpredictable. But plan on leaving with much more clarity.

AGE: 36 years and six days.

RELATIONSHIP STATUS: In process. Barf. I hate the word *process*.

COST: It's not cheap ($3,000). And you need to travel to them and take four days off.

HUMILIATION FACTOR: I'm trying a tad too hard, don't you think?

LOCATION: Evergreen, Colorado.

I am finally getting the kind of marital counseling I needed in my marriage. The fact that I am divorced, getting marital counseling with Laird—to whom I'm not even close to marrying, let alone not even currently dating, but essentially dragging him out of Miss Live-in-the-Now's bed—well, that seems like a wee bit of an oversight, like getting marital counseling via proxy. A Washington Trust Bank business loan and I paid for the tuition, the dog-friendly motel, and, yes, Laird's time off.

Miss Live-in-the-Now told Laird, "She's buying you."

"You didn't buy me," Laird assured. "I come here with an open heart and mind." But I thought Miss Live-in-the-Now had a beyond-fair point. Had I not made it financially burden-free, I doubt he would have come. I'd bet the tuition.

But if I was going to win back his adoration, it would all come down to underdesiring him and outdifferentiating her. She had no idea with what or with whom she was dealing, my pulling the *differentiation* card and all—highbrow therapeutic tactics for such a lowbrow, ego-driven desire. I knew that the minute she started grasping for him as I had, she would lose. Take *that*, you boyfriend snatcher. I wasn't so sure I even wanted this guy, so much as I wasn't going to lose him to some nearly-cross-eyed-bad-Taoist philosophizer with her two-bit analysis of Laird's and my relationship, all the while keeping her hands and mala beads in the prayer position. Let her watch me blast right past desperate and pathetic bush-dweller to caller of the romantic shots.

I myself came to Passionate Marriage with one tiny ass and two tons of EMDR crammed into my brain. I felt centered. I would survive if we stayed broken up (although privately trying to quell that obsession to make *this one work no matter what*).

But I was so successful *appearing* strong and clear (being *differentiated* and all that, not needing Laird to make me whole blah blah blah) that Laird wanted me back.

Drop the mic.

Turns out it's as *they* say: the I'll-be-fine-without-you-so-you-are-free-to-choose attitude suddenly made me hugely attractive. When we weren't having counseling, we sexed it up in our dog-friendly lodging (I, so mature and differentiated, rented accommodations with separate bedrooms). I (with a metric ton of work and possibly faking it till I was making it) magically appeared to be the low-desire partner. I don't mean low-desire sexually. In any couplehood, there's a high-desire and a low-desire partner (this can flip-flop), but the low-desire partner has the control. Like being willing to walk off the used-car lot when negotiating. The salesman can smell it. Then suddenly you have a deal.

"Are you sure you're not on something? You're so relaxed, so *in* yourself, in a good way. It's almost weird."

"Nope, I'm not on anything, seriously. I just did some good work with Majie." (And got depossessed—or de-obsessed—four times. According to the newly differentiated me, that was *my* business.)

I called Coco to update her.

"Maybe I'm using Laird to get to the kind of help I wanted with Tim. Is Laird like a stand-in? Marital counseling with a stunt double?"

"I honestly don't think he's your guy, but as long as you're there, just learn what you can."

The only positive spin I can find on the merits of marital counseling with (and I mean no offense) the relational equivalent to an Oscar ceremony seat-filler is that I saw it as a testimony to my resolve—to bring clarity to what the bounds of marriage are meant to be, in hopes of taking that learning into this or my next relationship. And I had done it with the person who most closely could be described as my partner. In a few months, Tim would take Vee to Passionate Marriage per my recommendation. Maybe he got marital counseling via proxy too.

Despite one waste-of-time conversation where Laird discussed why I needed to learn to sip water out of a bottle without letting it touch my lips, most of it was productive. Although, come to think of it, maybe this was the most valuable moment.

"Yeah, Megan does this thing with her mouth. She looks like a trucker," he tells Ruth, our guru (like a Rocky Mountain Mrs. Claus). "I tell her she should drink like they do in India."

"India? What's this about India?" Ruth asks.

"In India they know how to share water bottles elegantly—to drink from a bottle without touching their lips to it. So they can share." Laird's smoky voice making his cross-cultural bottle argument. As was often the case, his words felt more like seduction than argument.

"And this is a problem for *you* about . . . *Megan*?"

"Yes, she . . . it's an example of where she is unconscious."

Ruth looks at Laird, then at me. Then down to her own water bottle, sitting to her right. Then back up to us. You can tell she doesn't quite know where to take the conversation from here: to the underpinnings of the relationship or the theories of how to ingest liquids internationally.

I watch her look back and forth once more between us and the bottle before she makes her move. She reaches for it, looking self-conscious as we watch, while she considers whether now is the time to sip.

"Careful," I say, grinning. I can't help myself. All eyes are still on Ruth as she slowly untwists the cap uncomfortably and lifts the bottle to her lips. She sucks it down like a trucker, just like I do. So *there*.

Maybe trying to differentiate—to not twist up in a man again—is like trying to quit smoking. They say the number of times you attempt to quit will eventually lead to your success. In that case, I'm one attempt closer to permanently differentiating—one more good college try at not shape-shifting for a guy. After our recoupled return to Bellingham, did Laird continue largely to just want to eat, putter and build, have sex, stuff animals, and walk the dogs—in that order? Yup. But he did pass out an extra business card or two. And did he try to hang in with committing? He tried that too. And did I try to not push so hard to make him/us *grow* (barf)? Yep. I really did. I called Majie at the end of the intensive.

"How'd it all go?" he asked.

"The one thing I know, Majie, I'll never again pay for marital counseling at 8 percent interest with a boyfriend who's broken up with me."

78

DRINK HOASCA WITH
THE UNIÃO DO VEGETAL

PURPOSE: A spiritual practice based on mental concentration for self-knowledge. Michelle (ever practical) thinks I'm looking for trouble with this one. Coco gets it.

DURATION: About five hours. Associate with the UDV church and you can do this twice a month.

EQUIPMENT NEEDED: The tea itself, of course. A picture of Mestre Gabriel at the front of the room. A circle of green Rubbermaid chairs.

AGE: 37. It's suddenly my birthday again. My, how time flies when you are kinda stuck and stumped.

RELATIONSHIP STATUS: I believe Laird would like me best if I were in a permanent state of having just come out of general anesthesia. I'd like him to stumble onto some ambition. Neither of us is winning an award for acceptance.

EMPLOYMENT: Acupuncturist, my vocation. Writing, singing lessons, studying interior design, reading about Alzheimer's and North Cascade hiking, all avocations.

COST: Free. By invitation only.

HUMILIATION FACTOR: *Humiliation* isn't the right word here. If the term were *intensity factor*, we'd be locked and loaded.

LOCATION: South Seattle, Washington.

If you have any inkling you don't want to go the whole way, I think it's better you get up and leave right now, because once you know, you cannot stop knowing and you might as well get on with it.

—*Ram Dass*

"Do you have the Force? Do you have the light?"

The answer to these two questions is either *yes* or *still waiting.*

"Still waiting," I say, in the butchered Portuguese I learned forty minutes ago.

I sit in an open session with members and guests of the União do Vegetal. Literally translated it means Union of the Plants: a Brazilian Christian religion based on the use of hoasca and the teachings of José Gabriel da Costa, or Mestre Gabriel, a doctrine that teaches the love of fellow humans and the practices of goodness, all in accord with the teachings of Jesus.

My friend Heather invited me, as I showed interest over a year ago. When the Supreme Court upheld the UDV's right to drink their tea as religious sacrament, a Harvard professor testified that he made it his business to educate himself on every psychoanalytic tool available and that, from his experience, hoasca was the single-most powerful. If that's the case, I'm in. I mean, I hear the stuff can make you sick, but what's a little nausea compared to one of the single-most powerful psychoanalytic/psychopharmaceutical tools one can legally take?

I'm no Timothy Leary, but I'm on some sort of quest, which I share with the group in the classic sharing circle.

"I'm still stuck. I do most of the things one does for balance: exercise, care for clients, eat healthily, have creative outlets, et cetera—but inside, some places in me are stuck."

Tim is getting married. Did I tell you? Not only did I find the therapy to salvage his relationship with Vee, but the *Passionate Marriage* duo salvaged it enough that they are to marry. What a helpful ex-wife. Full-service situation. And get this: he's going to marry Vee using the wedding ring I gave him.

"You're doing *what*?" I asked him to repeat.

"We're getting married and I plan on marrying her using the ring you gave me."

What about a clean slate? Didn't they want their own ring?

"Really? I mean . . ."

"Yeah," Tim said matter-of-factly.

The thing is, I bought the damn thing. And it wasn't your average guy's $100 gold band. It's platinum and gold swirls and cost $4,000. And, given my recent education of Tim's tiny oversight about how much he'd spent in the prostitute department, I would have reevaluated our little divvying up of debt. So much for our do-it-yourself divorce and happy division of property, which didn't account for the hundred or so XYZs, the phone sex, the probation fees, or the waste-of-time Don hours. I would have happily taken the ring back to sell on eBay. Instead it was going to be some symbol to live on into his next marriage.

"Why? Why *this* ring?"

"Well, I've always liked the ring."

"Would you consider not using it?"

Silence.

He wouldn't have it. Maybe they liked the idea of wedding ring recycling or something. To transform it, they were going to have the ring hammered.

"Hammered?"

If I had to drink this tea to let go of the man I had married and the Laird to whom I couldn't quite commit, and who couldn't quite commit to me, well, then drink I would. The only person who could make these changes was me—to unhook from Tim's business, to let Laird go, to accept my mother's illness and my father's return to Christian Science and whole new life. He's living in Tahoe now, teaching Christian Science Sunday school, and it challenges me that he's still chasing some new business idea—this time involving tilapia fish, cold-fusion or fuel-cell something-or-other, and organic farming in prisons. Not all together, mind you (well I'm not totally sure), but of equal interest, I guess. And it hooks me that at this age I still fantasize about a dad who's more interested in Renee and me than farmed fish. Some traits, like his dream chasing, I could set my watch to. Others, like the Christian Science revival, catch me off-guard. Renee, on the other hand—and unlike me—is not about to ingest hoasca, and instead is doing a very nice job creating a more traditional relationship with a husband and baby. She got baptized a Lutheran, joined the NRA, and practices her accuracy at the gun club. I hear they have pretty good music on the weekends. At the other end, I'm drinking some sort of psychotropic tea and bracing to vomit my brains out so I can make better choices. *Go figure.*

If hoasca could help me let go of fatherly or male relationship challenges, or the guilt I feel over Mom, well I'm totally *totally* in.

I told the group: "I have certain beliefs and a certain lack of optimism that doesn't serve me. And while I know this, I can't seem to change my mind. I suspect I'm not so much stuck on a guy, I'm stuck on *being stuck* on guys, and hold unrealistic expectations about my family—a fantasy that I must end to make room for what's real. I promise you, if there were a magic pill to take, I would *take* it; an incantation to say, I would *say* it. Perhaps it's mere stubbornness and I need to find someone with a big enough sledgehammer to strike a titanic blow to my head."

The group nodded kindly.

"And hoasca sounds the most like a sledgehammer than anything I've heard about." More nods.

Letting go—you just have to do it. Like leaping out of a plane. My general relationship with it, however, mostly involved being on very good terms with its opposite: holding on. In fact, barring a workshop or violent crime that literally chopped off my hands, I wasn't so sure I could ever learn letting go.

And at some point, it only makes sense that I try at least one church, right? To be fair or something? Okay, so the UDV isn't exactly a classic church experience, but it's as close as I can come.

In the beginning, my main worry was that I wouldn't be given enough tea. I remember being handed my glass (like cloudy apple juice) and trying to lick every last drop out of it. I feared they would underestimate given my relatively small size, when really, I figured the size of the dose should be determined by the stubbornness of one's spirit.

We approached the front and Mestre William for our tea, one at a time, then returned to sit in our duck-duck-goose-arranged green lawn chairs (apparently, the Rubbermaid lounger is the chair of choice). We sipped. It was the single-most disgusting ingesting experience I've ever had—like drinking rotten dead animal mixed with ammonia mashed together with the bitterness of a thousand aspirin, sprinkled with some garbage and peppered with a hint of battery acid. And then we wait.

A half hour in. Nothing.

Argh. I really am too stubborn; I'm just someone it won't work on. Maybe I should ask for more. Hmph.

And then.

It. Comes. On.

A buzzing in my ears arises like a million insects on a hot Midwestern afternoon mixed with as many model airplanes and Husqvarna chain saws rising and falling violently inside my ears. No question this sound can be adopted immediately as a new torture device.

Holy shit. I am going to die. Like, really. Make it go away. Make it go away. I gotta get out of here.

I launch out of my green lounger, through the French doors to the yard and the nearest tree to commence vomiting something that looks more like brown sea foam than the can of Progresso chicken noodle soup I had for lunch.

For the next five hours I alternate between unabating nausea and vomiting mixed with a high-speed tour of the emotional (not the positive) underbelly of my life. Heat. Buzzing. Throwing up. Between retches I kick myself for jumping in so blindly. Michelle was right to worry. But all I can do now is hang on. Experienced UDV counselors support the guests. If you feel like you are going to be sick, you are encouraged to vomit outside. So most of the guests have exploded into the yard while the haunting Portuguese prayers continue to be sung right inside the doors.

One guest all in white shuffles in the courtyard like a fast-moving penguin in a lockdown ward with a load in his pants. At the moment, this big guy is unaccompanied, but this UDV group is organized enough that in moments a counselor will come to his aid. I see Heather's boyfriend, Arthur, ass-up, moaning in a flower bed. Arthur is a highly rational, sharp, witty tax attorney. I'm guessing this is his first bout moaning ass-up in a flower bed. I myself have taken a great fondness to vomiting and rolling around in sap under a particular pine tree, the location closest to the French doors. I can't be bothered by the sappy pine needles stuck to my brown Juicy Couture sweatpants. I keep trying to leave my tree. But mostly, I can't move without throwing up again.

Beautiful Portuguese prayers, called by Mestre William, continue to reverberate out of the session room. Guests in various positions continue to vomit in the yard. Who knew church could be like this? I still cannot move. Soon, a counselor comes to encourage me to try to come back into the room. Her name is Erin.

"Megan, how are you doing?"

Somewhere between ass-up and the full fetal, moaning, I reply, "I'm . . ." That's all I can say. Vomiting has kidnapped my voice box.

I know they prefer you stay in the session room, but they also don't want you vomiting in the room. I'm torn, as I want to do it right. Even feeling like I am about to die, I want to follow the rules.

"I'm so sorry, so sorry, so sorry," I eke out.

Erin lightly rubs my back, reminding me of her presence when I can't look up (which is most of the time). She stays beside me for hours.

Somehow I end up on the other side of the yard. I guess I crawled (or rolled) there. I'm not sure. No recall whatsoever. Erin offers me a rubber band so I'll stop puking on my hair.

"How long has it been?" I ask.

"You are about two hours in. About three to go."

"Oh, Godddddddd." I try moaning to see if it helps. Then a new position. A curled-up roly-poly.

My life and a whole string of sense memories rumble through like a train with a decided course. And not the good sense memories; the ones that remind me of the ways I grew smaller, not bigger.

"You're doing fine," Erin says.

This woman is a saint. I know Erin is battling Stage Four cancer and, even with all that, she chose to spend her Sunday this way, to help people like me.

Imagine what it would be like to completely fall apart. Like, completely. To be irrationally, vomitously, unpopularly, emotionally overextended so extensively that you can't be polite or together or conscientious or insightful, and that then this person, this stranger, seeing all that, comes to your aid. I was exactly all those things and Erin never left me. Meanwhile, the *Clockwork Orange* version of my life keeps barreling through me. You know that part where they put toothpicks under his eyelids or something so he can't not look at whatever he doesn't want to look at? It's like that.

Because of Erin I experienced far more than a chemical brain experiment. I will be in love with her for the rest of my life. If I had to get that sick to experience such patience and kindness, I'm the better for it. Kind women to help me out of the holes I take myself down with undependable men. I'm starting to notice this.

Erin has to help another guest. I hear her say to another counselor, "Arthur's stuck on the toilet. Can you help me get him off?"

Tax attorney Arthur, stuck on the toilet. After the apparent toilet triage, counselor Darren returns and sits down next to me in the grass.

"Do you know what this experience is about for you?" he asks. "It's important to not just let this blast you, but understand it for yourself as much as you can."

I nod. I do understand.

Another hour passes, largely in Darren's company. Enormous, kind brown eyes above me as I continue on my runaway train. Erin returns to ask, "Mestre William would like to know if you could return to the group. Can you walk with me?"

Erin and I take the world's slowest walk back to the room. I walk hunched with my hands on my knees. For all I know it took half an hour to walk what would normally take ten seconds.

After five hours and a now gradual return to Earth, I hear singer Israel Kamakawiwoʻole's Hawaiian version of "Somewhere over the Rainbow" in the background. Mestre William asks us how it was. The appropriate answer is: *"Fue boa. Graças a Deus."* (Well, thanks to God.) But upon sitting up to say this, I have to vomit again and run to the yard. So my reply from my pine tree is:

"Fue [retch] *boa."* (Well.) I can't get that last "Thanks to God" bit out before I have to heave again.

"Graças [retch] *a Deus."*

Then William asks us to share our experiences. A heavyset guy with a gray ponytail, rock band T-shirt, and rings on every finger goes first: "During my session, I called and met with all my Angel Guides and communed with them."

I can tell he is one of those *spiritual experts* guaranteed to rub me the wrong way. He appears to talk mostly to make sure we know about his previous trainings that allow him to call on his various forces and gods: "It's all about us dancing together. My gods danced with me. I chose to engage them—interact with them."

I couldn't fathom how someone could drink this and still have any sense of identity, authority, not to mention dancing ability. Maybe they hadn't given this guy enough tea. I myself had just tried to hold on for dear life, while feeling head-to-toe blown apart.

So what did it do to me? First, I've come to realize that it's virtually impossible to talk about any experience all that successfully when there is an urge to use the term *life-changing*, largely because almost any person who would hear that (including me) tends to think you are a chucklehead, bought the snake oil, drank the Kool-Aid, or D. All of the above.

Look, if having a completely normal life—maybe I had a boat, or was a big skier, or loved to watch movies, or enjoyed having a beer with my buddies on the weekend while holding down a regular job, or had 2.1 kids and a dog—would have sustained me, believe me, I would have done it. It sounds lovely, really. But my ticket didn't get punched that way. Instead I find myself spending my birthday vomiting my brains out.

But what does the hoasca do? My theory? It's not one thing but a combination of many. The tea is brewed for days in the Brazilian rain forest, highly ritualized, surrounded by people supporting the community and its making. When the tea is drunk, it's done in an intimate, safe setting. Nothing casual about it. The session director, trained to sense what people need, selects the prayers called particularly for that group. And the overwhelming message of the calls and the music and the prayers? Hold on, people. It might sound corny, but I have to say it. The message: love. Unadulterated, unconditional love directed to the goodness and the force and light of each person.

I have drunk the tea a few times since and this is what I have figured out so far: it isn't the tea itself that unsettles me, it's the power and intention of the group in combination with the tea In subsequent sessions, every time I would leave the circle to vomit, I knew if I sat and waited the session out in the bathroom, I could ride it out no problem. But to reenter the circle of participants with the music and the emotion rising like a cathedral, accompanied by this feeling of love in the room—that's what seemed to make me sick. As if my system had been trained to not take in too much love or a strong belief in my own goodness for fear I wouldn't be enough, *it* wouldn't be enough. But the power of the tea is that it forces my nervous system to receive more, more of what is actually here—a group of people gathered to wish one another well and find communion with themselves and that unexplainable sense of something larger.

And, lo and behold, each time I left the circle to barf, I would feel a smidge more like my *normal* less drippingly positive self, and this would make me feel less sick. And each time I would reenter the circle, I would feel the calls pulsate my body to the point of uncontrollable nausea. I would try to sit as long as I could to take in this kindness I could feel—up until the point of retching—waiting till I couldn't bear it another minute, and then would set my mind to bear it a minute more. When it got too much, off I would go to the bathroom or to the little plastic-lined trash cans dotting the entryway. But I would eventually return to the group, taking in tiny bites of kindness one at a time.

Now, don't get me wrong, it's not that no one had shown me kindness in my life—far from it. It's that there seemed to be resistance in me or a lack of recognition to know how much I could receive.

And the new information I could take in was that there was love here for no other reason than my being exactly as I was.

Hoasca felt like strong enough medicine for someone like me. As if the tea said, *I don't care what sort of fight you put up, you are going to take this in.* Like I got force-fed some really good food, and I screamed and yelled and barfed my way through my first meal, but then suddenly I could taste. Sometimes it's after you start eating that you realize how hungry you are.

After that first session, Heather drove Arthur and me home. While we were all together, a storm had passed through Bellingham and my favorite tree now lay fallen in my yard, split open right down the middle. I stepped over that tree and walked inside. I knew that Laird would be leaving, and I knew I needed to go too. Not to flee Bellingham, the boneyard of my major relationships, but to go toward nourishment, whatever and wherever that might lead.

What I would take with me: a memory. About three hours into the session, this image began repeating itself: me flat on my back, being pulled up to the sky, getting to the top and trying to open my chest, to offer myself up to that sky. But right at the moment I should open, I would recoil in fear and tumble back down, only to try to rise up and try again. Each time at that apex, I would feel this desire to splay myself open, and then this automatic terrified recoiling. The best gift I could give myself or any of them—Tim, Laird, even my mother—would be to stop the recoiling. To rise up out of myself. To open my chest and take flight.

CONSTELLATION

Start close in,
don't take the second step
or the third,
start with the first
thing
close in,
the step you don't want to take.

—David Whyte

79

CLASSICAL HOMEOPATHY

PURPOSE: With more than five thousand remedies in three classes (animal, vegetable, and mineral), homeopathic medicine seeks to enhance physical, mental, and emotional health by gently strengthening our innate ability to heal. Founded on the principle *like cures like*, the goal is to increase a patient's immunity in the least invasive, most rapid, and most permanent manner possible. Unlike most medicine, which tries to counteract a condition, the remedies work on the opposite principle.

DURATION: About an hour. Taking the remedy takes moments. Then you wait for the effect.

EQUIPMENT NEEDED: A heck of a lot of training by the homeopath and the remedy (in a tincture or infused in little sugary pellets under the tongue) are key.

AGE: 37.

RELATIONSHIP STATUS: Post-Hoasca-Anti-Stage-Five Clinger Wannabe.

HOMEOPATH: Krista Heron, ND.

REMEDY: Dog milk.

COST: $90.

LOCATION: Ravenna, Seattle, Washington.

Like treats like.

—*Samuel Hahnemann*

I had gone to Krista years ago with success. She was worth the drive. I thought the recent insights with the UDV might help her strengthen my constitution further. I hoped a subtle remedy boost (the less they are given, the more powerful, so it's not something to overdo) could help me continue to change things up in a positive manner. While my previous remedy had been the riparian parsley-like plant conium, Krista has now decided to give me dog milk. She only shares the remedy name weeks after I feel its effect.

"Milk," Krista explains, "is about nourishment. And the personality of the dog-milk remedy, in particular, is for the individual who may feel shame associated with needing that nourishment. Picture a cat. You can't shame a cat for being hungry—for anything, really. But you can shame a dog. Think about it."

I look down at Isabelle, who had snoozed through that appointment between Krista and me. I think of my mother's favorite expression of her father's growing up: *sucking a dry tit*.

Now I find myself ingesting the tiniest amounts of milk. Milk from some kinda dog. Nearly imperceptible doses are considered more powerful than more concentrated ones. If like treats like, apparently that's my kindred spirit: a dog in need of more nourishment, but ashamed to need.

Krista's Notes on Dog Milk:

1. The milk remedies struggle to cut the umbilical cord with their mother or with their family as a whole—learning to individuate.
2. To prescribe *Lac caninum*, you must have someone who tries to behave as you would like, not how they would like.
3. *Lac caninum* struggles to express anger freely. They'd like to be furious with rage: "I would like to bite these people." But they never do.
4. There is a part they want to vomit or wash out: something they cannot integrate. They feel a sense of disgust and self-loathing.
5. Often, the experience of a loss of an important relationship can be the starting point of their decompensation—losing something they longed for

before they could manifest the relationship. They have based their life on trying to secure a love relationship, so when they lose it, they do not want to admit the ways they did not like their primary love, or their mother or father, or admit that now they can be free.

6. The isolation of *Lac caninum* is very peculiar: they present as if they are isolated, but often find themselves in the center of things.

7. Some confusion in them and their family exists about the needs of the parents versus the needs of the child. These projections can prevent the mother or father from truly seeing the child's needs, desires, and individuality.

8. They struggle to know what they want. They are floating, feel inconsistent. If a child's own needs are not validated, how can they know who they are or their own desire? This lack of acknowledgment turns into anger, directed inward to become self-loathing. They suppress their anger and hide their aggression.

Thousands of remedies (not just dog milk) exist in homeopathy. Each client has a unique manifestation of a pattern. And two people helped by dog milk won't look alike, in the same way one orchid is distinct from the next.

Without knowing any of this at the time, drinking dog milk helped me gain momentum, to feel myself not as a failed daughter or failed wife, but to look for a full, rather than a dry, tit. Within hours, and through the subsequent weeks, I felt like a big ship with a decided course, cutting through strong seas with a powerful wake. I packed my car and headed out toward fullness.

80

CADAVER LAB/
YOGA TEACHER TRAINING

PURPOSE: To come face-to-face—body-to-body—with impermanence. This is acupuncture continuing education, as well as part of Richard Freeman's yoga teacher certification. Cadavers, you say? And yoga? Yes. Richard takes the body quite seriously. Dead and alive.

DURATION: Monthlong training. Before I started treating breakups as my cardio, I loved yoga. I want to remember that.

EQUIPMENT NEEDED: A lab containing the requisite cadavers. To donate your body requires much more paperwork than your standard organ donation. (Somehow this helps me.) Relative to other options (namely, living), these donors wanted to be here.

AGE: 37.

RELATIONSHIP STATUS: Single. Not looking. I'm quieter in this training than normal.

EMPLOYMENT: Acupuncturist.

COST: $100.

LOCATION: Boulder, Colorado. Fresh start.

Richard Freeman is what I would describe as the most intellectual, contemplative combination of yoga philosophers with the most advanced of asana practices. Not only can he recite and interpret the Bhagavad Gita with utter splendor, but he can do so (if required, which he never is) while wrapping his leg around his head fifteen times. And perhaps it's because he can wrap his leg around his head fifteen times that he knows it's not about that at all. It's about a deeper practice—a constant return to the breath. And today's instruction has us not in the studio breathing deeply but instead in this cadaver lab trying not to. There's a bit of a smell.

With lavender essential oil smeared under my nose as some pathetic attempt to lessen the formaldehyde odor (impossible), the bodies are more still, more empty, more fleshy than I imagined.

I find myself holding somebody's entire large intestine in my hands. It's hard to keep it all from spilling out of my palms. While I handle the organs with respect, they are awkward and inelegant. As we pass the rubbery thick digestive tract around, we then peer into the stomach, and then are handed one lobe of the lung. It is heavier than I imagined, and smaller. Like a thick, stiff, fully absorbed sponge.

I look at these bodies and think of my father, about how he doesn't believe in death. To him, death is that misunderstanding and mere concept. That idea, driven into me to somehow not take myself or difficulty or even something as obvious as physical form more seriously. But these bodies don't look like "misunderstandings." It's very clear. Death has passed through these forms and they are now empty.

We isolate an ovarian cyst. On the next cadaver, one student fails to recognize a particular appendage as a penis. We're all kind of embarrassed for him. I'm just thankful I'm not the one who made the gaffe. We peel back the layers of the perineum—the pelvic floor, a multistory trampoline structure of thick fibrous muscles. There are at least three levels to peel away. Maybe the midwife was right. Maybe there *are* four layers of the labia.

The cadaverist unpacks the brain and hands some of it to me. I remove the pituitary from the midbrain held between two bones. It looks like a little cave right behind the nose—an impressively small sucker of a gland, no bigger than a shriveled pea. As the master gland, it governs all hormones. This speck of a speck is responsible for every bad mood we ever have, each bout of PMS and

breast tenderness and bloat, our reproduction, our emotional life, our metabo-
lism. All that, run by this here pea. It boggles the mind—that mind, that brain,
that I will be lucky to use for another seventy years, tops. I'm curious to see the
plaque tangles associated with Alzheimer's brains. The cadaverist can't find any.
I think of those tangles and then of the little memory quizzes my mother has
started to give herself secretly and record in her diary. How many names, and
whose, she couldn't remember; how long it took to recall the name, all recorded
in minutes and hours; the failed hunts for names of objects she couldn't conjure. No friend or spouse to tell these secrets. Just this beautiful leather book
with her increasingly shaky writing within. I don't have the stomach to snoop
through the diary again. All because of some tangles I can't see.

I ask the cadaverist if he can show us where in the body the sensation of
butterflies emanates. I meant this as a purely technical question. He points to
the tissue above the diaphragm, the spot he believes responsible for every case
of nervous stomach and jitters we've had; frankly, the responsible area really
isn't all that near the stomach. I touch my belly and think of every love butterfly
or sinking piece of information that came from that spot.

I wish I could drag Dad in here. But I would literally have to drag him,
having knocked him unconscious first. This room and its educational mission
goes against everything he believes. Here, a physical end point is understood:
that last station stop for that train, that final eddy in the river before you are
washed out to sea.

The irony: Mom would have loved to see all this but now no longer would
understand these bodies. Dad would understand it but refuse to see. Renee
would likely be gagging under a gurney with an eye mask she quilted herself
and with sharpshooter earplugs stuffed in her nose. And here I stand, the genetic crossing of both those parents who made a woman with particularly dense
breast tissue; an anxious mind; at times, a goiterlike neck, other times an ag-
gressively thin frame; and, so far, no known tangles in my brain. Well, not of
plaque.

81

ADVANCED HAKOMI MEETS NEUROSCIENCE

PURPOSE: Majie now lives in Canada, so he's referring me to Phil—Majie's teacher—a nationally recognized Hakomi psychotherapist and trainer. Phil says his role with clients is to be an ally to their unfolding. I like that.

DURATION: Once a week. One hour and ten minutes. Phil is generous with the clock.

EQUIPMENT NEEDED: A highly trained professional.

AGE: 37.

RELATIONSHIP STATUS: It's obvious, right? *Sola.* Single. Alone. Solitudinal. *Independiente.*

EMPLOYMENT: I've been busy trying new things in addition to acupuncture. Been writing short stories. With all this, I need more passive income. Getting into Airbnb and renting out my Bellingham house and where I live in Boulder. People seem to like how I design things.

COST: $100 a session.

LOCATION: Boulder, Colorado.

Phil's big, warm eyes look at me. He keeps asking me the same question.

"What's it like between *you* and *you*?"

This is the strangest question. I much prefer to analyze what it's like between two *other* people or anybody else and me. Mom and Dad arguing over what love really means and my offering up trite toilet-book aphorisms; avoiding conversations about spirituality with my well-meaning stepmother; why my very presence in any room seems to drive Renee to the other side of it; why my wanting alone time occasionally with Dad is still considered heresy (and that adult postdivorce trip to SeaWorld doesn't count); what I tried to analyze about any man I'd ever been with and how I could be different so we could share in X, Y, Z. Even with girlfriends, I'm not one of those types to give the "I Need to Ask You for What I Need" speech.

I had these fantasies that if I were articulate, insightful, or funny enough, or likable or accomplished enough, I could pull my father out of his next project or his Highest Sense of Right. If I were clever enough, I could decipher my mother's disappearing language and pull her out of her sadness. If I were nonthreatening enough, I could get my sister to want to spend time with me. If I were yogic enough, I could get Laird to be different. If I were tough-love enough, I could have gotten Tim the help he needed earlier. If. If. *If.*

But when Phil asks, "What's it like between you and you?" I go blank.

"Uhh."

Literally blank. I don't even know where in my brain to go look. When I feel this blankness, I know I must turn toward it. So I do.

It is awkward and uncomfortable. But Phil insists I find those answers for myself and encourages me to experiment. These final experiments are of my own making, not from anybody else. Just me.

82

ACCIDENTALLY WRITE AND PERFORM A ONE-WOMAN SHOW

PURPOSE: Try to find a narrative arc in your life that, even if it makes you look like the biggest chunk-shlub in the world, still might help a stranger have a laugh and get through their own challenges a bit faster and more gently.

DURATION: Eighty minutes (about).

EQUIPMENT NEEDED: Simple props. My stage looks like an acupuncture treatment room/therapy office. What a surprise.

AGE: 37.

RELATIONSHIP STATUS: Special to have family and friends come. Quite the reunion. My aunt Donny and her kids came. And my kind stepsibs. Coco wore a name tag that said *Renee*. Coco hoped she'd show. So did I.

COST: You won't believe how cheap it is to rent a little theater in Boulder, Colorado.

HUMILIATION FACTOR: Some excellent risk factors: a roomful of strangers, a lot of words, and me. Weirdly, I was more nervous to treat my first patient. The good news? Embarrassment isn't dangerous.

LOCATION: Boulder, Colorado.

Coco and I not only bonded philosophically over acupuncture styles. We also seem to have stomached our own losses in parallel. She, her eyes. Mine, my marriage, and possibly my SSRI seven-day mind. And two mothers with Alzheimer's. Coco coped with lots of stillness and time alone, listening to audiobooks, trying to distract herself from thinking about what she could no longer see. I coped with dramatic gestures and relational antics. And Coco would say that, like with acupuncture, it was her dogged curiosity that kept her from dumping me as a friend when I was so man-obsessed, kept her trying to understand why somebody (me) would make such polar-opposite decisions than she would. Like watching (absurd) reality TV.

On my end, I felt this urge to distract and amuse her by turning the day's/week's/month's antics into stories: the eggs, the sticks, the doula births, the surveillance. So I wrote them down and read them to an audience of one, Coco, hoping to create a counterpoint to her reality—encroaching blindness—from which there was no escape. I'd be lying if I didn't admit that writing was a place to let my freak flag fly. Perhaps the stories helped us both feel rooted, to mark that we were both still here—even as we lost our mothers word by word, helped us see and be seen not just by others, but each other.

The stories became quite a pile.

"Now that you aren't obsessing over Laird anymore, maybe you should take that energy and *do* something *new*."

"Well, I've been thinking," I say shyly, "of stringing them together and speaking them. Like a long version of that *Moth* performance thing I did in Bellingham, mixed with that singing-lesson recital in my acupuncture office I did with my singing teacher. You know, like one long story . . . like a *show* . . ." I'm embarrassed to say the word *show* out loud. Even to Coco.

"A show . . ." Coco is thinking. Not judging.

"Kind of like putting on a play with friends when we were little, no?" I ask Coco. She then replies with a burst, laughing around her words:

"You know what you should *do*? You should go to the Boulder Dairy Theater. They converted an old dairy into performance spaces. You should go rent a theater and do it!"

"A dairy? That sounds amazing." I laugh with delight. I picture cute cows and milk pails and straw, with shows in little horse stalls. *My kind of theater.*

"Well, maybe . . . maybe only if you would critique me? And Leah too?"

As luck and irony would have it, Leah—my Bellingham singing teacher—had moved to Coco's town of Fort Collins.

"It could be like the fun of putting on an eighth-grade play, but as adults, right?"

And that was exactly what it was like. My grade-school friend, actress, and writer Spencer in New York helped me string the stories together, and then Leah, Coco, and I would gather in Fort Collins parks, Coco's living room, and Leah's backyard, and I would memorize and tell the stories. An unknown benefit/skill of acupuncture school was how many role-playing scenarios we had to do, so we were experienced at critiquing each other and our authenticity as we practiced our patient-interviewing skills.

I walked into the Dairy in May. They had a week open in July.

"How much is the Black Box Theater?"

"A hundred bucks."

"Are you kidding? A hundred-seat theater? One hundred dollars a night? Christ, everyone should host a show. I'm in."

I took all the open nights they had. I had six weeks to get it together.

So, should writing and performing your own show be a calling, here's a high-speed list of the *how* of it:

Write some stuff down that you think matters or, in the very least, you think worth retelling; have friends help you cut out the useless/poorly written/dullard parts; memorize your stories while walking your four-legged in circles around your neighborhood, saying your whole show out loud; find some props from your living room and office—massage table, stability ball, therapy chairs; practice some more; laugh really hard at idiotic mistakes; accelerate toward embarrassment—it makes the whole thing easier.

Don't care if you are *profound* or good at it, just do it; get really panicky that you will host a show and not a single person will buy a ticket except maybe your dad and some pervy old man with loud plastic bags in his lap eating a sandwich; take yourself and your furry Isabelle to Boulder County Farmers Market and, while they pet her (she loves strangers of all kinds), pass out flyers while saying, "Come to a funny show with a funny woman" and when they ask, "Who is this funny woman?" say, "I am the funny woman," and try to keep a straight face at how foolheaded this sounds, and not die of humiliation; be grateful for terror as a continued motivation; run an ad on Craigslist for a lighting designer; meet lighting designer (petite Korean woman named Sophia) the night before the show; when your co-director Leah's husband is rushed to the emergency room with nausea and stomach pains during the dress rehearsal, try not to take this personally; be grateful he turns out okay and that she can still come for the real thing.

Try not to worry when your blind friend has to hold a very tall ladder in the dark theater with the pint-sized Sophia teetering at the top, adjusting gel lights (too bad Isabelle lacks opposable thumbs and prefers snoozing on the cool cement floor); forget that you need to rent sound equipment and watch Coco try to hide behind the curtains to see if holding up a Bose boom box is loud enough (turns out it isn't, no matter where Coco thrusts out the speaker from behind the black velvet curtain); realize you will need to rent sound equipment, which is maybe why the theater is so cheap; find comfortable shoes and a dress; be shocked when you oversell your tickets and have to bring in extra chairs; practice your narrative again; pray you don't go blank once you hit the stage and see the hundred-plus faces in front of you; practice the small bit in the middle and the end when you sing.

Keep going even if you mess up; never point out your mistakes, even if you've been pointing out your mistakes your whole life to everyone; be grateful that a friend could fly with your mother so she could see it too; be aghast your mother asks whether you've had implants (no); realize that your chosen dress might have been cut too low and try to fix it; thank Michelle and Scott for the Dairy party they throw on the last night; have it go well enough to take it to a little festival in New York City, where you, Coco, Leah, and Sophia enjoy being the most wide-eyed, least-trendy people in the festival; be thankful that you and your friends haven't lost that enthusiasm for putting on plays and telling stories you believe in, a combination of qualities your little troupe shares that comes from the innocence of youth peppered with a hearty appreciation for finding the good in the hard knocks.

83

DATE YOURSELF

PURPOSE: Call it a refresher on the real you. Although I hate that phrase. Like all relationships, the one with oneself merits special attention. Consider the classics: the Friday and Saturday nights, the Sunday brunches.

DURATION: Unclear. Maybe I'll get lucky tonight.

EQUIPMENT NEEDED: I recommend full pre-date antics: the shower, the special outfit, the shave, the wax, whatever does it for you. Although if I get a Brazilian, I'm pre-dating with tequila.

AGE: 38.

RELATIONSHIP STATUS: Single. Whatever.

COST: Dinner tab.

HUMILIATION FACTOR: Say your best self-loathing things to yourself for, like, five minutes. Then ditch all that and have fun.

LOCATION: Denver and Dolores, Colorado.

It's embarrassing (at first) to go on a date with myself. Because a cultural assumption exists that because you're solo, you couldn't get anybody better to join. Ridiculous. So I'm taking that one down. Killin' it. Whether married or single, straight or gay, very few of us get all that much pleasurable downtime with ourselves in the same way we get it with other people.

Also, it's kind of like orgasms: helps to know solo what a good one feels like so you'll recognize who's giving you an excellent one. If I don't know what I am looking for . . . well . . . you see where I'm headed. So I'm backing up. The simple date. I had solo and partnered orgasms down fine. The self-enjoyment (not in bed) thing? Not so much. It had been a very long time since I got any really good social kick out of myself.

I started out with a romantic dinner. Okay, a lightly romantic dinner. Okay, not romantic at all: the Cheesecake Factory. *What can I say, I happen to love their Caesar. Which—by the way—can easily feed a family of ten. Cheap date.*

I brought a book. And a pad of paper to draw. While the book made me feel like a spinster, with the doodling I felt like a dining rebel. It felt kinder to fancy myself a doodling, self-dating, dining rebel. I ordered my favorite Caesar salad, my favorite margarita with my favorite tequila.

It's not as if I'd never eaten alone in a restaurant before. This was more like going on a date with somebody who, for years, had just been a friend, but we wanted to check out the deeper potential, so we stepped it up. The same motions: the appetizers, the wine, the food, but now very consciously on a *date*.

There's the question of what to talk about with myself or, for that matter, what else to do. I've always been a fan of eavesdropping. Lucky for me, I have a gift for eavesdropping and doodling simultaneously. I ate. I drank. I joked with the waiter. Polished off the marg and headed home. No good-night kiss.

But I *just might* call me the next day. I thought she was sort of interesting.

After a few more dinner dates, I step up my level of commitment: the weekend getaway. I pick the very special Dunton Hot Springs outside Telluride, Colorado. The place is built for couples, but I'll sort that out. Technically, with Isabelle, we're a party of two. The Dunton bar allegedly served Butch and Sundance their first beers after they robbed their first bank. The fact that a female drunk sales executive from San Diego is dancing on the bar to keep her geriatric date interested frankly gives the Butch-Sundance thing a run for its money.

After full bellies and an endless ball session in the twilight (Isabelle could and would, if asked, happily retrieve till dawn), Isabelle and I head to our cabin, which is where Bilbo Baggins and Robert Redford would honeymoon, should they marry. Original Western log nineteenth-century chinking, but with tiny arched doors to duck through to get to the bathroom.

With a hot spring a stone's throw from my cabin—but without someone whose eyes I could gaze into with oogly-googly longing—I didn't want to blow the best activity at the get-go. (I also brought my taxes, in case I couldn't gut out the leisure stuff.)

By morning, after a hike with Isabelle (including a few uphill off-trail sprints to prevent Isabelle's out-of-her-mind-I-must-chase-and-say-hello-to-those-whitetail-deer), I thought the whole dating thing was going pretty well. I mean, I wasn't ready to make any marriage proposals, but I'd do me.

At nightfall, I crawled via ladder down into a large, sunken, barrel-like hot spring to take in the night sky. Turns out, I wasn't so good at taking in the night sky alone. None of that, "Are you sure that's Orion's Belt?" Or, "Ever seen the northern lights?" I knew the answer to both. Yes, that's really Orion's belt; I'm sure of it. And, yes, I've seen the northern lights. They were greenish and brief.

So in lieu of soft talk, I gaze up at the stars and find myself feeling shy and a little awkward to be with myself. I feel young and vulnerable, and kind of sweet. Like I can remember this soft part of me that is still very much in need of care. I try to sit through the discomfort of feeling this shy-sweet-what-am-I-really-about-sort-of-thing. When I think I can't bear it one more second, I bear it one second more. Turns out this kind-softness to myself feels rather delightful. Delightful enough that I start trying to drag the date out.

The small valley looks like a miniature old town, with the quaintest dotting of cabins right out of the most idyllic Western. I decide to go for a stroll. Isabelle and I walk through the oil torches that illuminate the road like a work of art. Her jangly turquoise collar is the only sound other than our footsteps. I head to the library and nestle into a wingback chair to peruse a German design book while sipping whiskey they leave out. I don't think I'll like whiskey, but it seems like an experience I should have. In lieu of a sexy foot massage, I remove my shoes and rub my feet on my first bearskin rug. Isabelle splays on her back there too, offering her belly for a rub and a scratch. I oblige. After a spell, I meander back toward our Bilbo cabin. I stop on the carless dirt road and lie down with my face up to the stars. I think: *If I were with someone, I would do this.*

I will never have this moment back. And so, I rest. I rest on my back and breathe in the night sky while scratching Isabelle's flank. I count three shooting stars. I stay until I'm too cold to stay any longer.

I gather myself, taking my own hand, my own heart, my own self back to the snuggly warm down comforter that Isabelle and I will burrow into. If I feel racy, I might do so naked. But only if it's extra toasty in the cabin.

I'm definitely going to marry this woman. This weekend clinched it. Turns out, she's a keeper. At least for me.

84

THE HOFFMAN PROCESS

PURPOSE: "An intensive residential course of personal discovery and development. The process allows you to examine your life and your behavior and empowers you to make lasting changes while increasing emotional intelligence and spirituality." I'm considering it. Harvard Business School recommends it.

DURATION: 8 days.

EQUIPMENT NEEDED: Luggage *and* baggage. With the willingness to unload both.

AGE: Marching toward 40.

RELATIONSHIP STATUS: I am almost never without Isabelle at my side. She bounds along wherever we go but seems to know when we have to use our inside voices too. I miss Taraco, but with Isabelle's mere thirty-five pounds and sweet nature, even a few places that don't allow dogs let us break some rules.

COST: $4,295.

HUMILIATION FACTOR: We will discuss.

LOCATION: St. Helena, California.

I'm back in touch with my childhood friend Kimberly's parents, Marilyn and Gary (the ones who did the EST children's training road trip with us, who also studied with Lawrence). We've spoken intermittently, as old friends do. They too have a mother with Alzheimer's and, like most people, have complicated family issues in dealing with such things. That's largely what we've been catching up about—the way our mothers look and feel so different. The way I can literally sense the ebbing of her consciousness and the volume of light decreasing in my mother's eyes, to the way her body has less force to animate her being.

And did I mention? They want me to do the Hoffman Process. I got the Big E-mail Plug about it. I know an E-mail Plug when I see one. I've heard about the Hoffman Process. And despite my conditioned practice of acknowledging there's *always more we can learn* (still one of my mother's favorite sayings, I might add; I would have no problem if she forgot that one), I'm willing to bet my right frontal lobe that I'm sufficiently familiar with the Hoffman terrain. I say this without pride, more like a checklist of sorts. Like traveling to Europe, but not just the top hits. I mean the thorough itinerary—beyond the photo in front of the Leaning Tower of Pisa. I mean like: slog to the top of Mont Blanc, check. Hijack a gondola in Venice, check. Tickle a Vatican guard, check. Lean into Stonehenge, like give it a really good push, checkity-check.

I hear Hoffman helps you map out your family of origin in some sort of exhaustive list/diorama so your family issues don't grip you as they once did. Check. I hear the idea is to take "time out of your life to examine your life" and talk about how it was formed. Check. Check. I hear you'll explore how to forgive your parents while understanding how you've rejected or adopted their negative traits. Check. Check. Check. I hear by treading in your own murky waters and getting more clear, the Hoffster will help you develop deeper compassion for your fellow humans. I hear you hit things with a big stick or baton, for heaven's sake. Christ, I'll volunteer to teach that one myself.

So I'm going to go against my conditioning and kindly decline the Hoffman Process. I'm putting my money on the Megan Process, without needing to recruit anybody to try it too. So God love 'em, even if Marilyn and Gary met Allah, Mother Mary, the Buddha himself, or if Kenny Loggins is a huge fan, I *ain't doing* it. I bet it's fabulous. And you know what? I'm still not doing it. You heard me. And any extra $4,295 that crosses my path, it's going into savings, or Alzheimer's research, or swimming the Arno, or, Christ, a much longer trip to Dunton.

It's not that I'll never try anything again. I just know that deferring to my own authority may mean saying a kind *no, thank you* more than in the old days. And while I may not get the same pleasure of thinking of myself as someone who's game for most any experiment, in exchange I garner the new pleasure of how it feels to trust myself. Although, if they *really* did meet the Buddha . . .

85

SPEND TIME WITH MAASAI SCHOOLKIDS

PURPOSE: I have been invited by the founder of the International Community for the Relief of Suffering and Starvation (ICROSS), a network of primary-care clinics across Kenya, to document the work of his clinics and visit corresponding Rift Valley Maasai schools. I'm writing for a new blog.

DURATION: Fourteen days.

EQUIPMENT NEEDED: Nothing.

AGE: 40.

RELATIONSHIP STATUS: I tried *taking a lover* in Brooklyn on my way to and from Kenya. Met him at Burning Man. Screams cliché. As for the *lover* part, what a bust. I'm not cut out for the casual deal. Casual kissing, maybe. Sex is apparently never casual to me.

EMPLOYMENT: Still an acupuncturist, but the Airbnb stuff is going remarkably well. Meanwhile I come to Kenya in a rather official capacity—as a freelance writer. Jenny, a professional photographer and friend, joins me.

COST: Plane ticket. Wasn't cheap.

LOCATION: Great Rift Valley and Karen, Kenya.

I now stand in front of a room packed with fifty Maasai schoolchildren. I get to interview them in small groups with my shy friend Jenny. I am interested in knowing what they imagine for their lives, what troubles them, what brings them joy. Before we get started, I figure it's only fair they get to ask anything they want of Jenny and me: two white man–less women traveling solo. This is what they want to know in this order:

1. What is the staple of our diet?
2. What do we think of Barack Obama?
3. How do we bury our dead?

I try to cover 1 and 2 simultaneously. I make a gross generalization saying much of the country is thrilled about Obama. The ones that are thrilled tend to eat more vegetables. The ones who are less thrilled tend to eat more meat and potatoes. The Maasai children find this confusing, as they—not just as Maasai warriors, but as Kenyans—are thrilled about Obama. But they also mostly eat meat (and the occasional potato), as they are a nomadic culture becoming less nomadic by the year. I try to clarify that I've made a bit of a stereotype that is more of a joke. It is thrilling to make these kids laugh—to feel humor crossing linguistic boundaries. They laugh before anything is translated. Like we all know the universal rhythm of humor without needing to know every word.

As for how we dispose of our dead, I rather simply explain we like to be buried, burned, or thrown into the ocean. Upon hearing my summary, Jenny—who is quite possibly as shy as I am extroverted—feels compelled to speak up. She mumbles to me that I need to clarify that we just don't wing our dead out of boats and into the sea. We burn them first. And we use a nicer word: cremation. And as for the burning idea (which seems to horrify the kids), Jenny would like to make sure I also clarify we aren't burning anybody alive. I am to stress we do this ever so respectfully and only after our loved ones have passed.

So while I stand here trying to tackle death, politics, and diet in a one-two punch, it occurs to me there are about five hundred things I'm grateful they aren't asking me about. To that end, I hope they haven't noticed the teensy-weensy (previously not so teensy-weensy) droop of my left eyelid. I'm praising some higher power that I don't have to explain:

1. Why I would willingly (aka enthusiastically) shoot Botox (aka the botulinum toxin) into my forehead.

2. How it is I became the lucky one in five hundred bastards to have my botulinum migrate into my left eyelid, rendering a me a one-eyed Quasimodo for about six sexy weeks. And while I've passed the phase of literally needing to prop up my lid with my index finger in order to make any proper use of my second eyeball, I still might not look quite right.

3. Should they notice my lingering subtle droop, this would shoot us directly into a far trickier conversation than death and burial: like why in the world do we in the United States hide our age? How did it come to be that I don't just shoot up Botox, but sleep in a bra, trying to keep everything north of town—quietly fighting aging like it's a high crime?

4. I'm also thrilled not to have to explain that I (and others) choose to purposely starve myself for up to twenty-one days a year—all in the name of longevity and anticancer research, peppered with the tinge of an eating disorder. I do so all the while surrounded by an endless supply of gorgeously colorful, antioxidant-rich, high-quality food. And even with access to such amazing food, how could I possibly explain to them we still die of nutrient deficiencies and diseases of excess rather than scarcity? But that's like a whole talk (or another chapter).

5. Why we feel a need to co-opt other cultures. Like why we asked a Brazilian shaman, a Buddhist, and a Native American to come bless my acupuncture school, but would never ask the Protestant pastor down the road to bless our former-dentist-office-cum-Taoist-acupuncture-school in Louisville, Colorado.

6. While on the subject of ritual, I'm thrilled I don't have to explain my Brooklyn-lover attempt at Burning Man. And regarding Burning Man, who wants to explain how you can't tell whether a giant tepee in the middle of the desert filled with sleeping people is an art installation or merely random attendees passed out, having lost their way back to their tents.

While we are at it, I can also say I'm thrilled to not have to explain therapy involving a bataka bat, talking to pillows, self-administered EMDR, going commando, and my experiments not wearing underpants as a means to find freedom; nor grocery-store therapy assigned by a licensed therapist, where I end up with corn dogs, potato salad, and gummy frogs in my basket as an actual exercise; nor my current musing whether first-aid military antishock pants can be used for emotional trauma as well as physical trauma (keeping the blood in your core when in shock).

I guess you can say that at least we are trying? To construct ritual and alternative culture in the face of a dearth of both? I suppose this circles us back to why I'm torn over our "documenting" these Maasai kids in the first place. We sense they've got something we don't, yet we can't help but visit with some air of superiority.

I think I should end this school interview and just give one of these kids Jenny's camera, a notepad, and a plane ticket, and say: "You want a really good laugh? Come see the trouble *we* Westerners have gotten ourselves into."

86

FACING DEATH

PURPOSE: Meet my mother wherever she is. Phil and I talk about this Sanskrit term *darshan* a lot. It means *to see*. That sometimes one needs to just go see—to see things exactly as they are, not need them to be different.

DURATION: One month.

EQUIPMENT NEEDED: Beyond hideous sweatpants, nothing but the intent to bring all of me.

AGE: 40.

RELATIONSHIP STATUS: I am alone. Solitude has been my other teacher. And it's not permanent.

EMPLOYMENT: Acupuncturist, aspiring writer, landlord, Airbnb host.

COST: Short-notice plane ticket. One phone session with Phil midmonth.

LOCATION: Langley, Whidbey Island, Washington.

I just got the call. Mom has fallen and broken her hip and neck at her farm.

"Head hit the safety railing. Her feet slipped out from under her on those river-rock steps in front of the house," Renee tells me. I find this ironic. The safety railing. "Mom was refilling one of the bird feeders."

Mom is single-handedly trying to feed the entire bird population on the small Northwest island where she lives. Renee still lives there too, just up the road with Rich and little Kelsey. Mom was at the heart of where Renee wanted to build her own family. Renee and Rich married on the farm in a stunning fall wedding. Conceived on a visit. And then Mom got diagnosed with Alzheimer's. Wasn't the plan.

As for this neck and hip break, postsurgery, she will be weeks in rehab. And then, as it often is with the elderly, there will be trips in and out of the hospital. This and the hospital stay itself will tax her. But this time, my sister's call tells me this could be it. They don't know. Nobody knows.

Now I am on a plane. Now I am waiting for Isabelle via kennel near the luggage carousel. They say Portuguese water dogs have an extra octave that easily identifies them. And it's true. I hear her distinct high bark (and her kennel) approaching. Now we are in the rental car driving north, both peering through the rainy windshield, wiper blades working overtime. I hate this soupy city and its weather. If I time it right, we can be through downtown catching the next ferry in forty-five, but I doubt it.

Two boats later, we are dumped onto the island, now chugging up the hill through the downpour. It's dark. I wished I'd figured out where I was staying tonight, but there wasn't time. Not with Renee. It's not that I'm uninvited, but I haven't been invited. I drive slowly through the village, looking for that right turn.

When I get there, I enter the living room/de facto lobby of the care facility. Renee is on the phone with a doctor. She waves, then waves me on. She looks tired. Apparently, my mother's room is at the end of the hall. My last thought before entering is: *Remember, she'll be smaller. She will look different. That's okay. Just go with it, whatever she looks like. Join her there.*

She is a miniature version of herself. And she is throwing up. The care provider is making sure my mother keeps hold of the large Tupperware bowl while saliva drips and hangs thickly from her mouth. Her eyes are watering. Here comes another retch. Small blurbs of bile seem to be the only thing coming out.

I know they haven't been able to keep anything down her in days. I understand the nausea has been unabating.

Oh, my little mama. My sweet mama.

"You finished?" Kathy, the care provider, asks. Mom sort of nods and looks over at me.

"Hi, Mom. It's Megan." I climb onto the bed. I can't really hug her with the neck brace. It's a Lilliputian neck brace—a child's small—but it's still too big for her. I lean in to kiss her cheek. She smells sour. Kathy, the care provider, wants to get in there and change the padding on her brace. This place is spotless. The owner was a colonel army nurse and that fact is obvious as I look around.

I curl up next to my mom. She can't look down at me, but I can move my head to get a good look in her eyes. She looks exhausted. I ask how she's feeling.

"Not good. Not good at all. I don't know about all this business, Megan. I don't know." She never complains. So this means something.

"I know, Mama. It looks rough. The worst, really. It looks like you are having a go of it."

Nobody knows what's causing the nausea. The inability to eat. Is it the pain medication or some sort of infection? The mystery will continue for weeks. I will find a rhythm here. Just not an easy one. When I am not in the room with her (the care providers don't like us here all the time; there are rules), Isabelle and I walk in the rain; I make phone calls. Although most of my life is on hold, the e-mails are backing up. But I don't care. I start reading *Winnie-the-Pooh* out loud to her. My own mother's reading cadences come back to me. Maybe I am channeling the memory. I am six years old now, stretched out on the giant leopard-print beanbag, with my mother next to me. Only today I am the one reading. I will read about Pooh and Piglet going searching for a Heffalump. My mother smiles in recognition. She knows this story like the back of her hand. While she couldn't recall it, she can ride the familiarity. And with Alzheimer's, it seems the oldest stories stay the longest. Maybe I'll stick with this one for a few days.

Sometimes I crawl onto the bed and ask the questions I know no one is asking. There's this assumption that she should be fighting to live. That she should get herself to eat at any cost. And fight the infection as hard as she can. I'm not sure this is what she wants. I've met the hospice nurse. Nobody knows if she's coming or going.

When I am alone with her again, next to her again, I take a breath and ask quietly, "Mom. Are you ready to go? Are you tired of this, or are you interested in what's next? Do you want to stick around? Do you know?"

She looks at me with wide-open, wet blue eyes, takes a big breath, and looks like she's really mulling the idea of leaving or staying. There is a flash of relief across her face. I imagine it as a fleeting flash of a sense of power or control. Like midfight, it hadn't occurred to her that it really still is all up to her. Maybe she's been so caught up in the fight, there'd been no time to consider this.

"That's a really good question. I don't like feeling like this anymore. I want it to be done. The idea of finding out what's next sounds nice, but I don't know. I don't know. I'll have to give that some thought . . ."

I want her to know that anything is okay. I don't know how to impart that sense of permission or freedom to her. So I talk about eagles. That's her animal. Her power animal. She read a book on a plane about shamanism once, flying to Chicago to help a childhood friend of mine in a shamanic ceremony. Mom met her power animal in, like, five minutes, after closing her eyes. This woman has the most unusual and unexpected gifts.

In my quietest voice, I conjure an eagle in my head and ask gently, "You wanna fly around up there?" And I start making those sounds like I'm the wind. Or like we are in the wind together. Like an eagle is catching wind under its wings. A faint whistle. She seems to like the sound. She closes her eyes. She makes a little of the sound herself. She's tired. I kiss her good night. I find myself touching her soft face and hair more bravely and tenderly than I ever have. And she lets me.

The days wear on. More vomiting. More measuring her fluid intake in teaspoons, not cups. Nothing seems to stay down. Between the vomiting, I read to her or she sleeps. *Winnie-the-Pooh* again. She laughs sometimes. Other times it is too much. I don't know if the reading makes a difference. But I think it might.

I close each night by reading Mary Oliver. Mom's favorite poet. Because of her memory, she won't remember that I read "Wild Geese" last night or the night before that or the night before that. But I have. And I will read this poem again tomorrow. We will read of the geese and their skyward return. Of all the landscapes we must move through to reach home.

. . .

This is her poem. Our poem. A poem between us. A poet that links her to me. And it fits here. I am sure it fits here. Wild geese heading home. Somewhere through the nausea, through the fatigue, I know this poem is talking to some part of her still here.

The thing is, she's not who she was. But at the same time, she is. Both here and absent simultaneously. I crawl onto the bed and look at her. And she looks back. Blue eyes wide open. So much expression in those eyes. Then, out of nowhere, she takes her index finger and starts ever so lightly tracing the contours of my face. Over my cheeks (I have her cheeks), around my nose (I have her nose). Her finger lingers at the tip. And she touches it a few times repeatedly. It's her way of telling me she loves me. As her finger reads my face, I know this is one of those moments that will never leave me.

But now, her infection is back. And she's weaker. I enter her room the next morning to find her mouth hanging wide open. Her face, a fixed stare gazing off toward the window. The caregiver looks distressed, wondering if it's a stroke. Her mouth was open all night and her tongue has dried out and now it is bloody. A bright, red raw spot right in the middle of the tongue. I ask the caregiver where I can find a glycerin swab to moisten her lips and tongue. I dab the spot, but it stays bloody. My mother officially looks like one of those people I remember seeing when I was a little girl volunteering at old-age homes. I tell myself that the Alzheimer's makes everything look worse. When an infection comes, the body is too taxed to complete normal cognitive functions. Her eyes won't stop watering.

Her fever rages. The *Clostridium difficile*, or *C. diff*, is back. But I won't learn this until later in the day. I planned to fly home today, but I can't leave her like this. I can't make contact today, and I won't leave without making contact.

I've been here now for a month, riding this line between life and death I've never been so close to before. When I was eight, my best friend Julie and I dug up her buried hamster to see what death had done to Miss Piggy. A week postburial and Miss Piggy's body was softer. It twisted easily as I lifted her out of the shoebox, her peach fur falling out in my hands and catching the wind like thistles. I had thought digging her up merited a second funeral, and so I sprinkled her shoebox coffin with mustard blossoms and placed her back in the ground. This is about all that I know.

But back at the care facility, we are still on the edge of life. But it's hovering. It could fall either way in this small, tidy room today. If it looked like death, I could follow it out. If it looked like her staying alive, I could join that too. I realize that somewhere inside me, I think I would prefer she go now while she still knows who her loved ones are. I wonder whether this one thought might make me a horrible person. There's also something quite natural about deciding not to fight, whatever way it goes. Even if it stays in a gray area. Hovering indefinitely—well, until it doesn't.

I've taken to sleeping in my clothes on the couch. I am staying in the barn we built together. I sleep right next to the wood-burning stove, with my back to the thirteen-foot-long cement table that always privately seemed—to the architects, my mother, and me—more sacrificial altar than kitchen counter. We loved that. And so each day with my back to the altar, my face to the fire, my wake-up call comes in the form of a temperature drop. When the fire dies out, the chill stirs me. I've also taken to sleeping with my shoes on. I think it's odd, but it seems easier. Why bother taking them off? I'll just have to put them on again. I haven't taken a bath in days, but my head is elsewhere. The barn well is having a challenge, so Renee tells me I can shower in her guest room, but I cannot take a bath in her yellow bathroom with the sunken tub. She tells me that my entering her bathroom would be an invasion of her private space. This hurts. I say little. I postpone the shower. It's become too loaded a topic. When the infection gets in check, I will head home. I recall the way Arctic geese drop down to accompany the sick and the injured until the birds pass or improve. Only then do the companion geese rejoin the flock.

And her infection passes. I know something will be back. Something will get all of us, just not today. I say my good-byes and try to make it like any other day, but I try to remember her face as it is, in case today is the last day.

I board the plane. As it takes off, we lift out of Seattle's gray cloud bank and hover far above the city's clouds, now flooded in sunshine. I can't really explain it, but amid the sunshine, I feel somehow turned toward life in a way I don't remember ever feeling. None of what happened here is good news, but I feel touched by the fleeting nature of what I hold dear. I just want to eat up everything I can while I am still here. I want to eat big meals, run long distances, and have a really good laugh. I act on the urge to ring up people I haven't spoken to in ages. Life is calling to me stronger than ever. Like wild geese.

87

CORD CUTTING

PURPOSE: A virtual boundary-establishing exercise to beat all boundary exercises. A shamanic practice of literally cutting your energetic cord with another.

DURATION: Takes three seconds. Correction. Something like a decade and three seconds.

EQUIPMENT NEEDED: A vivid mind's eye.

AGE: 40+. I've decided from here on to make this my permanent age.

RELATIONSHIP STATUS: Single and happy. Not happy to be single or unhappy to be single. Happy. Single. Two separate facts.

COST: Financially, free. Emotionally, depends on the relationship.

LOCATION: Boulder, Colorado. But technically this is the locationless location of all locations. The Internet: everywhere, somewhere, nowhere.

Idiot Compassion: Something we do a lot of and call it compassion. It's the tendency to give people what they want because you can't bear to see them suffering. Instead of offering a friend medicine, bitter though it may be when ingested, you feed them more poison—at the very least, you don't take it away from them . . . This is not compassion at all. It's selfishness, as you're more concerned with your own feelings than attending to your friend's actual needs.

—*Pema Chödrön*

For the longest time I wanted to think of myself (not that I would admit this) as the Mother Teresa of ex-wives. It was *really* important to me that Tim think well of me.

Perhaps (and I can barely admit this to myself) I wanted the last word, which was (silently): "Despite all the shattered trust from Hookergate, and the level of risk you exposed me to, I will show you that I am kind until the end. And I hope that makes you feel bad." Maybe I wanted to outnice him. Sometimes I've thought that was what I was doing. Other times, I just think I possess a hearty dose of understanding. The world is not easy, and some of us, injured in deep early ways from which recovery may be impossible. I hope he is not in that group. Mostly I didn't think Tim should be punished more than the internal torment he was likely still living—day in, day out—with a problem so much larger than himself. And I truly still love this man, flaws and all. I had grown up with him. It was complex, and yet, still that simple.

But I wondered if I had taken the Mother-Teresa-Possible-Ego-Trip-in-My-Own-Mind thing too far. Somewhere between me and me, it had been more important to be likable than authentic. And between me and me, I wasn't sure I liked that about me. For whom was my continued friendship with Tim? For me? For him? Did it even make sense in this stage of my life? Did I even want it? Did he? Or was he staying friends out of guilt, and was I just dragging him through some occasional social niceties so I could feel all good about myself? All puffed up like a blowfish, like, no matter what, I was kind? I suspected as such. Yuck. So I changed my mind. And through my travels, I had harnessed enough of myself to do so.

Quietly, on a day like any other day, in a gesture far more powerful to me than our divorce, I cut ties. From the cutting of an invisible cord that still connected us in my mind's eye to the social feeds we even just lightly shared. I imagine he didn't even notice. I just slipped away. I wished him no antagonism—quite the opposite. I knew that our time or, better said, my time, was done. I had loved him deeply and love him still. But that day, I laid down the burden of helping him peripherally navigate his life. Not that he asked me to do that exactly. It's just we never figured out new terms—how or why to be in each other's lives after a rupture like that. Not a lot of closure there. So I made my own. Now, with all I knew of myself, I no longer needed to be his friend in any public way. And if laying down my Mother Teresa Habit eased some or *any* of his pain, and my idiot compassion, all the better.

I know what we had, know how I behaved, and am proud (albeit critical) of all I tried, and I know he tried his best too. Truly. He gave what he could, the best that he could. And I, him. Phil taught me that.

I know he is a beautiful man, an accomplished man, a kind man, a lying man, a playful man, a dedicated man, a secretive man, a generous man, a haunted man, an intelligent man, a sensitive man, and, like all of us, flawed. And now, he was an important man in my life to whom I could say good-bye. I felt born again and also as if something had died. Some tether loosened and I let it go. Like cutting an internal cord. A brain wire. A snip out there in the ether.

On Tim's and my first trip to Patagonia, we were part of a river rescue. At a crucial part of the river crossing, the rope that was to pull the stranded students to our side of the river fell right out of their hands, and we watched that tiny cord float down the river, untethered to anything or anyone.

One minute I was holding the rope. The next minute it was gone.

88

SING HYMNS

PURPOSE: Not what you'd think, exactly.

DURATION: In this case, less than an hour.

EQUIPMENT NEEDED: A computer that can both play music and display lyrics. Like a karaoke hymnal.

AGE: 40+.

RELATIONSHIP STATUS: I've started mulling about thawing an egg. In the meantime, I still love dog-parenting my furry four-legged. She has personality bursting at the seams of her curly self. If she were a tarot card, she might be the trickster, helping me not take myself too seriously.

COST: More plane tickets. Three, to be exact.

LOCATION: Whidbey Island, Washington.

My father is flying up to see Mom. He did not ask. He announced. What he means by this is he will fly up with Margie for an administration of Christian Science at Mom's bedside. Despite it coming from a well-meaning place in them, it's hard not to feel the unspoken sentiment, which is, if Mom still practiced Christian Science, she wouldn't have run into this tricky Alzheimer's business in the first place. He doesn't say this, but this is what he thinks and plans to remedy. I know him.

When it comes to Dad and Mom, I lived not only as the nosy eavesdropper on their endless velvety-chair talks, but as a self- (or de facto?) appointed intermediary. And in my pursuit of balance between them, it usually seemed more important to help Dad hear Mom than the reverse. That was my bias. And so, for good or bad, I've acted as my mother's energetic interpreter.

"When they get here," Renee says, pausing to take a sip of wine over her fabric table. She's sipping and measuring. I get the feeling we are going to quilt and Côtes du Rhône our way through this thing. Twenty-two table runners and counting. Two runners for Mom each month. This one is Fourth of July flags. I say, whatever gets you through.

"I just can't . . ." She trails off, moving pieces of fabric out of the way for another pour. I look at her handiwork. An interesting Americana theme is starting to emerge: Benjamin Franklin place mats, George Washington quote posters, Glenn Beck T-shirts. What with her newish love of guns and flags, there's something here about her sense of security. I'm mulling what it means. She hadn't made a firearm quilt yet. I'm tempted to request one. But this is not a time to poke the bear in the zoo.

"I nominate you to talk to Dad. You're better at these things," Renee says.

This is one time I wish we didn't agree.

When it comes to Dad, I will say the uncomfortable things that Renee cannot or will not say. When it comes to Dad, I'm the Emperor-Has-No-Clothes Kid. I am the Joker in the King's Court, whose job it is to give the king the bad news as kindly and likably as I can. When it comes to Dad.

And now Dad is coming.

I talk to Mom in her little room, still struggling to keep her fluids down and do things like negotiate a straw with that mini neck brace.

"So Dad is coming. He'd like to see you. He's bringing Margie. What do you think? It's up to you. I can manage it."

She takes a large sigh, looks around the room. Her eyes fill with tears—of sadness and complication, still aware of herself as the spouse who was left. And yet there's a tether between them, and only she and he truly know its shape. *Is it curly? Knotted? Kinked? Taught? Shredded?* Thirty-five years and two children.

She looks at me. Takes another big breath.

"Yes," she says. "He can come."

When Mom moved to the farm, Dad and Margie had sent her a huge, fancy rooster plate. They'd heard she got chickens, so they sent the plate. Mom didn't know what to do with it. For years, she kept it. And then—I don't remember the trigger. *Was it the photograph they sent of the two of them at her old home on Lake Tahoe? Or the way he insisted he bring all Margie's children and spouses we'd yet to meet to Renee's farm wedding, despite polite discouragement on behalf of Renee's wishes? Or the way he gave the tour of the barn Mom and I built as if it were his by extension?* All I know is, at some point, Mom grabbed the rooster plate and, with all the force her dainty self could muster, she threw it to the ground, sending shattered pieces flying. And because she never leaves a mess, proceeded to go in search of the broom and dustpan.

And now they were to visit.

"Yes, he can come, but I would only like to see him."

"I totally get it, Mom. I've got this."

Nausea, a broken neck, fading words, intermittent vomiting, infections they don't believe in, antibiotics they wouldn't take, the humiliation of their judgment on disease hovering above all of us, a broken hip, incontinence, and now a visit from her former husband and his unrequited college love he planned to marry even before his divorce was final.

Two days later Dad and Margie have cozied into the guest room of Renee's home. He is to head over directly. I hear the door.

It's not just him. But them. The one thing Mom had not agreed to.

"Hi, Dad. Hi, Margie. So nice to see you both." This is true when viewed with a wide-angle lens. Less true with a zoom. My job just got ten times harder.

Margie takes my hands and squeezes. Christian Scientists don't typically ask after someone who is ill because it means you're *buying into this illness stuff.* So they don't ask how Mom is doing.

She squeezes my hands some more.

"So nice to see you too, dear Meg." She means it. She has a big smile, lots of sparkle in her eyes and cheerful laugh lines framed by her stylish blond coif.

Despite not seeing the world as she sees it, I've always respected her lifetime of religious orthodoxy. She studies every day. But this seems an onslaught of misplaced intentions. I look down at her hands as she holds mine tightly. I see her large emerald wedding ring glinting in the light of the narrow hallway of the care facility. I think of the tiny emerald ring and only jewelry my dad ever bought my mom. It's a tiny chip. Mom loved that tiny emerald.

"Well, here's the thing, Dad, Margie. I believe you mean well. But, Margie, as I explained previously, Mom prefers to just see Dad. I hope you understand."

"Yes, honey, whatever your mom needs."

"Oh, Megan, that's just baloney." Dad pushes back. All powerful 230 pounds and six feet of him towering over me. "She is my wife and we want to come say hello. Don't get so dramatic. That's just bunk. Let's all move beyond that."

"Dad, I'm not being dramatic. I'm just representing what Mom has told me."

"We want to come in. Don't dwell on that old stuff." He says *stuff* like it's toxic waste. His angry voice.

"I'm not dwelling. I'm trying to respect two points of view, and one of them doesn't feel well right now. Wait one moment, Dad. And again, Margie, I mean no disrespect. It's just up to Mom."

"Of course, honey." But she does not leave. If I were her, I would have gone and sat in the living room out of respect. Instead the two of them stand there, holding hands. I return to Mom.

"Mom, he wants to bring in Margie too."

Mom sighs, then sighs some more. Her eyes look around the room.

"Just tell them they can come in," she whispers.

"I can just tell them to go," I say. "Or give him the choice to see you alone or not at all. Really. It's up to you."

"Let them in." She looks like she's going to cry. But doesn't. I search her eyes, touch her tired face.

"Okay," I utter.

I let the dam go. Or the floodgates. Or the barrier. Or whatever I might be obstructing between Dad and Mom. *Perhaps this is their karma, their path.*

Maybe this is a completion they've needed. I kiss her head and exit to get them, so whatever is to happen can happen.

My father gusts by me, his ever-present yellow tablet of notes in hand. Margie follows.

In moments, they are at Mom's side, no makeup, hair brushed back, her face gray. The twinkle she normally has, absent. And they start. About *Principle and Truth. All is infinite mind and its infinite manifestation . . .* Margie takes my mother's hand and closes her eyes while she talks. My mom looks uncomfortable.

"Dad?" I ask. "Any chance you have those gorgeous Christian Science hymns with you?"

Maybe this could work. Mom and Dad used to sing together. Not hymns. But it's got to be preferable to this.

My father snaps out of his talk and—to my eye—condescension toward the woman on the bed. The broken neck, the brain, the hip. All because, in *his* mind, she lost connection to Divine Truth.

"I do, actually. I have some hymns on my computer." His boyish voice, back with excitement.

"I think that would be wonderful. Singing can be quite a healing. Why don't we all sing?"

My mother looks at me and then back at them and breathes a little easier. If I'm about to traumatize her, I hope to minimize it. So I hoist an attentive Isabelle onto the bed for Mom to feel next to her. Isabelle curls up and, as if reading my mind, starts nuzzling Mom's hand to instigate some behind-the-ear scratches. On instinct, Mom starts a gentle pet. Both look more peaceful now despite the awkward company and sterile surroundings. Dad heads back out of the room toward the car and computer, and Margie and I wait for the hymns.

We sing.

> One in the freedom of the Truth
> The freer step the fuller breath

I try to figure how *few* hymns we need to make them feel heard, and how *many* she can tolerate if they are upsetting to her.

I go with three.

For a moment, Dad leans down and talks just to Mom, and I hope they have a special moment of peace. With my eye still on my parents, Margie leans into me and says softly, "You know, your mother can be healed from this. In Christian Science—it is a *science*, you know—and in this *science* we understand that there is *no* separation from God . . ."

"Yes," I say. "Thank you so much, Margie. And from the Christian Science view, isn't it true that we are all whole, perfect, and complete at all times?"

"Yes, Megan."

"Well, then, my mom is whole, perfect, and complete, exactly as she is."

89

TRUDGE THROUGH THE RAIN

PURPOSE: Transition my family.

DURATION: A month-plus.

EQUIPMENT NEEDED: Moving materials. Tape and the like.

AGE: 40+.

RELATIONSHIP STATUS: Single. I've seen some dating action. A few wooers. A whitewater boater, a fighter pilot. The first likes PBR and a green leafy plant a little too much for my taste. I don't need to substitute one man's compulsions for another. The pilot will be a lifelong friend. Because honestly, can you see me as a military wife?

EMPLOYMENT: Aspiring writer with bridge jobs. Renee is buying the farm from Mom. I will receive a portion of the sale. I'm putting it into an Airbnb multiunit operation, larger than what I've already been doing. I think Mom would approve—hosting both travelers and people in transition. This is a more profitable profession to combine to make writing possible. Plus, the space-designing comes naturally to me. I've landed a few design covers.

LOCATION: Whidbey Island, Washington.

It's raining on Whidbey Island and I'm packing up boxes. I'm here at my mother's house. I'm packing up all that she's left behind. She never got that modern woodsy refuge for women she imagined. Renee and I couldn't sustain the dream. Well, at least not together. It became more about how to not let this fairy-tale spot fall apart without going bankrupt. We attempted to shape the place as a wedding venue, but when discussions about where to move the couch became the Battle of Stalingrad, I knew that without Mom, the together-farm would never be. Instead it became about where to put the new dishes my mother kept buying for the gatherings she would never have. That's one of the things the plaque tangles did to her. She couldn't stop buying dishes.

So I want very few of those newer stacks and stacks of tangled-plaque dishes. Hurts too much. But before I leave, I will style the barn—her barn, our barn—and the wooded landscape that surrounds it in the way I believe she would have wanted. It will be impermanent, a temporary exhibit. And I will take pictures and get it on the cover of a magazine. Isabelle will grace the cover too.

We photograph it all: the picnics we never had, the piles of cheeses and fruit on vintage linens we never laughed around, campfires we never lit, marshmallows we never roasted. I will style gorgeous pretend fresh eggs from imagined chickens pretending they live in the old coop. I will drag out every extra Hoosier cupboard and strange object that my mother bought from a dead woman she never knew but heard about from one of those lawyers who wants to make money on elderly clients, no matter the harm. Tables, chairs, portraits of this stranger. Even her shoes. I should say shoe. My mother also bought one singular shoe from this old woman courtesy of the scoundrel attorney, straight out of the children's story. Loyal to her books to the end.

"Mom, why just the one shoe?"

"Well, because I couldn't buy two." She says this like it's the most logical thing in the world. And in a certain light, it is.

I will send these pictures of the life that never happened here to the young architect Thomas who loved this place. Like Renee, he married here too. He deserves to see it as we envisioned. I don't want him to feel the residue of her illness on his work. I think she would want to give him the vision come to life. If only for a moment.

Mom lives down the road now at the care facility where they dress her and feed her and brush her teeth and give her pills and set her in front of the TV. I hate the place. She's too alone. My sister loves it. It's close. And this is one thing we needed lawyers to talk about and never found a compromise. But where I pack is the farm that my mom can no longer even imagine still exists. And so I'm wrapping up stacks and stacks and stacks of dishes and vases and containers and tiny trinkets that mean something to her once. I will not save the newer ones, only the ones I believed truly mattered to her.

It's raining on Whidbey Island and I'm packing up silver. The silver that told us when a special event was really special. It doesn't feel so special holding it now. I think I count seven butter knives, and I don't eat butter. And only six escargot forks, but I don't eat snails. I'm to be out of here by the thirty-first. Not that I ever lived here, but traces of me did. And now all those traces need to be sorted, packed, labeled, and stacked and put in a pod. That's how moving works now. It's about pods. I'm to put these echoes of a life in this pod and make it all invisible. No trace of me or these objects by the thirty-first. Put into boxes and tubs and labeled like it all makes sense. even though none of it makes any sense. She's still alive and living down the road. But that's how the disease works. You say good-bye to those with it; you say good-bye to them in pieces.

It's raining on Whidbey and I'm packing up Beatrix Potter dish sets. Renee and her family will be moving in by the thirty-first. And she will call this place home. I am happy for her. But that does not translate. And so Renee wants all traces of me gone by the thirty-first. I don't know why this is. It just is. I suspect I'm a safe place to pack the anger. A reminder of a family that got fractured. By divorce, by disease. And one particular face (mine) and hers to me, an echo of that family that didn't quite work.

It's raining on Whidbey again and I'm packing up wedding china. I'm splitting up gray and white plates with tiny pink flowers. Almost Asian in their delicacy. Mom loved those tiny pink flowers. Delicate like the heart she kept so hidden. Delicate and wrapped in Bubble Wrap to prevent breakage.

I'm packing up boxes and cooking big vegetable meals for the woman who spends the most time with my mother, a Buddhist named Heidi. I have to feed somebody who needs to eat. I need to have good memories of this kitchen. This kitchen that never got used as it was designed. Mom got sick first. And this fine woman, for whom I cook, she takes my mother to the library for new books that my mother can no longer read but recognizes the covers. She takes my mother on undersized walks (you can hardly call them walks anymore). She takes my mother on small shuffles. Small shuffles to and from the car. I couldn't make this woman enough food to thank her. I serve these meals on Beatrix Potter plates. I want to put a new memory or two to these plates. I will load up Peter Rabbit and Benjamin Bunny with piles of kale and chard.

I'm packing up boxes, now of Christmas dishware and Mrs. Tiggy-Winkle tea sets. For a childhood that is no longer mine. I wrap these dishes in Bubble Wrap and wonder if I will ever have the sort of life that gathers large groups around a holiday table with Christmas tree plates. My Christmases don't so much look like that and I wonder why that is. I wonder if I mind.

I am not yet packing up the blue and white Meissen china. So it sits out. My sister has divided it in half but covered it all with Post-its, labeling dish subgroups with codes marked *A*, *B*, *C*, *D*, and *E*. It appears I'm to do something about these groups, according to some secret division system only Renee understands. I don't know what any of these Post-its mean. Her order doesn't match how my brain works. Never has. And so I will repile the dishes without subgroups and Post-its. And this will offend her. And I will feel bad about it. And so I will leave out my redivision for her approval. And she will disapprove. That's how it's mostly gone. I've never fit neatly into a subgroup. But not for a lack of trying. I can tell you I stared at those Post-its for a good long while, trying to decipher their meaning, all the while wondering how her language became the one I tried so hard to defer to. And why mine has so often repelled.

Instead, I now pack up my uncle Ted's cutting board, which he made in the shape of a pig in woodshop. My mother had him autograph it because it was one of the only things he made with his hands other than laying bricks. She couldn't take her brother's bricks with her. So I pack the pig.

I won the pig when the lawyers flipped a coin for who got what object. Yes, it came to lawyers and lists in order of priority, and coin tosses. An expensive way to divvy up stuff, especially when none of it really seems to matter. My mother is gone. The part that cared about dishes and rabbits and cutting boards is gone. And I'm packing it all up anyway. Maybe someday I will cut vegetables on my uncle Ted's pig. I add the tiny milk pitchers and large colored goblets from a trip to the Madonna Inn—quite possibly the tackiest place on Earth. I can picture Christmas with the tacky glasses easier than the Christmas tree plates. The goblets are so ugly, so garish and bright, I find them beautiful.

I don't know why life is asking me to release those I have held most dear:

a fading mom, a distant sister. But it is. It is asking me to do this. This life is asking me to do this. And I am obeying. And hoping some new version of us will rise up. Like a phoenix from the ash.

I'm packing up boxes slowly. I've never been particularly good at good-byes. And I'm doing it anyway. Despite being awkward and clumsy and having to say it more than once. When it all gets too much, I put down the Bubble Wrap. When it all gets too much I get in the wagon Mom used to drive and pull up to her care facility where she lives. I often bring Isabelle. The only thing I like about the place is that they understand how much four-legged friends help their residents. I knock on the door and head in, where she is watching *The Sound of Music* again.

"It's a good story," she says, petting Isabelle while she watches.

Wait two minutes.

"It's a good story," she says again.

Everything works out in *The Sound of Music*. The whole family climbs that damn euphoria-inducing-happy-hill and escapes the Nazis together. The care provider, Kathy, tells me she cared for the youngest von Trapp after she suffered a stroke. She says at the end, the woman (I think it was Gretl) had no contact with her family. I guess a few things happened they didn't cover in the movie.

So when I'm not packing up boxes or driving her old car or running trails with my furry sidekick to shake these blues and mean reds, I'm at the facility climbing in next to my mother on her Tempur-Pedic adjustable bed.

Sometimes life changes on a dime and you just can't make sense of it. I am a happy person, but this is not happy. I am often a joyful person, but today I do not feel joy. I laugh a lot now in my normal life. But today is not normal. These are sad parts that I will pack up and try not to let linger longer. I don't need to make these grooves of loss any deeper than they are. They are deep enough.

I haven't forgotten that despite the rain on Whidbey, the rain over the Olympic mountains, the rain in the North Cascades, it is sunny many places I love other than right here. It is sunny in the Wind River Range of Wyoming; and in Watamu, Kenya; and in Newport Beach, California; and on my new pint-sized porch in New York City. And I will return to those places once the boxes are stacked and podded.

I will try to trust that one day I will get to love and be loved by a man again. The Mom thing, I don't know where that love goes, only that this is not how I want it. I will tell myself I have too much love to give to not share. And I hope my self will believe it. I will tell myself to insist that all this tenderness go somewhere good, to someone who knows he wants it. And I will tell myself (more than once, in hopes it will stick) that just like the rain that falls to the ground, love has its own natural course. That I can remember how it moves outward from my chest and can touch and be touched. I tell myself it will work like that again, that my heart will not live a life in Bubble Wrap. I tell myself that my heart likes the sun too much, the fresh air too much, the heat. And I hope my self will believe that too.

In the meantime, I will love on my mother even though she may no longer recognize the timbre of my voice or the nose on my face. For all this forgetting, my mom's disease would come in handy. But you can't retrofit it. It doesn't let you pick and choose the memories to take with you and those to leave behind.

I kiss my mother on the cheek and head back to my boxes. I will let her get back to Maria and the Baroness. Like I said, I'm not so good at good-byes. Especially with her.

I don't know why life comes in waves like this. Like it's saying: "Just free-fall. Let go and let what is meant to come to you, come. Let it take you. You can't wrap it all up," it says.

It tells me, "Some things will be broken. Others, lost. Not everything can be shipped off in a pod. Some residue will linger. She will linger. But sometimes, to get back to the brightest of light, you must trudge for a bit through the rain. And sometimes you must do so alone."

I look down at my pile of empty boxes I have yet to fold and tape like stiff origami. I know only two things to be true at this large kitchen table of objects yet to be sorted: I have no box for her. To keep her safe. To keep me safe.

So free fall, please take me. For now, you will be my lover, my teacher, my workshop, my mother, my companion. We will travel for a spell. I fall willingly. But if you can, please fast-track me. Quick as a bunny.

I believe I have a plate of hers somewhere here that says just that: *Quick as a Bunny*. Wait one second, and I will show you.

GROUND

"And now," cried Max,
"let the wild rumpus start!"

—*Maurice Sendak*

They say things happen in threes. I don't know if it's true, but I know how soothing it can feel to find those arcs within our own lives, with three of anything making it possible to feel a beginning, a middle, an end. They can help give one a sense of completion. To make sense of the difficulties.

My arc came in fours.

My beloved four-legged Isabelle has died. And with this, I no longer feel that wordless, albeit very communicative, furry companion riding next to me—nearly always shotgun in my car, or curled at my feet on planes, or tucked behind my knees in the middle of the night when we both sleep. She can no longer make her playful wagging introductions everywhere we go—splaying her belly to strangers at any bookstore or hiking trail or city street, hoping for a rub or a scratch to her perfectly pink tummy.

Her cancer came fast and hard. Coco and her husband were with us both when she passed, Isabelle curled in my lap, taking her last breath. We lit candles and said things we thought she would want to hear. Or that we needed to say.

And not knowing anything concrete about an afterlife, and because I wanted to cover all the bases that mean something to me, we sat both shivah in the Jewish tradition and followed Buddhist practice for the deceased—for shivah, we covered mirrors, sat low to the ground. And in Buddhist fashion, we didn't move her little brown body for three days. Buddhist thinking suggests this helps the spirit of a sentient being travel as it needs, by keeping the body as still and quiet as possible. My childhood friend Nessa would check in now and then, making sure I didn't get too comfortable spooning—in her words—a dead dog. By the morning of the fourth day, Isabelle's presence actually felt different. On that fourth, she now felt like a body, not like a soul. This made it far easier for me to bring her to the crematorium, where the undertaker explained how it would all work. The temperature, the time it would take, what would remain. All to transform her into ash with her favorite stuffed froggy next to her.

As for the second, my father's kind wife, Margie, the devout Christian Scientist, has Alzheimer's. Not that she will ever call it that. Nor will my father. Nor will I ever push to label it as such. But a far too familiar disease process is passing through our family again. I am heartbroken for them both. She has loved my father deeply and well. And he, her. They are going on twenty years of marriage, but he's loved her far longer. The disease is moving faster with her. Margie would never take a medication for a condition she doesn't believe in.

So without ever giving the situation a name, I can still love on her. I know how to help support her through the confusion. And I know a thing or two about how to help Dad navigate this loss, as I have learned via trial by fire how to get through.

From my point of view, my father sits with this all in an awkward place—between refusing to acknowledge that something is happening, yet having to vent and plan and work to help his loved one when things he says aren't happening are happening. All this is softening my father. With this new challenge he needs friendship, a laugh, a break. To tell a difficult story to a nondenying ear. And I want to and do offer that help wherever I can. For now, it is dealing with the level of one who can't remember how to put together a puzzle, or forgets whether a bath mat goes inside or outside a shower, or whether we just ate, or where someone has just been yesterday, or where they will go tomorrow. And if or when she worsens, I will be there for both of them: as she forgets how to dress, to talk, to feed herself.

I'm open to a miracle. I just don't think that's how it will go.

Regardless, I will *never* say, "*See*, there *are* some things that even the most dedicated of religions can't protect you from." What I will stay instead is, "Margie, Dad, tell me about your favorite hymns. I would love to sing them for you."

This next one has no number.

My mother has passed.

As with Isabelle, I was with her there too.

Down to the last days, she could still respond to yes-or-no questions with a blink system she and I developed. Very long, deliberate winks for a yes.

"Are you scared?" I asked.

"Yes," she said with one decidedly lengthy close of her eyes.

When I asked, "Are you ready to go?" She answered with a far more tentative blink. But that made sense to me, to be less sure of a decided end.

After the first night that we thought she was near the very end, with her fluid-filled breaths and huge silences between those breaths, Renee and I spooned one another through the night next to Mom's bed in a wildly uncom-

fortable La-Z-Boy. By morning, Renee and I watched a giant bald eagle perch
in the yard of the care facility for a half hour. When I answered a call from
Coco while we watched Mom's power animal, Renee told me, "The eagle took
a huge dump just as you answered the phone. Mom hated when Dad took his
phone calls. I think she's telling you to get off the phone."

"Don't you think we are taking this eagle thing a *tiny* bit too literally?" I
asked. We giggled. Then laughed hysterically. It felt good.

And then the final day came. Somehow, we knew that this was the day.
Renee sat meditating and in prayer in the La-Z-Boy, and I searched for Mom's
and my shared favorite song, Sarah McLachlan's "I Love You." As I pushed *play*
and the song began, her breaths got further and further apart still. We went
from our chairs to her bed. Renee sat on her left holding Mom's hand. And I
sat on her right with my hand on Mom's heart. Her breaths became wider and
wider still. So wide, I was sure no human could hold her breath that long.

"She's going," I said.

"I know," Renee said.

And then she took that last breath, to the song's words, "I forgot, to tell you
I love you . . ."

Her eyes rolled up and to the left. Renee and I curled up around her and
cried in silence for the next two hours, holding her, holding each other, playing
softly all the music that reminded us of her, her most beloved songs. As for her
memorial, we made her favorite books as centerpieces, stacked and tied in giant
burlap bows—Barry Lopez and *Blueberries for Sal*. By the end of her life, when
Mom couldn't recall any names, she still wanted to speak of Lopez. She called
him *Our Man*. And I always knew of whom she spoke. We only had one.

For the walls, we hung a quilt of Mom's favorite books that Renee had
made. Mom's vintage toys and figurines of Beatrix Potter, Winnie-the-Pooh,
and other characters made a beautiful showing on the tables, welcoming guests
and old friends from nearly every modality she ever tried, from Christian Science to Lawrence studies to the Children's Bookshoppe. For her, I invited
Tim, which felt right. He declined with a very kind note about her, which felt
right too.

The eulogy that slayed me was unexpected—as if it emerged from the ether.
I suppose the best ones do. It was given by the librarian—a veritable stranger—
from the abused children's home out in the desert. She still ran the program my

mother built, and had made it flourish. Mom had charged this woman with a new idea: that a trip to the library and a book weren't just a reward but could help heal what's broken. It was like Our Man had taught us:

Sometimes people need a story more than food to stay alive.

The librarian spoke of the ripple effect one ordinary person could have on so many. In this case, it was my mother. And the librarian wasn't just talking about the kids. She was talking about herself. She couldn't stop crying. It felt as if her gratitude came from that deepest well—the one where you feel the generations of all who came before you in your bones. Mom, who had driven out to the desert, week after week, having never been asked, started with just a little box of books and a story hour. To the librarian it was as if she'd said: *Take this. Run with this. Run with this and then fly.*

Alexa says Mom came to the memorial. And that she loved it. I like to imagine she was there, cross-legged with the Maharishi. Alexa says now her energy will visit me when I am doing something particularly creative. I like to imagine this too.

As for the fourth, now two months after my mother has passed, Phil has told me he is retiring as a therapist. Nine years of work together, coming to an end. In all ironies, as I am learning to land, Phil wants to spend the next phase traveling with his wife, no longer defining his primary role in the world as a therapist, nor primarily rooted in one geographic location. But for the first time in my adult life, in the face of these changes, I have my own center to which I can return, and invite others into as well. This center comes in the shape of a perfectly round house. I have built myself a yurt alongside twelve other yurts surrounded by Grand Teton National Park. It's quite beautiful—beautiful enough that a new resort ranch has asked me to design a group of them in the Wasatch Mountains. Now the fact that I choose to reside in a structure created and used by a nomadic people scattered across Mongolia, this irony is not lost on me. I'm doing my best here. Perhaps it also made landing more gentle that I raised my yurt in the wilds of Wyoming—the landscape of my mother's most precious dreams. But my version has more unexpected delights than either of us could have imagined. I am surrounded not just by the pack of rescued dogs she imagined, but by elk, bison, moose, coyote, wide braided streams, spectacular night skies, and a perfectly framed view out my window of the seven-thousand-foot rise of the jagged, young, and majestic Grand.

I often wake with the sun streaming through the dome, and end with the moon cresting over a late-night fire. Sometimes alone, sometimes with friends and family passing through. I have the coziest little guest tent to welcome those, as I have been welcomed—like Coco in Fort Collins, and Michelle and Scott in Lander, and Nessa in Newport. It's a good spot. What Wyoming may lack in convenience, it makes up for in large open spaces.

Tonight, it's a full house. Dinner on the deck in the height of summer; a strand of Italian twinkly lights; bellies full of pesto pasta and giant hot chocolates. A small constellation of friends dots my camp. Michelle and Scott have turned off the small chandelier in the guest tent; their young daughter, Magda, reads by headlamp on my couch inside the yurt. And the last, a new friend, is deck-side, curled up in the womb cocoon of his sleeping bag, his face under the stars, embarking on his very own first solo astro bivy. I am honored that he chose this spot for his first bivy.

Protection. Nourishment. Comfort. In the end, it's not that complicated.

(P.S. I did the Hoffman Process. Couldn't help myself. *Loved* it.)

ACKNOWLEDGMENTS

It is called *The Book of Help*, after all. I am profoundly grateful to have been the beneficiary of countless gestures of kindness and help in this book's making—far more than I'll be able to capture here. To the community of Bread Loafers who gave me inspiring friends, readers, and teachers like Nina Swamidoss McConigley, Rachel Starnes, Bret Anthony Johnston, and David Shields. And to the early reading and generous notes from Pam Houston. To Vanessa Chong for being the steady you-can-do-it bossy force on this (or frankly anything) since second grade. And to the Griswold-Shepard-Bacigalupi crew for our Blended-Extended from Atlanta to Kauai. Vermont to Virginia. The Washoe Valley to Whidbey.

To Michael Anastassiades for being my role model in how to keep at it. And to Sandy Burt for your perfect comedic tone on everything. In my head, I often write what I think would tickle you. To inspiring friends and cheerleaders and readers: the very dear, gifted, and multi-talented Jay Knowlton, Dana Scanlan, Christin Helander, Anne Paulu, Christa Hubbell, Stephanie Pastor, Mary Taylor, Anne and Don Polkingharn. And to my dear Ellen Silva, who keeps teaching me how the little things are the *big* things (like how to make lavender blackberry jam and enjoy the delicacy of a garage-sale teacup) just the way Joyce would. And to Kevin-*I-Say-It-All-the-Time-and-I-Have-No-Idea-What-It-Means*-McLaughlin for being the best early comedic-riff wellspring to bounce paragraphs off of and craft a beat for. And to my Dad, who insisted I read him the entire manuscript (and laughed a lot while I was at times holding my breath) as he sat cross-legged in the yurt's meditation tent, no less. He even endured the chapter on cadavers (a bit squinty eyed, but he did it).

A beyond enormous thank you to my extremely skilled and generous editor Alyse Diamond. I couldn't be more fortunate to have a home with her. And for the incredible art by Aitch that the incredible PRH team brought to life. And to my anything-is-possible-believing friend Liz Gilbert. Thank you to Watamu for bringing you to me. And to Alex Polier for your unwavering get-'er-done confidence. And to Jenny Pfeiffer for telling stories with me, with the help of your lens. And to the best tiny apartment neighbor and book lover and insight generator, Sarah Shatz. And for the gently nudging words and hands of Emily Griffin and Liz Connor. And the book smarts and hearts—and Yellowstone floats—of Rob and Jen Campbell. And to the Wind River Hiking Posse who remind me to get my feet and lungs and head back out there: Aileen Brew, Kathy Brown, Missy White, Molly Absolon, Holly Copeland, and of course our fearless leader to be mentioned later. I love those long days, often with me at the back, thinking book stuff while you are talking natural history, races, fiddle camps, and training rides. And to Phil del Prince, Majie Lavergne, and John Travis for your dedication to your work and the work you've helped me do. And to Alexa Robbins for your otherworldly sensitivity. And to the words of Barry Lopez, to which I will always return, by way of a compass of sorts.

Thank you to Alexandra Fuller. In what special universe was it my luck to have you move into the yurt next door? Your expansive mind, raw kindness, and protective sisterly care, as well as your faith in me, hit me deep. Not to mention, there's nobody I'd rather clean a yurt bathhouse with. And thank you to the generous readers and beings in the form of the inspirationally trailblazing Sarah Ross and shiny bright star Cecily Ross, two very special young women who were brought by luck—and yurtville—into my life. To my Patagonian family, Molly Doran and Andrew Cline, and the Escudero-Kanes. Thank you for being there for those first big river crossings, and then there for the even bigger waters. Molly and Andy: there's nothing like laughing with you while sipping out of tiny ceramic cups surrounded by Mehari, Z, and those blessed times with Joyce. All our times together—on and off the trail—informed these pages. And to Tim, who taught me so very, very much. About how to grow up and out, and learn from our steps and missteps.

And thank you to my mother, Joyce. You gave so much light and infused me with your insatiable curiosity. For the way you could make me laugh at myself and make anything fun. You are missed. Thank you for giving all of yourself that you could to me. And to my sister for being my blood tribe as we each bushwhacked and broke trail both independently and with each other. And for giving us the gift of Rich and of one Miss Kelsey Bean.

And to Michelle Louise Escudero. Thank you for being my dear sister from the beginning, when we were just barreling down a Patagonian dirt road in a cattle truck or you were insisting we simply must attempt to spin wool on Lago Cochrane. Thank you for your unwavering love. My art-loving, community-dedicating, better-world-believing, route-finding, trip-planning, women-supporting, compulsive-*New Yorker*-reading, what-time-does-your-plane-land-asking (not to mention, my medical emergency contact on health forms) hermana. I thank the Southern Cross and the Baker River for bringing you and Scott and Magda into my life. You are my touchstone.

And truly, from the unfathomable depths of subterranean tectonic plates to the glaciated, sky-touching Grand Teton heights, I thank you, Bill Clegg, for being a lantern, a champion, a shepherd, a fellow traveler. Thank you for your sincere humanity and love—not just of books but for people and that larger unexplainable thing that connects us all. And how the way you care for your incredible family and community informs your work. The word *agent* doesn't even scratch the surface of your gifts, your intelligence, and heart. Not even close. We really do need a new word. You are a champion for so many of us. And the world of literature is more wonderful for your participation.

And madly, deeply, and finally to Pam-Pam-Pammy DeVore. There are no words for what your mind, heart, and truth-revealing friendship have given me. For all that PXE took, you gave back to me tenfold. You are the best listener, challenger, questioner, critic, editor, pregnant-reflective-pause taker, trixy-reveler I never could have imagined I'd be blessed to bump into at a tiny rare acupuncture school. Come to think of it, maybe we should have named you Trixy. Trix for short. Thank you for *always* making time. You have thought and felt your way through this material with boundless generosity and insight. Thank you for every place you let us discuss and let me read to you: deafening hails storms in Wyoming, library basements, hospice rooms, parking lots, riverbanks, construction sites, ferryboats, tucked-away closets, airports, hospital waiting areas, motel rooms, parks, I-80 in high winds with dropping signals, hiking trails, subway platforms, and subletted apartments. There's nothing I know quite like the words we've shared. And there's nobody whose terrifying, record-breaking pregnant pauses I will ever love more. Your fierce beautiful ears see more than any two eyes could ever dream of. And that's a fact.

And to anyone still reading this: whatever poem, painting, invention, cartoon, picture, recipe, purpose, story, mission, obsession, garden, flow chart, novel—whatever idea so special that you are maybe even too nervous to talk about—just know that the world is calling to you to bring to life your treasure, whatever that may be. Only you know. So get going. We can't wait to feel it.

ABOUT THE
AUTHOR

Megan Griswold went to Barnard College, received an MA from Yale, and
went on to earn a licentiate degree from the Institute of Taoist Education and
Acupuncture. She has trained and received certifications as a doula, shiatsu
practitioner, yoga instructor, personal trainer, and in wilderness medicine,
among others. She has worked as a mountain instructor, a Classical Five Element acupuncturist, a freelance reporter, an NPR *All Things Considered* com-
mentator, and an off-the-grid interior designer. She resides (mostly) in a yurt
in Kelly, Wyoming.

   Visit her at www.megangriswold.com.